WITHDRAWN

UNCOVERING THE PAST

UNCOVERING THE PAST

▶A History of
Archaeology

WILLIAM H. STIEBING, JR.

PROMETHEUS BOOKS • BUFFALO, NEW YORK

Published 1993 by Prometheus Books

97 96 95 94 93   5 4 3 2 1

Library of Congress Cataloging-in-Publication Data

Stiebing, William H.
    Uncovering the past : a history of archaeology / by William H.
Stiebing, Jr.
    Includes index.
    ISBN 0-87975-764-7
    1. Archaeology—History. I. Title.
CC100.S75   1993
930.1—dc20   92-40446
                                                                    CIP

Printed in the United States of America on acid-free paper.

For Professor James B. Pritchard,
archaeologist, biblical scholar, teacher, and friend

Contents

Maps

12   UNCOVERING THE PAST

Figures

Preface

For almost twenty-five years I have taught the history of archaeology as part of an introductory course in archaeology at the University of New Orleans. But throughout that time, there has been no satisfactory text on this subject. Popular and readable books like C. W. Ceram's *Gods, Graves and Scholars,* Leonard Cottrell's *Lost Cities,* or Brian Fagan's *Quest for the Past* were too selective. They did a good job of describing a few great discoveries, but they omitted whole fields of archaeology. On the other hand, the few general histories available, such as Glyn Daniel's *Man Discovers His Past* and *A Short History of Archaeology,* tended to be too brief. Thus, I decided to write this book.

Uncovering the Past is intended primarily for college students studying archaeology, anthropology, or ancient history. But there are many general readers interested in these subjects as well. So I have tried to keep professional jargon to a minimum and to make the material as readable as I can. Thus, I hope that a wide audience will find this book useful and informative.

As I see it, archaeology has had four major phases of development. The two longest ones were part of a "heroic age" during which the discipline was born and grew to maturity. Two shorter phases comprise the modern era in archaeology. So I thought about dividing the book into four sections, each covering important archaeological developments around the world during one of the discipline's phases. This is the way Glyn Daniel organized *A Short History of Archaeology.* However, such an approach makes it difficult, if not impossible, for the reader to recognize the developments within and the differences between separate fields of archaeological research. On the other hand, if the author emphasizes the individual growth of different archaeological subdisciplines, then the reader may not recognize similarities and interrelationships between the fields.

In the end, I decided to try a compromise between a chronological organization and a topical one. Separate chapters cover the origins and growth of archaeology in different areas of the world during the "heroic age," when the discipline had its roots in many diverse disciplines and interests. Each of these chapters is divided chronologically into two parts, however—the two phases of infancy and then early maturity. On the other hand, I have treated the more unified modern period chronologically with a chapter for each of its two phases. I hope this arrangement will help the reader appreciate the diversity as well as the common ground of this discipline known as "archaeology."

Naturally, I owe a debt of gratitude to many people who assisted in the production of this book. My students and lecture audiences through the years have made me aware of the lure and interest this subject holds for many people. Their statements and questions helped me select the material to be presented here. Michael Clark and Jerah Johnson, professors of history at the University of New Orleans, and Malcolm Webb, professor of anthropology at the University of New Orleans, all read portions of an early version of the manuscript. James B. Pritchard, emeritus professor of religious thought and emeritus curator of biblical archaeology at the University of Pennsylvania, read the entire first draft. The comments, advice, and constructive criticism of these scholars improved this work in many ways. Of course, I am solely responsible for any shortcomings that remain despite the best efforts of my colleagues. Mark G. Hall and the staff at Prometheus Books also made many valuable contributions to this volume. Finally, I want to say a heartfelt "thank you" to my wife, Ann. She has endured dust, heat, rain, and other discomforts while accompanying me on visits to many archaeological sites. Throughout our years of marriage she has provided love, friendship, support, inspiration, and even an occasional nudge when I needed it. Anything that I accomplish owes much more to her than she will ever know.

New Orleans, Louisiana
August, 1992

Introduction

For the moment, time as a factor in human life has lost its meaning. Three thousand, four thousand years maybe, have passed and gone since human feet last trod the floor on which you stand, and yet, as you note the signs of recent life around you—the half-filled bowl of mortar for the door, the blackened lamp, the finger-mark upon the freshly painted surface, the farewell garland dropped upon the threshold—you feel it might have been but yesterday. . . . Time is annihilated by little intimate details such as these, and you feel an intruder.

H. Carter and A. C. Mace
The Tomb of Tut.Ankh.Amen

What Is Archaeology?

What image comes to mind when you hear the words "archaeology" or "archaeologist"? Many people picture a romantic figure like the fictional Indiana Jones exploring exotic places in search of treasure and adventure. Novels, movies, and many popular accounts of archaeological discoveries have made this concept of archaeology and archaeologists quite widespread. Tales of abandoned cities, ruined temples, primeval monuments or mysterious ancient tombs tend to kindle the urge for adventure, exploration, or treasure hunting that seems to lie beneath the surface of even the most timid and conventional individuals.

21

As the following chapters will show, there was once some truth to this popular image of archaeology. The nineteenth century produced a number of archaeological explorers whose escapades could almost match those of Indiana Jones. But the fabulous treasures and exciting adventures that so captivate the public's interest are no longer the primary reasons for archaeological research. Today archaeologists seek knowledge rather than objects that are intrinsically valuable. Their ultimate goal is to sweep aside the mists in which time has enveloped the past and, thus, to help us understand vanished peoples and cultures. As we come to understand those who have gone before, we recognize our common humanity, our oneness with them, and we understand ourselves a little better.

Of course, this goal is not unique to archaeology. Both history and anthropology also seek to understand and empathize with past cultures and civilizations. As a result, archaeology is often regarded as a sub-discipline of one or the other of these two fields of study. What sets archaeology apart, however, is not its final purpose, but its method of achieving that purpose.

Historians, anthropologists, linguists, and other scholars derive information about the past from written records, myths, language, folklore, or oral traditions. However, the archaeologist attempts to deduce facts about bygone societies and events from the physical clues they have left behind. Tools, pottery, houses, temples, art, campfires, roads, and any other remains that show the results of human activity (including such unromantic items as garbage heaps), as well as the skeletal vestiges of humans themselves, all have stories to tell. And these stories might never be learned through written or oral sources. Archaeology attempts to extract from these physical objects as much of humanity's story as possible. Simply put, archaeology is the study of mankind's past through the recovery and analysis of its material remains.

Stages in Archaeology's Development

Archaeology's origins can be traced to a variety of different sources—Renaissance humanism, interest in biblical history, the emergence of a scientific understanding of the world and the universe, early ethnographic and ethnological studies, and art appreciation, among others. From such diverse roots archaeology has passed through what we might characterize as four general phases or stages of growth and development. The first two phases, which saw archaeology's birth and growth to maturity, I have called the "heroic age." The last two phases, from after World War I to the present, represent the modern era in archaeology.

It should be kept in mind that this four-stage division is simply a convenient system for understanding multifaceted and interrelated trends through time. The dates given here are also only approximate. They are "averages," so to speak. As the chapters that follow will show, different fields of archaeological study moved from phase to phase at times that varied somewhat from these "average" dates.

PHASE I—EXPLORATION, ANTIQUARIANISM, AND EARLY EXCAVATION (CIRCA 1450-1860)

The first period in archaeology's development was also the longest. It could be said to stretch into the ancient past itself, since various individuals in ancient times were aware that still earlier civilizations had preceded theirs. On occasion, ancients even conducted what amounted to archaeological excavations as part of building renovations or restorations.

However, it was not until the early modern era (the fifteenth to seventeenth centuries) that such awareness of the past began to blossom into scholarly study of bygone cultures. Humanists wanted to learn all they could about ancient Greece and Rome. Biblical scholars began to seek information about the original contexts in which the Holy Scriptures had been produced. Art connoisseurs searched for examples of ancient sculpture, painting, and other arts. European antiquarians became interested in the past of their own nations. Furthermore, the contemporaneous development of the sciences gradually forced scholars to recognize that prior to the early civilizations there had been a prehistoric era. By the middle of the nineteenth century archaeological excavations were being undertaken in the Near East, America, and various parts of Europe in efforts to obtain antiquities and to learn more about the past.

PHASE II—ARCHAEOLOGY COMES OF AGE (CIRCA 1860-1925)

The early nineteenth-century archaeological speculations and excavations laid the foundation for widespread archaeological activity during the latter half of the century. Unfortunately, national rivalries and an emphasis on possession of antiquities often led Westerners to pillage and loot sites in less developed parts of the world. However, reports of these excavations and the arrival of major antiquities in Europe and the United States helped stimulate widespread interest in and support for archaeological research.

Gradually, those who saw archaeology primarily as a source of information about the past and not simply as an antiquities-collecting enterprise began to exercise some influence. During the decades at the end of the nineteenth and the beginning of the twentieth centuries, stratigraphical excavation techniques, typological sequence dating and stratigraphically based pottery chronologies were developed. During this era archaeology became an academic discipline rather than an adventuresome hobby. While antiquities continued to be gathered, what they told us about the past began to be valued more than the objects themselves. Leading scholars in most fields of archaeology had adopted this new professional approach by the outbreak of World War I. By the mid- to late 1920s it had become practically universal.

PHASE III—SYSTEMATIZING AND
ORGANIZING THE PAST (CIRCA 1925-1960)

During this period widespread excavation continued in most areas except during and immediately after World War II. The multitude of digs using the now generally accepted stratigraphical method of excavation made it possible for archaeologists to better date and interpret their finds. Scholars were able to synthesize data to define individual cultures and trace their development through time. Unfortunately, many of these cultural "histories" were little more than descriptions of changes in the types and distribution of pottery and other artifacts. Nevertheless, they laid the foundation for the more complete understanding of cultural development that would follow.

As archaeology became more systematic, its practitioners began to express its theory more explicitly. Was archaeology basically a hand-maiden of history or was it a form of cultural anthropology? What should archaeologists be striving to accomplish? Naturally, in this discipline with many diverse origins there was little agreement on such theoretical issues. Various attempts to delineate the theory of archaeology led to widening differences between the historically oriented fields of Old World archaeology and the anthropologically oriented New World archaeology.

This period also saw more widespread use of scientific instruments and procedures to locate, date, and interpret remains. Archaeologists learned to use aerial photography, machines that measured electrical resistance, metal detectors, and other scientific devices to locate walls, artifacts, and other archaeological features still buried beneath the earth.

As a result, archaeological surveys became more complete and more useful.

The best known and most important scientific aid to archaeology, however, was in the realm of dating remains. Radiocarbon dating, tree-ring chronology, and other scientific dating methods revolutionized our understanding of prehistoric chronology. They also helped make archaeologists aware of the importance of wood, charcoal, grain, and other natural materials encountered during excavations. Thus, excavation methods had to become even more precise and careful than before.

PHASE IV—TOWARD A SCIENTIFIC ARCHAEOLOGY
(CIRCA 1960-PRESENT)

By the 1960s some archaeologists recognized the need for a more complete understanding of ancient cultures, including their ecology. But a few went further. Instead of simply describing ancient cultural phenomena, these scholars sought to explain why the phenomena had occurred. Led by Americans schooled in cultural anthropology, these archaeologists became even more scientific in their approach, proclaiming the advent of a "new archaeology." They emphasized careful formation and testing of hypotheses, a cultural evolutionary approach, the use of systems theory, and quantitative analysis of data. They were confident that they would discover basic laws governing cultural change that not only would enlighten our understanding of the past but better enable us to shape our future.

The ideas of the new archaeologists prompted much criticism and debate. But in time even historically oriented archaeologists accepted some of the elements of the new archaeology, including the use of quantitative analysis of finds.

This change in approach and emphasis has been accompanied by the continued development of scientific aids to archaeology. Better survey devices such as ground-penetrating radar and robotic underwater cameras have been used to locate sites and artifacts. Scientists have also continued to discover and improve scientific methods for dating archaeological remains. But the most important scientific development has been the computer revolution. Over the past decade and a half computers have become commonplace in almost every profession, including archaeology. From providing statistical analyses of pottery sherds to plotting the locations of excavated remains, computers play a major role in modern archaeology. Moreover, it is likely that their importance will continue to increase as time goes on.

Part I

Archaeology's "Heroic Age"

Phase I—Exploration, Antiquarianism, and Early Excavation (circa 1450–1860)

and

Phase II—Archaeology Comes of Age (circa 1860–1925)

1

The Discovery of Prehistory

Phase I—Exploration, Antiquarianism, and Early Excavation (1450–1860)

THE SIX-THOUSAND-YEAR HISTORY OF THE EARTH

One of the most popular hobbies in America today is collecting Indian arrowheads. But this is a new interest, new at least when considered in terms of the centuries. For hundreds of years Europeans seem to have been oblivious even to the existence of such things. Millions of people must have seen stone axes, spear points, and arrowheads in plowed fields and dried-up stream beds or on eroded hillsides, but they did not notice them. To them such things were just so many more rocks. However, by the sixteenth and seventeenth centuries many people in Europe began recognizing the differences between ordinary rock formations and ancient stone artifacts. They then felt the need to explain the origin of the stone implements found throughout the continent.

These objects were commonly called "elf-stricking" or "fairy arrows," and many believed that fairies, on occasion, shot them from the heavens to injure humans. Others of a less superstitious mentality believed them to be freaks of nature, "thunderbolts" produced in storm clouds and rained upon the earth.

However, narratives by New World explorers often described the stone tools and weapons used by American Indians. These reports led a minority of scholars to argue that "elfshot" or "thunderbolts" were really implements produced by ancient people. Sir William Dugdale, an early British antiquary, declared in his *History of Warwickshire* (1650) that they were "weapons used by the Britons before the art of making arms of brass or iron was known."[1]

In 1699 another antiquary, Edward Lhwyd, wrote,

> I doubt not but you have often seen of these Arrow-heads they ascribe to elfs or fairies: they are just the same chip'd flints the natives of New England head their arrows with at this day; and there are also several stone hatchets found in this kingdom, not unlike those of the Americans. . . . They were not invented for charms, but were once used in shooting here, as they are still in America. The most curious as well as the vulgar throughout this country, are satisfied they often drop out of the air, being shot by fairies, and relate many instances of it; but for my part I must crave leave to suspend my faith, until I see one of them descend.[2]

A few years later, a German historian named Johann von Eckart also recognized the true nature of stone tools. But, in addition, he presented for the first time a clear description of the Three Age system of archaeological chronology. Eckart had been investigating the rise of the ancient Teutons, and as part of his research he had examined many burial mounds in Germany. To his great surprise, he found that none of them contained iron weapons or tools. Rather, many barrows (as such mounds are often called) produced bronze swords, shields, pins, and jewelry while others contained only bone and stone objects with no trace of metal. Eckart correctly interpreted his finds as evidence that there had been a Stone Age when metal was not used followed by a Bronze Age and an Iron Age, each heralding advances in technology and civilization. Dugdale had suggested a similar idea, but he did not go on to develop its implications as Eckart did. Unfortunately, the publication in which Eckart set forth his theory did not attract wide notice, and it was soon forgotten. A century would pass before the Three Age hypothesis would be proposed again as a system for understanding the development and relative chronology of European antiquities.

Not even those who accepted a human origin for the stone tools and weapons found in Western Europe realized just how ancient they were. These scholars thought that the peoples who had occupied the

---

1. Quoted in Glyn Daniel, *The Idea of Prehistory* (New York: World, 1963), p. 47.

2. From a letter to Dr. Richard Richardson on December 17, 1699. It was later published in the *Philosophical Transactions of the Royal Society* 28 (1713): p. 97.

Fig. 1. An eighteenth-century drawing of Stonehenge as a Druid temple. (From William Stukeley, *Stonehenge, A Temple Restored to the British Druids*, 1740.)

northern and western portions of Europe when Rome was ruling the Mediterranean world had made all the stone implements. Scholars also believed that people of the classical period had built the megalithic monuments such as Stonehenge that were also being studied at that time.

Europeans derived their knowledge of ancient history from only two sources, the Bible and the accounts of the classical Greeks and Romans. Chronologies based on these writings allowed the earth such a short span of existence that there simply was no time for prehistory. Most scholars agreed that the world was only about six thousand years old, though there was considerable disagreement over the exact date of the creation. Jewish rabbinical calculations from the Hebrew Massoretic Text showed that the world began 3,740 years before the Christian Era. Roman Catholic tradition, based on the Latin Vulgate translation of the Bible, placed the creation in 5199 B.C. And most English-speaking Protestants accepted the seventeenth-century Archbishop James Ussher's calculation of the time of creation, 4004 B.C. Ussher's dates were placed in the margins of early eighteenth-century editions of the King James version of the Bible, making them seem even more authoritative.

The conflict between supporters of science and those who believed in the complete accuracy of all parts of the Bible had not yet begun. Most seventeenth- and eighteenth-century scientists saw nothing in their work that contradicted the Bible. They agreed that science, in uncovering the truths of nature, would produce deeper reverence for nature's God. Thus, anyone who interpreted scientific or archaeological evidence in a way that challenged religious doctrine or the historical reliability of the Bible had to fight an uphill battle for acceptance, not only among the general public, but also within the scientific community.

Throughout Europe scholars fit pre-Roman antiquities into the presumed six-thousand-year-long history of the world and assigned them to people known to have occupied various areas during the classical era. Many monuments (including Stonehenge and Avebury) were thought to be the work of Druids, the priestly class of the Celtic peoples of France, Spain, and Britain in Roman times (Fig. 1). Other remains were credited to the Slavs or Teutons. A few people might have wondered about the many different kinds of artifacts that antiquarians assigned to the same people and time. However, most scholars continued to believe in a six-thousand-year history for mankind until the middle of the nineteenth century.

HINTS OF HUMAN ANTIQUITY

Developments in the field of geology eventually forced scholars to recognize the antiquity of the human race. Like stone tools, fossil remains of plants and animals were often found in Europe in early modern times, but their true nature and importance was seldom realized. As early as the fifteenth century Leonardo da Vinci recognized that fossils represented once-living creatures. He also saw that the occurrence of marine fossils on dry land showed that areas of the continent had once been beneath the sea. But during the next two centuries few investigators continued along the path blazed by Leonardo.

Many educated persons of the sixteenth and seventeenth centuries accepted the theory of the medieval Arab philosopher Avicenna. These people argued that a "plastic force" was at work in nature shaping stones in imitation of living things. A few supporters of the vis plastica theory combined it with the concept of spontaneous generation, an idea popular since the days of Aristotle. They claimed that fossils were nature's "false starts," so to speak. Supposedly the creative force within nature modeled creatures in stone and, when the formations were complete, generated life within them. If the process was interrupted or faulty in some way, fossils rather than living beings resulted.

Other people interpreted fossils of large prehistoric creatures as the remains of unicorns, giants, or dragons (Fig. 2). The fossil ivory from the skeletons of such fabled beasts commanded very good prices from apothecaries. These early druggists ground up the material to produce potions believed to have miraculous healing properties or mounted fragments of it in gold or silver to make amulets thought to possess exceptional power.

But the most popular explanation of fossils was that they were the remains of living creatures killed and fossilized during the biblical Flood. Skeletons of fish or other marine creatures found far inland or on mountain slopes were thought to provide evidence of the absolute veracity of the Genesis account.

Among the earliest and most perceptive of the pioneers in geological theory was the seventeenth-century scholar Robert Hooke. Like Leonardo da Vinci, Hooke was interested in all aspects of knowledge. Besides dabbling in painting, music, and architecture, Hooke worked seriously in chemistry and biology. His *Micrographia* (1665) suggested several promising lines of investigation in microbiology. He proposed a wave theory of light, discovered the fifth star in the constellation Orion, worked with Sir Isaac Newton in optics, originated a kinetic theory of gases, invented several scientific instruments, devised a

Fig. 2. A seventeenth-century reconstruction of a unicorn from bones found in Germany. The eighteenth-century philosopher Leibnitz and other scholars accepted the validity of this fanciful reconstruction. (From G. W. von Leibnitz, *Protogaea*, 1749.)

practical system of telegraphy, and was the first to use spiral springs to regulate watches. When he turned his attention to the study of fossils, Hooke perceived "that there have been Species of Creatures in former Ages, of which we can find none at present; and that 'tis not unlikely also but that there may be divers new kinds now, which have not been from the beginning."[3] He also noted that fossils consistently differed from one rock stratum to another. This fact led him to suggest that fossils could be used to formulate a chronology for the earth much longer than that suggested by Genesis.

Even more important than Hooke's geological observations were those published in Florence in 1669 by a young physician named Nicholas Steno. Like Hooke, Steno believed that fossils were the remains of once-living creatures. Also like Hooke, he noted that successive strata of sedimentary rock contained different types of fossils. More significant, however, was his demonstration that the flora and fauna represented

3. Richard Waller, ed., *The Posthumous Works of Robert Hooke* (London, 1705), p. 291.

in each layer of rock were types that could be expected to occur together in the same environment. Fossils of animal families inhabiting shallow coastal waters were found with those of plants growing in shallow water; remains of animals living in the depths of the sea occurred with fossils of deep-sea vegetation (if remains of vegetation were present at all).

Furthermore, the type of sedimentary rock in which each group of fossils was found tended to suggest the same environmental conditions as those suggested by the flora and fauna. Sandstone would have resulted from deposits near shore, shale from deposits in deeper water, and so on. Thus, the strata and their fossil contents suggested deposition by a natural process and could be used to show changes in the earth's climate and in the positions of the oceans in the distant past. Steno ascribed many of these changes in the earth's crust to natural causes, though he thought some were the result of the Flood described in Genesis. However, the time was not yet ripe for widespread public acceptance of Steno's geological principles.

Meanwhile, various discoveries suggested that humans had been contemporary with some of the extinct species of fossilized animals. But generally these finds were misinterpreted, explained away, or ignored. In 1690 John Conyers, a London apothecary, made the first such discovery of which we have a record. While digging for gravel near London, Conyers came upon several pieces of "fossil ivory" with a flint spearhead lying nearby. After an examination of the bones he concluded that they weren't those of a unicorn, but rather those of an elephant. How had an elephant gotten to England, he wondered? Were these the remains of beings that had lived before the Flood?

Scholars had not yet recognized the mammoth as an extinct species of elephant, so there seemed to be little reason to posit great antiquity for the bones or stone weapon. Conyers took the objects to his shop in London where one of his friends examined them. The man remembered that according to ancient Roman historians the Emperor Claudius had used elephants during his conquest of Britain in A.D. 43. He speculated that a heroic ancient Briton having no bronze or iron weapons had used a stone-tipped spear to kill one of the Romans' elephants. This explanation satisfied Conyers and the public. The bones and spearhead were stored away and forgotten.

Over three quarters of a century passed before another discovery again raised the question of human contact with extinct species. A priest named Johann Friedrich Esper spent much of his free time searching the caves near Bamberg, Germany, for proofs of the Deluge account in Genesis. In one cave he found a layer of clay containing bones of a large animal that Esper recognized as an extinct type of bear. In the same clay stratum near the remains of the cave bear he dug up an unquestionably human lower jawbone and shoulder blade. The priest carefully removed his finds and continued to examine the nearby caves making notes and drawings of all that he uncovered. Finally, he dug up a well-preserved human skull. In 1774 he published his discoveries, claiming that he had found the remains of humans who had lived before the Great Flood.

However, Esper did not conclude that the human remains were as old as the bones of the extinct cave bear. Genesis made no mention of the disappearance of many species as a result of the Flood. In fact, the biblical account stated that Noah saved representatives of all species so that no such extinctions would take place. Thus, the extinct creatures represented in the fossil record probably had been destroyed long before the time of Noah.

In the first half of the eighteenth century scholars had also discovered that the earth was hot at its center. This fact suggested that the earth had once been in a molten state and that its surface gradually had cooled and hardened. However, experiments showed that the amount of time needed for a body the size of the earth to cool to its present state was much longer than the roughly six thousand years allowed by biblical chronology. So, by the time Esper made his discovery, scholars were coming to recognize that the Genesis account of the world's early history was not complete.

In 1778 such considerations led French naturalist Georges Louis Leclerc, Compte de Buffon, to postulate a series of "epochs" in the earth's history, each lasting a considerable period of time. He reconciled this view with the Bible by arguing that the "days" of creation mentioned in Genesis were six time periods of unknown duration, not ordinary twenty-four-hour days. According to Buffon, fossils, coal, and other geological deposits had been formed in earlier "epochs," thousands of years before the creation of human beings. He insisted that the six thousand years of biblical chronology were valid for the history of mankind, the end of the creative process, but not for the world itself.

Other naturalists proposed similar ideas. One group, the Neptunists, agreed that there had been stages in the creation of the earth, but held that all geological formations had been precipitated out of a primeval briny sea. Another school of thought, known as catastrophism, argued that there had been cataclysms separating the various epochs in the earth's history. The lack of overlap of fossil species from one rock layer to another seemed to prove that total destructions separated the geological periods these strata represented. After each great catastrophe, these theorists argued, God recreated living beings similar to (but not identical with) those from the previous era. Present-day species, including human beings, belonged to the last of these creations, the one described in the Bible; fossils belonged to earlier ones. While these naturalists and geologists disagreed over the details of how the earth's features had been formed, they agreed that the Genesis account of the last stage of creation was essentially accurate. They also agreed that present-day species, especially humans, could not have been associated with any of the vanished forms of life exhibited in the rock strata.

Thus, when Esper's account of his discovery of human bones in the same layer as remains of extinct species began to circulate in scholarly circles it was surmised that humans must have buried their dead in the caves long after the bones of the extinct creatures had gotten stratified in the clay layer. Even Esper concluded that there was not sufficient reason to presume that the human and animal remains were of the same age; they must have come to lie together by chance. So, the significance of Esper's finds generally went unrecognized.

Opposing the ideas of Buffon, the Neptunists, and the catastrophists were a few scholars who accepted the principle of uniformitarianism. This doctrine stated, in the words of its founder, Scottish geologist James Hutton, "No processes are to be employed that are not natural to the globe; no action to be admitted except those of which we know the principle."[4] In his major work, Theory of the Earth (1788 and 1795), Hutton described the earth as a delicately balanced system in which some forces constantly destroyed the land surfaces while others were slowly building future continents. Rivers carried the sediments worn from land masses to large bodies of water and deposited them there. Eventually the deposits would be consolidated into strata of sandstone, limestone, shale, or other types of rock by the pressure of the water and the weight of other material above them and by heat from the core of the earth. The heat would gradually cause the rock strata to expand and the pressure from that expansion would uplift them until they rose above the surface of the waters to form new land masses.

It was known that there had been little change in the geography of Europe since classical times, so these operations must take exceedingly long periods of time to complete. "The result, therefore, of our present enquiry," concluded Hutton, "is that we find no vestige of a beginning—no prospect of an end."[5]

---

4. Quoted in Glyn Daniel, The Idea of Prehistory (New York: World, 1963), p. 44.

5. "Theory of the Earth; or an Investigation of the Laws Observable in the Composition, Dissolution, and Restoration of Land Upon the Globe," Transactions of the Royal Society of Edinburgh 1 (1788): p. 304. Hutton revised this work, added rejoinders to his critics, and republished it in two volumes in 1795.

Attacks were hurled against Hutton both by Neptunist and cata-strophist geologists and by theologians who classed Hutton's theory with the atheistic materialism of various Enlightenment philosophers. As the geologists tried to explain away the evidence Hutton had pre-sented to support his views, it became clear that their objections were not based primarily on scientific considerations but rather on religious ones. Richard Kirwan, president of the Royal Irish Academy and leader of the scientific opposition to Hutton, explained his long attack on *Theory of the Earth* by stating, "I have been led into this detail by observ-ing how fatal the suspicion of the high antiquity of the globe has been to the credit of the Mosaic history, and consequently to religion and morality."[6]

In vain did Hutton and his few supporters argue that his system did not deny the existence of God nor did it state that the world had no beginning. Hutton claimed only that the earth must have originated an extremely long time ago and had gone through so many changes that one could discover no mark of that beginning. He had simply ap-plied to study of the earth the same scientific assumptions and mechan-ical principles that Copernicus, Kepler, Galileo, Newton, and others had already incorporated into astronomy and physics. But while sci-entists had accepted mechanistic views to explain the operation of the rest of the universe, the areas of geology, biology, and human cultural development were still studied on the basis of miracles and biblical history.

Hutton's views were opposed, but at least they were read and dis-cussed. A different fate awaited a discovery made in England nine years later, in 1797. John Frere, a Fellow of the Royal Society, found many flint tools and weapons at Hoxne in Suffolk county. He wrote a letter to the Society of Antiquaries of London to announce the results of his excavations, stating that the flints were "evidently weapons of war, fabricated and used by a people who had not the use of metals."[7]

However, Frere realized that these artifacts were important because of the position in which he had discovered them. He had found them in a gravel deposit twelve feet from the surface and under three other clearly differentiated layers of soil. The sand layer immediately overlying this gravel deposit contained marine shells and bones of large extinct animals. Frere stated the conclusions to be drawn from these facts:

---

6. "Examination of the Supposed Igneous Origin of Stony Substances," *Transactions of the Royal Irish Academy* 5 (1793): p. 307.

7. "Account of Flint Weapons Discovered at Hoxne in Suffolk," *Archaeologia* 13 (1800): p. 204.

Fig. 3. Two of the stone hand axes found by John Frere. (From J. Frere, "Account of Flint Weapons Discovered at Hoxne in Suffolk," *Archaeologia* 13 (1800).)

The situation in which these weapons were found may tempt us to refer them to a very remote period indeed; even beyond that of the present world; but, whatever our conjectures on that head may be, it will be difficult to account for the stratum in which they lie being covered with another stratum, which, on that supposition, may be conjectured to have been once the bottom, or at least the shore, of the sea. The manner in which they lie would lead to the persuasion that it was a place of their manufacture and not of their accidental deposit; and the numbers of them were so great that the man who carried on the brick-work told me that, before he was aware of their being objects of curiosity, he had emptied baskets full of them into the ruts of the adjoining road.[8]

Frere realized that his conclusions contradicted the prevailing theories. So he met in advance the charge of "accidental association" that he knew would be used to explain away his finds. He carefully pointed out that the flints could not have been washed into their present position

---

8. "Account of Flint Weapons," pp. 204–5.

and then covered by earlier material eroded from higher ground. The strata he had found were *higher* than the surrounding terrain and were themselves being washed away by erosion. Furthermore, the earth strata were horizontal, ending abruptly at the place where the high ground sloped down to the surrounding bog. If the weapons and fossils had been eroded from another area and carried to the spot where Frere found them, they would have been deposited on the slopes of the hill in an uneven pattern and not in the successive horizontal layers he had observed. There seemed to be no way to avoid the conclusion that people had existed before or during the time that some types of extinct creatures had flourished.

Current geological theory and a six-thousand-year history for mankind could not explain the materials he had uncovered. As he had stated, they must have belonged "to a very remote period indeed, *even beyond that of the present world*" (that is, the world known from Genesis). Frere's letter appeared in 1800 in *Archaeologia*, the journal of the Society of Antiquaries, but the response he expected never came. His conclusions were not attacked or explained away. They were simply ignored.

RESOLUTION OF THE CONFLICT

The validity of uniformitarianism, evolution of species, and the extremely long prehistory of the human race was not generally recognized by scholars until the third quarter of the nineteenth century. That victory for these ideas did not come sooner was largely because of the vast influence of one man, the great French natural scientist Georges Cuvier. Cuvier's lectures and writings brought catastrophist geological theory to its zenith both in popularity and in the scope and persuasiveness of the evidence presented to support it. His ideas dominated thought in biology and geology during his lifetime and for more than a decade after his death in 1832.

Based on his study of comparative anatomy, early in his career Cuvier formulated his "Law of Correlation," which stated that when one organ of an animal develops along certain lines, a corresponding development will be noted in its other organs. For example, hoofed animals will always have teeth suitable for eating vegetation while beasts with the interlocking teeth and fangs of carnivores will possess claws as well. Cuvier insisted that so detailed was this correlation that he could usually reconstruct the form of an entire animal from only one or two bones.

The well-known story of his encounter with the "devil" illustrates his commitment to the absolute validity of this law. Some of Cuvier's students decided to play a prank on their normally imperturbable professor. One night one of them dressed in a devil outfit complete with horns and shoes resembling cloven hooves. The others waited outside Cuvier's window to enjoy his discomfiture when this apparition burst upon him. Into the room rushed the devil roaring, "Wake up, thou man of catastrophes! I am the Devil. I have come to devour you!" Cuvier opened his eyes, glanced at the intruder, then calmly replied, "I doubt whether you can. You've got horns and hoofs. According to the Law of Correlation you only eat plants."[9] Upon hearing this, the students outside who had come to laugh at their professor instead burst into admiring applause.

To previous statements of catastrophism, Cuvier brought his thorough knowledge of fossil remains, which has earned him the title, "founder of vertebrate paleontology." Cuvier noted that there was only a small amount of variation between individuals within given species (either living or fossil). Because of this fact he could see no means by which one species might gradually change into another. He, therefore, affirmed that species were immutable, and steadfastly opposed hypotheses (such as that of his contemporary Lamarck) that suggested an evolution of present forms of life from extinct species found in the fossil record.

Cuvier found additional support for his views in the work of an Englishman, William Smith, who in 1816 published a table of thirty-two strata, each containing different fossils. The lack of overlap of species from one stratum to another, Cuvier argued, proved that the geological periods represented by these layers of rock had been separated by total destructions and that life had been created anew after each great catastrophe. The fact that fossil life, like living species, had been subject to the Law of Correlation seemed to suggest that an intelligent Creator, following laws which he himself had laid down, had recreated life along similar lines several times in the past. Like Buffon, Cuvier claimed that Mosaic chronology and history were correct, but that they applied only to the present geological period in which presently existing species, including humans, had appeared. Cuvier confidently asserted that human fossils did not—could not—exist!

So firmly established was Cuvier's reputation as a paleontologist and so obviously valid was his Law of Correlation that many scholars came to regard all of Cuvier's conclusions as unquestionably correct. But the evidence stubbornly refused to conform to catastrophist

---

9. Herbert Wendt, *In Search of Adam* (Boston: Houghton Mifflin, 1956), p. 149.

Map 1. Early discoveries in European prehistory.

doctrines. In 1828–29 M. Tournal, the curator of the Narbonne Museum, announced that in a cave in France he had found human bones and pottery with the remains of vanished species. Furthermore, some of the bones of the extinct animals even bore the marks of cutting tools. At about the same time other scholars made similar discoveries in Austria and in other southern French caves.

The most significant such finds, however, were made in Belgium by a physician named P. C. Schmerling and in England by a Roman Catholic priest named J. MacEnery. Dr. Schmerling investigated several caves near Liège. In one of them under a stalagmite crust he uncovered seven human skulls, other assorted human bones, and flint implements.

Furthermore, he found these human remains lying with the skeletal remains of cave bears, mammoths, and rhinoceroses.

Father MacEnery's excavations in Kent's Cavern, Torquay, from 1824 to 1829, produced almost identical evidence. Under an unbroken floor of stalagmite was a layer of soil containing flint implements along with remains of extinct animals. In both instances, the stalagmite covering above the remains seemed to provide irrefutable evidence for the great antiquity of the finds. It also precluded the possibility that recent human material had been accidentally mixed with ancient animal remains.

However, most scholars ignored Schmerling's publication for a quarter of a century, while MacEnery decided against publishing his results at all. MacEnery had written about his discovery to William Buckland, the leading geologist in England and a strong supporter of Cuvier's catastrophism. Buckland informed the priest that ancient Britons must have dug ovens in the stalagmite floor of the cave, allowing some of their tools to fall through those holes and become mixed with the antediluvian skeletons of extinct species. MacEnery had found no such holes in the cave floor. But what was the word of an amateur explorer against that of a professor of geology at Oxford? He continued to dig in Kent's cavern until his death in 1841, but his manuscript remained unknown and unpublished until after other discoveries proved the antiquity of human beings.

The turning point in the battle against catastrophist and Neptunist geology came with the publication of Charles Lyell's three-volume work, *Principles of Geology, Being an Attempt to Explain the Former Changes of the Earth's Surface by Reference to Causes Now in Action* (1830–33). This work supported uniformitarianism and provided such a wealth of geological data to illustrate that principle that even its most unyielding opponents were impressed.

Lyell pointed out that geologists had failed to note gaps in the succession of strata and to appreciate the duration of past time. This failure had led them to misinterpret the breaks between strata as evidence for global cataclysms and violent convulsions. If the events of thousands of years of human history were compressed into the span of a few centuries, the appearance would also be one of constant and unnatural change and revolution rather than of slow and gradual development. Once one accepts the immensity of geological time, Lyell argued, there is no need to postulate supernatural catastrophes to explain the shaping of the earth's features. Given millions of years in which to operate, the agencies of wind, water, ice, and volcanism were sufficient to produce even the most dramatic alterations of the earth's surface. Of course, Lyell's arguments did not convince everyone. But they did force most geologists to reevaluate their positions, and they had a strong influence on the generation of young scientists (including Charles Darwin) who in the early 1830s were completing their education or just beginning their careers.

One aspect of the geology of Europe that seemed to support the views of the catastrophists was the occurrence of huge boulders or piles of smaller stones on the plains, miles away from the nearest mountains. How had such stones gotten there if not by the agency of some tremendous upheaval, such as a cataclysmic volcanic eruption or a universal Deluge? Soon after the appearance of *Principles of Geology* the question was answered by Swiss professor Louis Agassiz, who led a team of men into the Alps to study glaciers. Through his investigations, Agassiz was able to show that ice sheets had carried the erratic boulders found on European plains. He also proved that the advance and retreat of one or more great glaciers had produced many other features of the European landscape. Geological features formerly attributed to the Flood were now seen to be products of an Ice Age that must have lasted for a very long time.

The opposition to evidence of the existence of human fossils now began to wane. In 1837 Jacques Boucher de Crèvecoeur de Perthes, a French customs official, started excavating in the gravel deposits of the Somme Valley near Abbeville. Like several explorers before him, he found flint tools and weapons side by side with the remains of extinct Ice Age creatures like mammoths, cave bears, woolly rhinoceroses, and bison. But this time scholars did not ignore the finds, and attempts to explain them away failed. Some opponents of Boucher de Perthes's claims went to France to examine the evidence for themselves or undertook their own excavations to prove him wrong. One by one they accepted the view that humans had been coeval with extinct animals of the Ice Age.

In 1859, two eminent British scholars, Joseph Prestwich and John Evans, were sent to examine and evaluate Boucher de Perthes's discoveries. After seeing the excavations for themselves, they returned to England and presented papers at meetings of the Royal Society and the Society of Antiquaries. In these reports, Prestwich and Evans stated their conviction of humanity's antiquity.

The year 1859 turned out to be decisive in the long conflict over the validity of Mosaic chronology and the biblical view of mankind's early history. It was the year in which Prestwich and Evans publicly accepted the finds of Boucher de Perthes. It was also the year in which William Pengelly substantiated the previous discoveries of Frere, Tournal, Schmerling, and MacEnery. Pengelly had excavated at Kent's Cavern in 1846, confirming the evidence found by MacEnery. But Buckland's suggestion that weapons of Britons had gotten mixed with earlier animal remains caused doubts to linger in many minds.

Virtually all doubt about human contemporaneity with vanished species was dispelled, however, by the evidence Pengelly obtained in 1858–59 from his excavations in Windmill Hill Cave overlooking Brixham Harbour, a coastal site about 165 miles southwest of London. Quarrying operations had accidentally uncovered this cave, and human occupants could not have used it since the Ice Age. From the beginning of the investigation a committee of prestigious members of the Royal and Geological Societies oversaw the work and could vouch for the accuracy of Pengelly's observations. Pengelly found the cave floor covered with a sheet of stalagmite from three to eight inches thick. Sealed within and just below this stalagmite floor he uncovered remains of lions, hyenas, bears, mammoths, rhinoceroses, and reindeer. In the layer of earth beneath the stalagmite, he found flint tools lying with the bones of Ice Age fauna. The antiquity of humans had finally been established beyond reasonable doubt.

Charles Darwin's *Origin of Species by Means of Natural Selection, or the Preservation of Favored Races in the Struggle for Life* also appeared in 1859. Lyell's arguments had strongly influenced Darwin and had removed one stumbling block encountered by earlier proponents of evolution, the short history of life on earth. If one accepted uniformitarian geological principles, then fossil remains in rock strata would suggest that life had existed on earth for a very long time—long enough to allow the slow development and modification of species to take place as assumed in evolutionary theories. Darwin cited a wealth of evidence from comparative anatomy studies and the fossil record to support the evolutionary hypothesis. But his major contribution to the theory was his presentation of a likely method by which evolution might occur. His description of the way "natural selection" and the "struggle for existence" determined which species or which individuals within a species would survive was extremely persuasive. Of course, many people, particularly some theologians and clergymen, objected to the theory of evolution because it eliminated the biblical concept of the special creation of living things. Nevertheless, in a short time the Darwinian hypothesis became the accepted view of most scientists and educated laymen.

Meanwhile, the first remains of Stone Age man had been found. In 1857 workmen digging in a cave in the Neanderthal Valley near Düsseldorf, Germany, found a human skullcap with prominently projecting browridges and a low, sloping forehead. A few supporters of evolution and the antiquity of man immediately recognized the find as genuine. Other scholars, however, argued that it was the congenitally deformed skull of an idiot, or that it belonged to an Irishman or a Cossack. But as acceptance of Darwin's ideas about evolution and natural selection grew, so did willingness to believe in the existence of humans with features more primitive than ours. Finally, when two more Neanderthal-like skeletons were found in 1887 in an Ice Age deposit in Belgium, almost all scholars were forced to accept the authenticity of Neanderthal man.

Within thirty years after 1859 the great antiquity of human beings, uniformitarian geology, and the evolution of species were all so widely accepted that their validity could be assumed in popular books on early man. Also, Neanderthal man and Cro-Magnon man (first found in 1868) had become recognized as our ancestors. The study of the past had at last been freed from the confinement of Mosaic chronology and a literal acceptance of the accounts in Genesis. Thus, the year 1859 marks a major turning point in the development of anthropology and archaeology. A new scholarly discipline, prehistoric archaeology, was born.

THE THREE AGES

While the battle over the antiquity of man was still raging, northern European scholars were showing that technological differences exhibited by human artifacts also had chronological significance. Much earlier Eckart had proposed that humans had passed successively through a series of technological stages, each more advanced than the preceding one. However, this idea wasn't taken seriously until a young man named Christian Jurgensen Thomsen applied it to Denmark's antiquities. Thomsen became the first curator of Denmark's newly created National Museum of Antiquities in 1816. Facing him was the task of organizing, labeling, and cataloging the royal collection, which at that time contained over one thousand pieces. When the museum opened three years later, visitors discovered that Thomsen had not followed the conventional practice of grouping artifacts primarily by their function or shape. Instead, he had grouped objects by the material of which they were made, producing three major classifications, stone, bronze, and iron. Within these groups, objects were subclassified in the familiar way by function and form.

Thomsen published a guidebook to the Danish museum in 1836. This work explained that his arrangement was not simply a convenient system for classifying museum collections, but represented three historical periods or technological stages through which early man had progressed. Thomsen's Three Age system began to attract the attention of antiquaries and museum curators in other areas of Europe, and soon museums in Sweden and Germany were using it. While it is possible that scholars in those countries independently developed the Three Age concept, it was not until Thomsen applied it to his museum collection and persuasively related

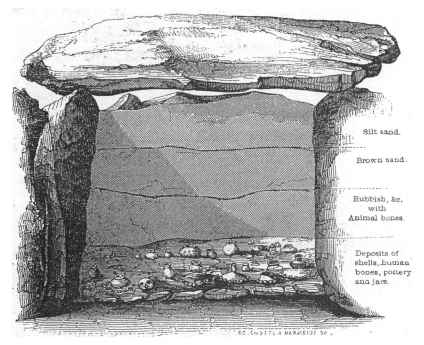

Silt sand.

Brown sand.

Rubbish, &c.
with
Animal bones.

Deposits of
shells, human
bones, pottery
and jars.

Fig. 4. Cross-section of an Iron Age tomb on Guernsey showing its stratigraphy. (From J. J. Worsaae, *The Primeval Antiquities of Denmark*, 1849.)

Danish artifacts to stages of cultural development that the idea of a Stone, a Bronze, and an Iron Age received significant support.

Jens Worsaae, a student of Thomsen, soon showed the usefulness of the Three Age concept for understanding the relationship between primeval monuments and the history of a given area. In an 1840 article on Danish burial mounds, Worsaae distinguished the types of mounds and burial practices characteristic of each period, producing for the first time a relative chronology for these prehistoric barrows. After two more years of excavation and study, the young scholar published one of the most important books in the history of archaeology, *Danmarks Oldtid* (1842). This work was translated into English as *The Primeval Antiquities of Denmark* (1849). It gave a convincing account of the evidence for the Three Age system and related all the then-known Danish antiquities to either the Stone, Bronze, or Iron Age.

The Primeval Antiquities of Denmark also showed how careful study of archaeological discoveries could produce information on prehistoric population movements.

In the stone-period and in that of bronze the funeral ceremonies and barrows were completely different; and we are therefore justified in concluding that the race who inhabited Denmark in the bronze-period was different from that, which during that of stone, laid the foundation for peopling the country. This is clearly shown by the antiquities, since there exists no gradual transition from the simple implements and weapons of stone, the beautifully wrought tools and arms of bronze.[10]

Worsaae also stressed the importance of careful excavation and record-keeping, becoming one of the first to state the importance of noting stratigraphy and the position of finds (Fig. 4). "Antiquities have a value with reference to the spot in which they are found," he stated.[11] In another place he remarked that it is "indispensably necessary to examine and compare with care the places in which antiquities are usually found; otherwise many most important collateral points can either not be explained at all, or at least in a very unsatisfactory manner."[12]

Perhaps Worsaae's greatest contribution to the development of archaeology was his recognition that the primary purpose of excavation should be to produce information on man's history and cultural development, rather than to gather specimens for museums or private collections. At a time when classical and Near Eastern monuments and antiquities were being plundered for the benefit of European and American collections, and more than fifty years before careful methodology would become common in excavations of European prehistoric sites, Worsaae declared,

A very important rule is, that all antiquities, even those which appear the most trivial and the most common, ought to be preserved. Trifles often afford important information, when seen in connection with a large collection. That they are of common occurrence forms no objection; for historic results can be deduced only from the comparison of numerous contemporary specimens.[13]

Worsaae traveled throughout western Europe studying prehistoric remains and museum collections, and at every opportunity he explained and defended Thomsen's Three Age concept. Soon, in excavations in the Danish bogs and in the newly discovered prehistoric stilt-villages in the lakes of Switzerland, stone tools were found beneath strata

10. J. A. Worsaae, The Primeval Antiquities of Denmark, trans. William J. Thoms (London: John Henry Parker, 1849), p. 126.

11. Ibid., p. 156.

12. Ibid., p. 76.

13. Ibid., p. 156.

containing artifacts of bronze or iron, providing stratigraphical proof of the Three Ages. By the middle of the 1860s the Three Age system had become widely accepted throughout Europe. Scholars then combined it with the concepts of evolution and the great antiquity of human beings to produce a clearer understanding of mankind's long journey from savagery to civilization.

As prehistorians began to compare the materials found in various parts of Europe it became clear that the ground and polished stone implements in the Scandinavian collections were quite different from the chipped stones found in France by Boucher de Perthes and in England by Frere, MacEnery, and Pengelly. This required the division of the Stone Age into two parts. John Lubbock in his *Prehistoric Times* (1865) named these eras the Paleolithic ("Old Stone") and Neolithic ("New Stone") periods. Specialists would gradually recognize subdivisions within each of these periods as well as within the Bronze and Iron Ages as they developed a more detailed picture of the movements and cultural history of pre-Roman groups in Europe. After a very long childhood, prehistoric archaeology now rapidly began to mature.

Phase II: European Prehistoric Archaeology Comes of Age (1860-1920)

RECOGNITION OF ICE AGE ART

If there were any lingering doubts about early man's association with now-vanished Ice Age beasts, they should have been finally dispelled in the early 1860s. In France Eduard Lartet discovered bones engraved with animal likenesses, the most dramatic being a piece of mammoth tusk containing a portrait of the hairy mammoth itself. These finds revealed that early humans had possessed considerable artistic talent.

However, as acceptance of the doctrine of evolution spread, many had come to conceive of Stone Age people, especially the Neanderthal variety, as ape-like, primitive brutes only slightly more intelligent than their simian relatives. It seemed difficult to fit the idea of Ice Age artists into the picture of human development then current. So some authorities flatly denied the possibility that Stone Age people had produced the carvings. Others accepted the authenticity of the engraved pieces of bone only with strong reservations.

Scholars were still debating the issue when, on a spring day in 1879, Don Marcelino de Sautuola and his twelve-year-old daughter

Maria set out to further explore a cave. For weeks the Spanish nobleman had been conducting excavations in the cave located on the de Sautuola estate at Altamira. He had found bones of bison, wild horses, a giant stag, and a cave bear along with flint and bone tools and mollusk shells with what seemed to be black and red pigment encrusted on their inside surfaces. While the amateur archaeologist renewed his digging in a side chamber of the cave, Maria wandered about, exploring the entire area illuminated by her father's lamp. Suddenly Don Marcelino's work was interrupted by a shout. "Papa, Papa, look! Colored bulls!"[14] Gazing upward in the direction his excited daughter was pointing, Don Marcelino was startled to see that beautiful paintings of great horned bison covered the roof of the chamber in which he had been working. In all the time he had spent exploring the cave, he had never before looked at its ceiling. Now, as he and his daughter examined the chamber's walls and roof more carefully, they discovered other paintings as wonderful as those Maria had first noticed. There was a charging wild boar, a large doe, a wild horse, and more bison—standing, running, crouching, dying.

Don Marcelino immediately reported his find to Vilanova y Piera, professor of paleontology at Madrid. After inspecting the cave and carefully questioning its excavator, Vilanova declared the paintings genuine. Vilanova's opinion was not enough, however, to stop the outcry of disbelief and ridicule that greeted the public announcement of the discovery. When they learned that Don Marcelino had befriended a penniless French painter a short time before discovering the cave paintings, many scholars accused the nobleman of perpetrating a clumsy hoax. Others of a more generous nature were willing to believe that Don Marcelino and Vilanova had been innocent dupes who had been taken in by the real engineer of the fraud. Even those prehistorians who had given unqualified acceptance to the previously discovered small engravings balked at crediting Upper Paleolithic inhabitants with the amount of artistic proficiency suggested by the Altamira paintings.

Don Marcelino's honor and Vilanova's judgment were not vindicated until 1895, when engravings were discovered on the walls of a cave at La Mouthe, France. Paleolithic and Neolithic deposits completely blocked the entrance to this cave, so no one could have entered it since the latter part of the Old Stone Age. Two years later excavators found paintings and engravings in another French cave at Pair-non-Pair. The discoverers noted that at several places in this cave Stone Age deposits

---

14. Geoffrey Bibby, *The Testimony of the Spade* (New York: Alfred A. Knopf, 1956), p. 59.

that had accumulated on the cavern's floor covered the lower portions of the animal representations. This circumstance proved the Upper Paleolithic date of the art. Unfortunately, these discoveries came too late to be enjoyed by the men who had been maligned. Don Marcelino had died at the age of fifty-seven in 1888, followed by Vilanova in 1892.

Emile Cartailhac, professor of prehistory at the University of Toulouse and president of the Prehistoric Society of France, had been the most adamant opponent of the authenticity of Paleolithic cave art. But even he was convinced when cave paintings continued to be found at various French and Spanish sites. In 1902 he published a public confession of his longstanding error. Furthermore, he paid a visit to Don Marcelino's now married daughter, Maria, to apologize personally for the wrong he had done her father.

STRATIGRAPHIC EXCAVATION AND IMPROVED DATING TECHNIQUES

The last decades of the nineteenth and first decades of the twentieth centuries also saw major advances in techniques of excavation and in methods of dating prehistoric finds. Between 1880 and 1900, a retired British general named Augustus Henry Lane-Fox Pitt Rivers developed the principles of modern archaeological excavation, recording, and publication. Pitt Rivers had become interested in the development of firearms while still in the army. This interest led him to amass a huge collection of weapons, which he arranged in typological sequences. Upon his retirement from the military in 1880 he shifted his antiquarian interests to the excavation of some prehistoric barrows and earthworks on his estate. In these digs he put into practice the principles he later stressed in his publications.

> Excavators, as a rule, record only those things which appear to them important at the time, but fresh problems in Archaeology and Anthropology are constantly arising, and it can hardly fail to have escaped the notice of anthropologists, especially those who, like myself, have been concerned with the morphology of art, that, on turning back to old accounts in search of evidence, the points which would have been most valuable have been passed over from being thought uninteresting at the time. *Every detail should, therefore, be recorded in the manner most conducive to facility of reference, and it ought at all times to be the chief object of the excavator to reduce his own personal equation to a minimum.*[15]

---

15. *Excavations in Cranborne Chase*, vol. 1 (privately published, 1887), p. xvii (emphasis added).

Pitt Rivers recognized the chronological value that seemingly worthless objects such as pottery sherds could have if their stratigraphical positions were accurately recorded. He insisted on careful, methodical excavation of entire sites instead of the grave robbing and tunneling which at that time often passed for archaeological excavation. He meticulously recorded all finds, and the publications of his results were models of archaeological reporting. Along with descriptions of his excavations he published drawings and lists of every object found, plans, and sections. He carefully cataloged the objects and exhibited them in a museum at Farnham with wooden models illustrating various stages in the excavation of each site. The achievement of Pitt Rivers is perhaps best summed up in the words of Glyn Daniel: "In fifteen years he transformed excavation from the pleasant hobby of barrow digging to an arduous scientific pursuit."[16]

While Pitt Rivers was improving excavation methods, others were developing better ways to date prehistoric remains. Using the Three Age hypothesis, Thomsen, Worsaae, and others had worked out a relative chronology that could be applied to most antiquities within a given area. However, scholars recognized that the use of bronze and iron had come to different parts of Europe at different times. While one could say that Bronze Age barrows in Denmark were later than Stone Age mounds in the same area, no one could determine whether Danish Bronze Age remains were earlier than, later than, or contemporaneous with Bronze Age materials in Britain, France, or other parts of Europe.

This situation was transformed by the research of the Swedish archaeologist Gustav Oscar Montelius. By 1890 Montelius had linked together the local relative chronological schemes of various parts of Europe into a single complete system. Furthermore, by 1910 he managed to establish absolute dates for European Bronze and Iron Age cultures.

Montelius achieved these impressive results through the introduction of typological sequence dating into European prehistoric archaeology. This method required first a careful study of all finds from a given area. Then Montelius made lists noting objects that always occurred together and others never found together. From this study he would gradually discern several groups of contemporaneous objects, each group characteristic of a particular period. Next, Montelius studied a class of objects such as swords or axes, comparing the form of these objects from one group to another. Usually he could spot similarities between objects in different groups and arrange these objects into a

---

16. *A Hundred Years of Archaeology* (London: Duckworth, 1950), p. 173.

1

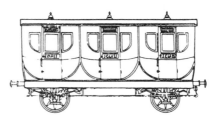

3

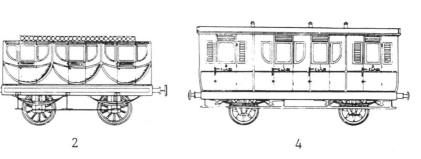

2   4

Fig. 5. The evolution of the railroad coach as an example of a typological series. Montelius used the development of the railroad coach to illustrate a typological series. The 1825 coach (1) looks like a contemporary horse-drawn carriage. The railroad cars of succeeding decades (2-4) change and develop, but retain vestigial features of the carriage, even though these elements have no practical function. (After O. Montelius, *Die älteren Kultur-perioden im Orient und in Europa,* 1903. The numbers were added.)

sequence in which the change from one group to another was gradual, even though the objects at either end of the sequence might have little resemblance to one another (Fig. 5). In order to determine which end of the sequence was the beginning and which the end, Montelius looked for evidence of technological advances or signs of vestigial features that had once served a useful function before degenerating into merely decorative elements. Once he had worked out several such typological sequences of individual objects and determined that the sequences were consistent with one another, then he could place the larger groups into sequential order. In this way he provided a relative chronology for the various cultures in a given area.

Trade items and mixtures of artifacts in border areas between cultures showed which artifact groups were contemporaneous with one another. This information allowed Montelius to connect the relative chronologies of two or more different areas. Such evidence also gave him the key he needed to determine absolute dates for the European

Bronze and Iron Age sequences. In the two decades between 1885 and 1905 archaeologists working in Greece and Egypt found many objects that evidenced Bronze Age trade between the two areas. Thus scholars were able to tie the Greek Bronze Age to the Egyptian absolute chronology, which was based on hieroglyphic inscriptions and ancient astronomical observations. Montelius was then able to use connections between the Greek material and assemblages in other parts of Europe to date European Bronze and Iron Age remains in absolute as well as relative terms.

During the early decades of the twentieth century another Swedish scholar, Baron Louis Gerhard de Geer, developed a method for dating past glacial movements. De Geer noticed that many clayey deposits were composed of many thin layers of soil. He discovered that these silt layers (called varves) were annual deposits caused by seasonal glacial melt waters flowing into quiet lakes or ponds. De Geer was able to relate various sequences of varves to one another and finally to a datable historical event. The chronology he created suggested that the last Ice Age ended about nine thousand years ago. Thus, artifacts found with remains of Ice Age animals had to be older. Varve chronology also provided the means for dating some of the Neolithic deposits in northern Europe.

Of course, over the years scholars have continued to improve these early chronological systems. The use of pollen analysis has allowed scholars to relate varve chronology to more archaeological deposits than had first been possible. Moreover, the development of dating systems based on the decay of radioactive material has provided absolute dates for much of the Stone Age as well as Bronze and Iron Age cultures. Nevertheless, the changes made in European archaeological chronology in recent years are minor compared to the great revolution in the scholarly understanding of prehistoric chronology wrought by Montelius, de Geer, and their colleagues in the late nineteenth and early twentieth centuries.

By the outbreak of World War I scholars had at last come to grips with the depth of mankind's past. Furthermore, with the development of methods for correctly recovering and interpreting that past, European prehistoric archaeology had become a mature discipline. The age of the amateur digger had ended, and the day of the professional prehistorian had begun.

2

Retrieving Egypt's Distant Past

Phase I: Exploration, Antiquarianism, and Early Excavation (1530–1858)

THE DAWN OF EGYPTOLOGY

The glory of ancient Egypt was never completely forgotten, for it was reflected often in the Bible and in the writings of classical Greek and Roman authors. However, detailed knowledge of the Egyptian past was lost after the late fourth century A.D. when Christian emperors made Christianity the only legal religion in the Roman Empire. The triumphant Christians closed (and often destroyed) the ancient temples, forbade the old religious rites, and banned the use of the traditional hieroglyphic writing. The monuments that once had teemed with life and activity were abandoned. They slowly crumbled from neglect, were covered by drifting sand, or disappeared entirely when their suitability as sources for building stone was recognized.

As the Renaissance revived Western Europe's interest in antiquity, a small stream of European travelers began to make their way to the Nile valley. They returned with descriptions of the magnificent monuments and other antiquities they had seen. Among the most notable of these early visitors were the Frenchmen Pierre Belon (1533) and Jean Palmerme (latter half of the sixteenth century), the German Johannes Helferich (1579), the Englishmen George Sandys (1610), John

Fig. 6. An Arab *dahabiyeh* on the Nile. Early European visitors to Egypt usually hired such a vessel in Alexandria to take them upstream to Cairo and the Giza pyramids. Only a handful of pre-nineteenth-century travelers continued on upstream to Thebes or Aswan. (From Samuel Manning, *The Land of the Pharaohs*, 1876.)

Greaves (1638), and the Rev. Richard Pococke (1737–38), and the Dane Frederick Norden (1738). But even the accounts of such travelers added little to what was already known. Unstable political conditions made travel to the southern portions of Egypt difficult and often dangerous. So, Pococke and Norden were among the very few visitors who went up the Nile as far as the first cataract. Furthermore, many travelers only stopped briefly in Egypt on their way to other parts of the Near East. As a result, most of the travel accounts published in Europe concentrated on the remains in the area of Cairo. As one might expect, they most often described the pyramids and Great Sphinx of Giza, long known from classical writings. By the end of the eighteenth century what little was known of ancient Egyptian history and civilization was still based on the accounts of ancient Greek and Roman authors supplemented by a few generally inaccurate drawings, measurements, descriptions, and inferences of European tourists of the sixteenth through eighteenth centuries.

This situation changed dramatically in 1798 when the French general Napoleon Bonaparte embarked on the conquest of Egypt. France was at that time at war with Great Britain. Presumably, Napoleon hoped to establish a base in the Near East from which he could eventually disrupt British trade with India and the East. However, besides being an excellent general, Napoleon was an enlightened individual who was aware of how little European scholars knew about Egypt, Palestine, and other lands that were then part of the Ottoman Turkish empire. So, besides his thirty-five thousand troops he took with him a Commission of Arts and Science consisting of 175 French astronomers, geographers, cartographers, architects, engineers, chemists, naturalists, physicians, orientalists, artists, and historians. While Napoleon's army was bringing Egypt and Palestine under French control, the members of this commission engaged in scholarly research. They surveyed and drew ancient monuments, produced the first modern topographical maps of the Nile Valley and the Levant, and studied the natural history, minerals, irrigation, and peoples of Egypt.

"Soldiers, forty centuries are looking down on you!" Napoleon reminded his troops before leading them into battle within sight of the massive pyramids of Giza.[1] With such inspiration, brilliant leadership, and modern weapons, the French had little trouble defeating the Mamluk forces that opposed them in Egypt. However, on August 1, 1798, a British naval squadron under the command of Admiral Horatio Nelson arrived off the Egyptian coast near Alexandria. In the Battle of the Nile it destroyed the French fleet that had brought Napoleon's forces to the Near East. Furthermore, when Napoleon moved through Palestine to besiege the coastal Turkish stronghold at Acre, the guns of British ships anchored just offshore helped break the French attacks. His dreams of Near Eastern conquest shattered, in August of 1799 Napoleon fled back to France. He left behind his soldiers and the members of the Commission of Arts and Science to fend for themselves.

It was while making preparations in 1799 to ward off British and Turkish attacks that the French made one of the most important discoveries in the history of archaeology. Pierre Bouchard (or Boussard), an officer of the engineers, was supervising the reconstruction of part of a decaying Arab fortification near Rosetta, about forty miles east of Alexandria. His crew was demolishing a wall when they came across a strange irregular-shaped stone. Three bands of different types of writing covered the slab of polished black basalt. Obviously the stone had been part of an ancient monument and had been reused as building material during an earlier repair of the fort. Bouchard recognized

---

1. *Correspondance de Napoléon Ier, publiée par ordre de l'Empereur Napoléon III,* vol. 4 (Paris: Plon et Dumaine, 1858–70), p. 240.

that one of the inscriptions was in the unreadable ancient Egyptian hieroglyphic characters. But he also saw that the bottom one was in Greek. He realized the importance that such a bilingual inscription might have in the study of the ancient Egyptian script. So Bouchard rescued the stone and had it delivered to the French scholars in Cairo. As fate would have it, this accidental discovery proved to be more significant than hundreds of hours of systematic, scholarly exploration and research.

The French forces in Egypt finally surrendered to the British in 1801. Under the terms of the Treaty of Capitulation all the collections, notes, and drawings of the Commission of Arts and Science were to go to England. But the British commander, General Hutchinson, backed down somewhat when the French scholars strongly protested and threatened to destroy the fruit of their labor rather than permit it to be stolen by the British. Hutchinson finally agreed to allow the French savants to keep their notes, drawings and collections of plants, animals, and minerals. But he refused to yield in his demand that all antiquities, including the Rosetta Stone, be surrendered to England. The French were keeping the stone in the house of General Menou in hopes that it could be passed off as his personal property. However, Hutchinson would have none of their argument. He sent a detachment of artillerymen with a cannon to take possession of the stone. The French grudgingly accepted the revised terms of the treaty. The surviving members of the commission and of Napoleon's army returned to France while the Rosetta Stone went to the British Museum, where it has remained one of the most treasured exhibits.

The educated public did not have to wait very long to learn what the French discovered in Egypt. The first information came from Dominique Vivant, Baron de Denon, an artist who had been a member of the commission. In 1802 Denon published *Voyage dans la Haute et la Basse Egypte* (translated into English later in 1802 as *Travels in Upper and Lower Egypt*). He used his detailed drawings to illustrate the two-volume account of his experiences with Napoleon's expedition. (A short time later Napoleon appointed Denon director-general of museums in France, a position he held from 1804 to 1815.) The official account of the commission's researches, the voluminously illustrated, twenty-one volume *Description de l'Egypte,* took a bit longer to prepare. It appeared between 1809 and 1828.

These works revealed for the first time to startled Europeans the monuments of ancient Egypt from the delta to the first cataract of the Nile. Interest in Egyptian antiquities began to rival that shown toward the remains of classical Greece and Rome. Though the French expedition

Fig. 7. Denon's drawing of a temple at Hermopolis. (From V. Denon, *Voyage dans la Haute et la Basse Egypte*, 1802.)

Fig. 8. A portion of the Temple of Karnak at Thebes. (Detail of a drawing in *Description de l'Egypte*, vol. 3, 2nd ed., 1823.)

to Egypt had been a military failure, Napoleon's foresight in taking along the Commission of Arts and Science had laid the foundations for the development of Egyptology.

THE SCRAMBLE FOR ANTIQUITIES

By the time the publication of *Description de l'Egypte* was complete in 1828, several of the monuments described and illustrated in it had disappeared. Some were broken up and burned for lime by the *fellahin,* the peasant farmers of Egypt. The Egyptian government demolished a well-preserved temple at Armant to make way for a sugar refinery (Fig. 9). Other monuments suffered because of the interest Europeans had shown in them. Many of the *fellahin* could not understand why anyone would go to the trouble of measuring, drawing, and clearing sand out of old buildings if not to find hidden treasure. Any wealth hidden in these ancient ruins, they reasoned, rightfully belonged to the followers of the Prophet who lived nearby, not to infidels from across the sea. The natives' treasure hunts produced none of the valuables they sought. But they did result in damage and destruction of remains that would have been priceless to later archaeologists and historians. Furthermore, since Western governments and individuals had begun to pay well for antiquities, other Egyptians devoted full time to robbing tombs and temples of all portable objects, little caring about the havoc they wreaked on immovable remains.

Europeans also participated directly in this pillaging of Egyptian antiquities. Mohammed Ali, who in 1806 became pasha of Egypt under the nominal authority of the sultan of Turkey, recognized the superiority of Western arms and decided to introduce European technology into Egypt. Realizing that his plans required the goodwill of the major powers as well as Western know-how and money, the pasha gave Europeans a virtual free hand to despoil Egyptian monuments and carry off antiquities.

Among the European explorers and adventurers who arrived in Egypt during the early part of the nineteenth century none was more remarkable than Giovanni Belzoni. Belzoni was born in Padua, Italy, but he lived for many years in England where he worked as a circus "strong man." (He was about six feet seven inches tall and powerfully built.) In 1815 Belzoni went to Egypt to try to sell Mohammed Ali a new hydraulic pump he had invented.

When the pasha didn't buy his machine, Belzoni accepted a commission to secure some antiquities for the British consul-general, Henry Salt. He only had a few simple tools and no power machinery. Never-

Fig. 9. Temple at Armant in 1798, later demolished to build a sugar refinery. (From *Description de l'Egypte*, vol. 2, 2nd ed., 1823.)

theless, in 1816 he successfully completed his first task—moving a colossal granite head and upper torso of a pharaoh (we now know it was Ramesses II) from a temple at Thebes to Alexandria (Fig. 10).

Besides several technical problems, Belzoni had to overcome disturbances among his workers caused by agents of Bernardino Drovetti, the Italian-born former consul-general for France. Drovetti would continue to plague Belzoni throughout his stay in Egypt. Despite all of the problems, the seven-and-a-quarter-ton colossus was levered onto a wooden platform, dragged to the river bank, loaded onto a boat and sent down river to Alexandria. The next year it arrived at the British Museum.

Another of Belzoni's spectacular accomplishments was the excavation of the rock-cut temple of Ramesses II at Abu Simbel in Nubia. Jean Louis Burckhardt, a young Swiss adventurer in the employ of an English exploration society, had visited Abu Simbel in 1812. There he discovered huge statues carved from the cliff-side but covered with sand up to their necks. He suspected that somewhere beneath the sand

Fig. 10. Belzoni's workers moving the head of Ramesses II from the Ramesseum. (From G. Belzoni, *Six New Plates*, 1822.)

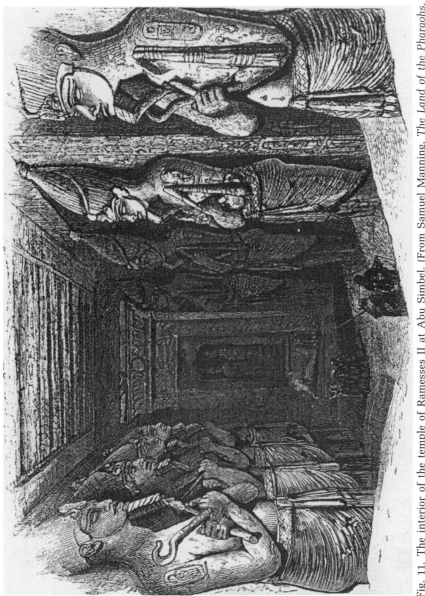

Fig. 11. The interior of the temple of Ramesses II at Abu Simbel. (From Samuel Manning, *The Land of the Pharaohs*, 1876.)

was an entrance to a temple, and he had told Belzoni of his ideas when he met him in Cairo in 1815.

During one of the periods of delay Belzoni encountered while trying to move the Ramesses II colossus down to the river, he and his wife took a trip up the Nile to Abu Simbel. Belzoni hired some workers and began trying to clear the sand that covered the front of the monument. However, he had not gotten very far when he had to return to Thebes and his task of moving the head of Ramesses. Nevertheless, Belzoni resolved to finish the work he had started at Abu Simbel.

In 1817 Belzoni returned to the Nubian site and renewed his excavations. He had to clear away forty feet of sand that covered the front of the monument, but finally he found the top of the doorway and wriggled inside. Belzoni thus became the first known European to view the interior of this spectacular temple carved out of the hillside (Fig. 11).

On his return trip to Alexandria Belzoni stopped at Thebes and explored the Valley of the Kings (Fig. 12). There he discovered several tombs, including the beautifully decorated tomb of Seti I, the most magnificent tomb in the valley. Then, after his return to the delta area he revisited the pyramids at Giza. By using logic and skill he discovered the hidden entrance to the second pyramid, the Pyramid of Chephren (or Khafre). He became the first person to enter it since medieval times, when the secret of its entrance was lost.

In 1819 Belzoni succeeded in duplicating his success of moving the torso of Ramesses II when he transported a twenty-two-foot obelisk weighing six tons from the island of Philae to Alexandria. William Bankes, a British gentleman and amateur archaeologist, had seen the obelisk during a journey to Philae. He had noted with interest that its base contained both a hieroglyphic and a Greek inscription. Bankes secured the rights to the monument from the pasha and hired Belzoni to get it for him.

However, Drovetti once again made the task much more difficult. The agents of the still-powerful former French consul hastened to Philae ahead of Belzoni. When they failed to convince the local governor that the obelisk belonged to their employer, they attempted to win the support of the local populace. Counting on the credulity of the illiterate *fellahin,* the leader of Drovetti's gang claimed to be able to understand hieroglyphs and proceeded to "read" the inscription on the obelisk. He boldly declared that according to the text on the monument itself the obelisk had belonged to one of Drovetti's ancestors! Belzoni arrived and foiled the plan by producing his official permits and a gift for the local governor.

Belzoni moved the obelisk to the river and loaded it upon a boat using the method that had proved successful with the statue of Rames-

Fig. 12. The entrance to the Valley of the Kings. (From David Roberts, *Egypt and Nubia*, 1846-50.)

ses II. However, the battle was not yet over. When the boat with the obelisk aboard reached Thebes, Drovetti and his hirelings were waiting. They ambushed Belzoni when he came ashore, threatening to kill him if he did not agree to yield one-third of the profit derived from the sale of the obelisk. Only the arrival of a large group of local villagers prevented violence and allowed Belzoni to proceed unharmed. The obelisk was eventually erected on the Bankes estate in England.

Throughout his explorations Belzoni continually looked for portable antiquities and papyri that he could sell to Consul-General Salt or other European collectors. He openly admitted that his purpose in entering ancient tombs was "to rob the Egyptians of their papyri."[2] From Belzoni's account of his experiences while exploring dark, unventilated tomb passages and chambers one can get an impression of the amount of destruction that must have taken place during this era:

> After the exertion of entering into such a place, through a passage of fifty, a hundred, three hundred, or perhaps six hundred yards, nearly overcome, I sought a resting-place, found one and contrived to sit; but when my weight bore on the body of an Egyptian, it crushed it like a band-box. I naturally had recourse to my hands to sustain my weight, but they found no better support; so that I sunk altogether among the broken mummies, with a crash of bones, rags, and wooden cases, which raised such a dust as kept me motionless for a quarter of an hour, waiting till it subsided again. . . . Once I was conducted from such a place to another resembling it, through a passage of about twenty feet in length, and no wider than that a body could be forced through. It was choked with mummies, and I could not pass without putting my face in contact with that of some decayed Egyptian; but as the passage inclined downwards, my own weight helped me on; however, I could not avoid being covered with bones, legs, arms, and heads rolling from above.[3]

It is only fair to point out that as an Egyptian archaeologist Belzoni was no worse than his contemporaries, and in many respects he was much better. He was a courageous, intelligent, good-natured individual who did not destroy antiquities willfully. More typical was the attitude of Col. Richard Howard Vyse, who arrived in Cairo in 1836 to "study" the pyramids. When he had difficulty locating the entrance to the third pyramid at Giza he used gunpowder to blast gaping holes in the masonry of the ancient monument.

---

2. G. Belzoni, *Narrative of the Operations and Recent Discoveries within the Pyramids, Temples, Tombs, and Excavations in Egypt and Nubia* (London: John Murray, 1820), p. 158.
3. Ibid., pp. 157–58.

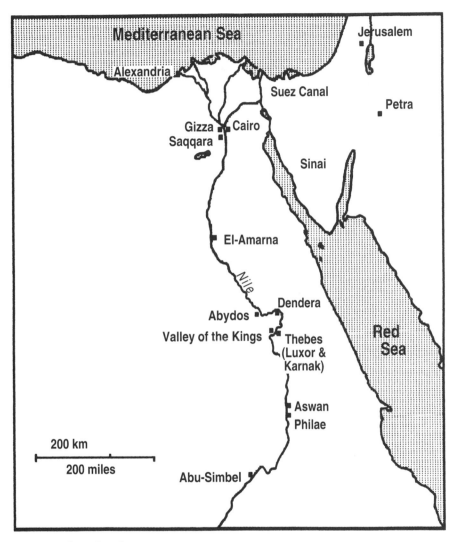

Map 2. Early archaeology in Egypt.

Drovetti's confrontation with Belzoni over the Philae obelisk seems
to have had a sobering effect on both Drovetti and Salt. They agreed
to end their cutthroat competition with one another by unofficially
dividing Egypt between themselves. Drovetti would have rights to all
remains on the east bank of the Nile while Salt laid claim to everything
on the west bank.

Only a short time after this agreement had been made, a young French engineer named Jean Lelorrain arrived in Egypt. A wealthy Frenchman, Sebastien Saulnier, had hired him to perform a difficult task. He was to secure for France an ancient zodiac that the Commission of Arts and Science had discovered on the ceiling of a temple at Dendera (Fig. 13). When Lelorrain learned of the pact between Drovetti and Salt, he realized he would have to keep the purpose of his journey secret, for the zodiac lay on the western side of the Nile in Salt's "territory."

The young Frenchman secured a general *firman* or permit. This gave him the right to conduct research or excavations on unnamed ancient buildings as far south as the Wadi Halfa. He then publicly stated on several occasions that he intended to visit Thebes to collect some mummies and other antiquities. In February 1821 he left Cairo on a hired boat and proceeded upriver. He stopped briefly at Dendera to make certain that the zodiac was still there, but the presence of British travelers kept him from spending much time at the site. He did not want to seem too interested in the zodiac and run the risk of having his interest reported to Salt.

Continuing on to Thebes Lelorrain set about obtaining a few portable antiquities, thus creating a blind for his real mission. He whiled away time until the visitors at "his" temple had left. Then, in the middle of April, while Salt's agents in Luxor were under the impression that Lelorrain was visiting the Red Sea, he secretly returned to Dendera and started to work.

The zodiac was carved on two three-foot thick roofing stones that would have to be cut out and lowered to the ground. Using small amounts of gunpowder, Lelorrain blasted a small hole in the roof through which he could insert a saw blade. To his chagrin he discovered that his saw could cut only about one foot a day through the hard stone. Lelorrain then made additional holes so that three saws could be worked simultaneously. Even so, it took twenty-two days to remove the carving from the roof. Sixteen more days were required for fifty Arab workers to drag the two stones four miles from the temple to the Nile and load them on Lelorrain's boat.

By that time travelers had brought news of the enterprise to Henry Salt. As Lelorrain's craft was descending the Nile another boat drew alongside. One of Salt's agents called to the Frenchman, ordering him to stop and yield the zodiac. Instead, Lelorrain immediately raised the flag of France, thus confronting the British envoy with a possible international crisis. Britain and France were then at peace, but what might follow a British attempt to board forcibly a French ship in neutral waters? Salt's hireling backed down and Lelorrain proceeded to Cairo.

Fig. 13. The Dendera zodiac. (From *Description de l'Egypte*, vol. 4, 2nd ed., 1823.)

Henry Salt appealed to the pasha. But Mohammed Ali, perhaps annoyed by Salt and Drovetti's presumptuous division of Egyptian antiquities among themselves, simply asked to see Lelorrain's *firman*. After reading it, he declared that Lelorrain had done nothing illegal. The zodiac was transported to France, where it became one of the treasures of the Louvre.

DECIPHERMENT OF HIEROGLYPHICS

While adventurers like Belzoni and Lelorrain were robbing tombs and legally pillaging Egyptian antiquities, many scholars labored at a less glamorous task. They were trying to wrest historical information from the monuments and objects sent back to the West. All their efforts, however, could produce little until someone solved the mystery of ancient Egyptian hieroglyphic writing.

From the outset the Rosetta Stone had been hailed as a possible key to the secrets of the Egyptian script, but little was learned from it for a long time. Of course, scholars had translated the Greek inscription almost immediately after the stone had been found. It turned out to be a proclamation of 196 B.C. praising King Ptolemy Epiphanes, one of the Macedonian rulers of Egypt, and granting him divine honors. But scholars still could not understand the other two scripts.

In 1802 the French Orientalist Sylvestre de Sacy recognized that the middle band of writing (in a late Egyptian script called Demotic) was simply a "running hand" version of the hieroglyphic text. He was even able to recognize the Demotic versions of several names mentioned in the Greek inscription, including that of Ptolemy. Other scholars also had suggested that the signs placed within ovals (called cartouches) in various parts of the hieroglyphic inscription probably represented royal names. But progress was limited because almost all investigators believed, as had the ancient Greeks, that hieroglyphs were symbolic pictographs. Most scholars did not investigate the possibility that hieroglyphic signs might represent alphabetic letters or syllables.

An exception was Thomas Young, an English physician and physicist best known for formulating the wave theory of light. Young made the first major advance in the study of Egyptian writing. He carefully compared the demotic and Greek texts on the Rosetta Stone and by 1814 had worked out the meaning of several demotic word groups. Turning to the hieroglyphic portion of the stele, Young applied to the signs in cartouches the letters of the name Ptolemy. He was thus able to show that hieroglyphs were at least partly alphabetic.

Additional study convinced Young that Egyptian inscriptions should be read from whatever direction the signs faced. He also concluded that the writing system used a combination of signs—some alphabetic, representing single letters, some phonetic, representing a complex syllable or sound, others pictographs, representing complete words. Young published an account of his discoveries in the 1819 edition of the *Encyclopaedia Britannica,* but he was unable to progress much further than his reading of the cartouches. In succeeding years he abandoned the study of hieroglyphics and concentrated on his research in physics.

The French had initiated the study of Egyptian antiquities, so it is perhaps fitting that a Frenchman finally deciphered the ancient Egyptian script. Jean François Champollion became interested in hieroglyphics in 1801 when, as a boy of eleven, he met the mathematician

Fig. 14. Jean François Champollion. (From S. Manning, *The Land of the Pharaohs*, 1876.)

Fourier, a former member of the commission in Egypt. He was shown drawings of Egyptian ruins and a copy of the Rosetta Stone. Champollion was saddened to learn that no one could read the ancient Egyptian writing, so he boldly promised that he would accomplish that feat.

Already the young Champollion had shown some linguistic ability by learning Greek and Latin. After his visit with Fourier the boy immediately began preparing himself for his self-appointed task by learning English, German, and Italian. Those modern languages were necessary for keeping abreast of current scholarship. In addition Champollion learned several Eastern tongues he might need in his researches: Hebrew, Arabic, Syriac, Chaldean, Sanscrit, Zend, Pahlavi, Parsi, Persian, and Coptic. He did all this by the time he was seventeen!

The young linguist applied for admission to a French secondary school at Grenoble to continue his studies. Like other applicants he had to submit an essay on any subject he wished. To the astonishment of the school's administrators, instead of the expected schoolboy theme, they received the outline for a book, *Egypt of the Pharaohs*. On September 1, 1807, after hearing the seventeen-year-old Champollion read the introduction to this proposed work, the professors of the school gave him a standing ovation and on the spot elected him a member of the faculty.

Champollion lectured in history at Grenoble for the next eight years and worked to perfect his knowledge of Coptic and Arabic. But the political crises accompanying the fall of Napoleon and the restoration of the Bourbon monarchy in France brought hard times for the young scholar, whose republican zeal and advocacy of academic freedom had made him many enemies. In 1815 he was accused of treason and dismissed from his teaching position, although he was not prosecuted. Without university duties he could now devote full time to the work for which he had so thoroughly prepared himself—the solution of the mystery of hieroglyphics.

Starting with the cartouches of the Rosetta Stone, Champollion, like Young before him, equated the individual signs with the letters of the name Ptolemy (*Ptolemaios* in Greek). He was able to prove the correctness of this reading in 1821 when he received a copy of the bilingual inscription on Bankes's obelisk from Philae, which had just arrived in England. The Greek text on the obelisk named two rulers, Ptolemy and Cleopatra. When Champollion studied the obelisk's cartouches he noted that the three signs they had in common were where they should be if his readings of the Rosetta Stone were correct. Furthermore, if the second cartouche spelled out the name Cleopatra, the sign for "a" should occur twice. It did so, strengthening the evidence for the decipherment. The last two signs in the Cleopatra cartouche could not be assigned a phonetic value, but Young had already pointed out that they almost always occurred at the end of the names of goddesses or queens. Thus, they probably represented a feminine ending. (This suggestion later proved to be correct.)

Encouraged by his success, Champollion went on to decipher other cartouches of Hellenistic rulers of Egypt. By 1822 he had determined the phonetic values of some twenty-two hieroglyphs, though there were still many uncertainties surrounding his readings. For example, the signs for "t" in the cartouches of Ptolemy and Cleopatra were different, as were the signs for "k" in Cleopatra (*Kleopatra* in Greek) and Berenice (*Berenike* in Greek). However, since all of these words were Greek names that the ancient Egyptians had tried to reproduce in their own script, some problems of this sort were to be anticipated.

Champollion received copies of hieroglyphic inscriptions from some Egyptian temples in September 1822. When he examined cartouches in them he found that he could read the names Thutmose and Ramesses. These had been native Egyptian rulers, so it was now clear that Egyptian names and words as well as foreign ones had been written in phonetic

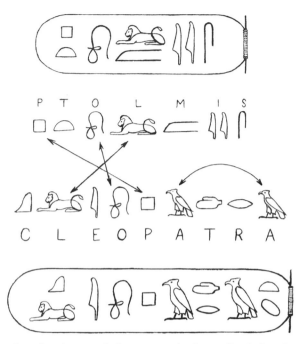

Fig. 15. Cartouches of Ptolemy and Cleopatra with Champollion's decipherment.

characters. Champollion waited no longer. He revealed his breakthrough
to the *Academie royale des Inscriptions* in Paris on September 29, 1822,
by reading his now famous *Lettre a M. Dacier . . . relative a l'alphabet
des hieroglyphes phonetiques.* The way to unlock the secrets of the
Egyptian past had been found at last.

Champollion had become an expert in Coptic, a late form of the
ancient Egyptian language written in Greek alphabetic characters. His
knowledge of this language now enabled him to make rapid strides
in reading hieroglyphic texts that had no Greek translations. By 1824
he was able to publish *Precis du systeme hieroglyphique* (*Synopsis
of the Hieroglyphic System*). This work proved what Young had
surmised—that the Egyptian writing system had used a combination
of ideograms, determinatives, and phonetic signs. As his knowledge
of the hieroglyphic system became broader, Champollion recognized
that many of the copies of inscriptions made by the great commission
and others were inaccurate. So, in 1828-29 Champollion and an Italian
pupil, Rosellini, accompanied by artists and architects, traveled to Egypt
to restudy the monuments and make more accurate copies of the inscriptions. The field work of this expedition produced many confirma-

tions of Champollion's theories and four large volumes of drawings.

Less than three years later Champollion died at the age of forty-two. He left two additional works to be published posthumously, a grammar and a dictionary of ancient Egyptian. In three decades of dedicated preparation and research, he had provided the means by which scholars would give back to Egyptians and others three thousand years of their history.

The decipherment of hieroglyphics made it possible to begin arranging ancient Egyptian rulers and monuments in chronological order, and gave Egyptian antiquities a new historical value. The great Prussian expedition of 1842–45 sponsored by King Frederick William IV displayed the new attitude the decipherment engendered. Karl Richard Lepsius, a linguist at the University of Berlin and an ardent supporter of Champollion's decipherment, led this important expedition. His goal was to fit each of its discoveries into the framework of the history of ancient Egypt.

Lepsius first studied the Old Kingdom cemeteries near Memphis, the ancient capital of Egypt that once stood near present-day Cairo. He excavated thirty previously unknown pyramids and many *mastabas,* the rectangular tombs of ancient Egyptian nobles. The expedition also excavated, surveyed, and copied inscriptions at el-Amarna, the Valley of the Kings, Thebes, Philae, Abu Simbel, and previously unexplored Nubian sites as far south as Meroë, the center of the Egyptianized Nubian culture that had given Egypt its Twenty-Fifth Dynasty. The expedition's return journey took Lepsius through the Sinai peninsula. There, at Wadi Maghareh and Serabit el-Khadem, he discovered inscriptions and other evidence of ancient Egyptian copper-mining activity.

Lepsius was not above collecting antiquities; he sent some fifteen thousand objects to Berlin. However, he sought primarily to understand the development of ancient Egyptian civilization. His publications, *Die Chronologie der Aegypter (Egyptian Chronology,* 1849), *Königsbuch der alten Aegypter (Book of Egyptian Kings,* 1858), and the still valuable twelve-volume *Denkmäler aus Aegypten und Aethiopien (Monuments of Egypt and Ethiopia,* 1849–58), became landmarks in the study of Egypt's past.

Phase II: Egyptian Archaeology Comes of Age (1858-1928)

ENDING THE PLUNDERING

The continuing pillage of Egyptian sites was often excused on the grounds that the West was saving the treasures of the past from the Egyptians themselves. Wasn't it better for these priceless antiquities to be in European and American museums where they would be properly appreciated than in their native land where they would suffer neglect or wanton destruction? This argument displayed the same paternalistic attitude that characterized nineteenth-century Western defenses of colonialism. It also ignored the destruction caused by "enlightened" Europeans and Americans during their quest for museum pieces. Nevertheless, there was at least some truth in it.

The Egyptian people and, more importantly, their rulers had as yet little appreciation of the ancient Egyptian cultural heritage or of the relics of the past. In 1835 Mohammed Ali had issued an edict forbidding the exportation of antiquities and creating a museum in Cairo to house future finds. However, this early attempt to protect the monuments was a failure. The law created no agency to enforce its provisions. Furthermore, Mohammed Ali's successor, his son Abbas, viewed the museum as a convenient collection of gifts to bestow on important visitors. It was largely in spite of Egyptian officials rather than because of them that the international looting of Egyptian antiquities was finally halted. The person who accomplished this was the first official to hold the position of conservator of Egyptian monuments, Auguste Mariette.

Mariette arrived in Egypt for the first time in 1850 on a mission to purchase some Coptic manuscripts for the Louvre. While visiting Saqqara one day, he noticed the head of a sphinx protruding from the sand. He examined it carefully and noted that it was exactly like several others he had seen in the gardens of various Egyptian dignitaries in Cairo and Alexandria. Had all the sphinxes he had observed originally come from this same spot? If so, he must be standing near an important ancient site which was now completely covered by sand. Into Mariette's mind flashed a statement by the ancient geographer Strabo that at Memphis there was a temple of Serapis "in a place so very sandy that dunes of sand are heaped up by the winds; and by these some of the sphinxes which I saw were buried even to the head and others were only half-visible."[4]

Abandoning his original mission to buy manuscripts, Mariette used his funds to hire laborers to clear sand from the buried sphinx even though he did not have a permit to excavate. Soon he uncovered an avenue of sphinxes with many Old Kingdom tombs on either side. In one of these tombs he found the famous statue of "the Seated Scribe."

Mariette felt that he was approaching the celebrated tomb of the sacred bulls mentioned by classical authors. The ancient Egyptians had believed that there was one bull, the Apis Bull, sacred to Ptah, patron god of Memphis. They kept this bull in a sacred enclosure near the temple of Ptah, and when it died they mummified and buried it in a special tomb with the remains of its predecessors. Priests then conducted a special search throughout Egypt to find a new Apis. In the later periods of ancient Egyptian civilization the Apis was identified with the god of the dead, Osiris. This identification produced the compound name Osiris-Apis, which the Greeks corrupted into Serapis. The temple of Serapis mentioned by Strabo was the funerary temple at the entrance to the tomb of the Apis Bulls, the Serapeum.

In February 1851, after reaching the doorway of a Thirteenth Dynasty chapel built in honor of the Apis, Mariette ran out of money. The time had come to announce his great discovery to his employers. Whatever the initial reaction of the Louvre's officials upon learning that the money they had allocated for purchasing Coptic manuscripts Mariette had spent on excavations, they soon realized the importance of his find. They immediately sent him thirty thousand francs to continue his work.

By November he had found the entrance to the Serapeum. However, before Mariette could enjoy his triumph, a day of reckoning arrived. Abbas Pasha, who was then the ruler of Egypt, ordered the seizure of all the antiquities so far discovered by Mariette's illegal digging. The French consul-general protested, and Abbas agreed to a compromise. The antiquities already uncovered could go to France, but any future finds would be the property of the Egyptian government.

Mariette informed the Egyptian officials that he was ceasing his excavations and would remain at the site only to pack the objects ceded to France. However, he had no intention of abandoning the Serapeum, whose investigation he had just begun. He constructed a trapdoor over the entrance to the tomb and covered it with sand. Each night a group of picked men continued the excavations. Then during the day Mariette

---

4. Strabo, Geography 17. 1. 32. The translation is from H. L. Jones, The Geography of Strabo (Cambridge, Mass.: Harvard University Press, 1959), p. 89.

Fig. 16. Subterranean chamber in the Serapeum with the sarcophagus of one of the Apis Bulls. (From Samuel Manning, *The Land of the Pharaohs,* 1876.)

visibly supervised the packing of his finds, hiding among them all the objects uncovered by the nocturnal explorers (Fig. 16).

After several months the French consul-general prevailed upon Abbas to relent and allow the "resumption" of excavation. Thus, Mariette was able to work openly once more. By 1853 he had cleared the three vaults of the tomb, ranging in age from the Eighteenth to the Twenty-Sixth Dynasties (the fifteenth through the seventh centuries B.C.), and reluctantly returned to France with his finds. In this spectacular fashion began the archaeological career of the man who only five years later would put an end to this kind of plundering of Egypt's heritage.

Abbas Pasha was assassinated in 1854 and succeeded by his brother Sa'id. Mariette wrote a memorandum to the new pasha urging him to create a governmental service to protect ancient monuments and to build a museum to house showpieces discovered in the future. Sa'id was no more interested in the relics of the past than Abbas had been, but he was interested in closer relations with France. So, when Napoleon III of France announced that he intended to visit Egypt, Sa'id decided to present some antiquities to his distinguished guest. Upon the recommendation of his friend de Lesseps (the builder of the Suez Canal), the pasha hired Mariette to undertake some excavations in order to secure an adequate collection of major antiquities for the French emperor. In 1858 Napoleon III canceled his proposed trip to Egypt, but by then Mariette, with the help of de Lesseps, had won the confidence of Sa'id Pasha. The Egyptian ruler created an antiquities service and named Mariette conservator of Egyptian monuments, or as the position was later called, director-general of the Antiquities Service.

Mariette received only lackluster support from Sa'id and his successor Isma'il. He had to continually persuade them to provide funds and almost as frequently restrain them from giving away antiquities or mortgaging them to secure loans. He also had to contend with the jealousy and opposition of antiquities dealers and minor officials. However, despite these problems, Mariette managed to organize Egypt's first department of antiquities and to create a museum that would develop into one of the world's greatest institutions. Henceforth, the museum could lay claim to all objects discovered in Egypt.

Because of his mistrust of other excavators, Mariette insisted on supervising almost all excavations himself. This made archaeological field work in Egypt virtually his personal monopoly. He dug at over thirty different sites, uncovering or clearing many important monuments, including the Table of Kings at Saqqara, the temple of Hatshepsut at Deir el-Bahri, the Ramessid temple at Medinet Habu, and the almost perfectly preserved Ptolemaic temple of Horus at Edfu. Mariette's excavation methods were no worse, but unfortunately also no better, than those of his contemporaries working in Egypt. He conducted his excavations in haste, with inadequate supervision and insufficient recording of stratigraphy and finds. Few of his discoveries were published adequately. Many (including his most important, the Serapeum) were only partially published long after his death.

Nevertheless, Mariette's accomplishments were imposing. He faced a constant shortage of funds and obstacles that would have defeated most individuals. But despite these problems, by the time he died in 1881 Mariette had managed to bring order to Egyptian archaeology. He ended the legalized plundering of antiquities and initiated among some Egyptians a sense of pride in their past and an understanding of their responsibility toward the remains of antiquity.

THE TRIUMPH OF CAREFUL METHODOLOGY

Under the tenure of Gaston Maspero, Mariette's successor as director-general of the Antiquities Service, Westerners were allowed to excavate in Egypt once more. However, they had to secure permits from the Antiquities Service. Furthermore, although some antiquities were normally awarded to the excavator or his sponsor, the rule that all objects must first be offered to the Egyptian Museum still prevailed. Unique objects and especially fine pieces remained in Egypt, while duplicates and common small finds were allowed to leave the country.

Interest in Egyptology had been increasing in Europe and America. When Egypt was reopened to foreign excavators, societies such as the Egypt Exploration Fund (organized in 1882) were formed to excavate promising sites. Much of the interest in Egyptian archaeology stemmed from a desire to produce evidence validating biblical narratives or as a result of claims that the ancient Egyptians had possessed advanced esoteric knowledge still unknown to modern man. In fact, it was because of the influence of a mystical religious interpretation of the Great Pyramid that William Matthew Flinders Petrie, the man responsible for introducing careful methodology into Egyptian archaeology, first came to Egypt.

Petrie's father, like many people of his time, was obsessed by the need to reconcile the revealed truth of the Bible, literally interpreted, with the facts being produced by science and archaeology. He therefore read with great interest Charles Piazzi Smyth's *Our Inheritance in the Great Pyramid* (1864), which claimed that the Great Pyramid had been built according to divinely revealed specifications. Supposedly, astronomical facts about the earth and predictions about the future were hidden within its measurements. Inspired by Smyth's volume, in 1880 the elder Petrie sent his son to Egypt to survey and measure the Great Pyramid with instruments more accurate than those used by Smyth.

Flinders Petrie had little formal education, but he had read widely and had developed special competence in mathematics, surveying, and measurement. For months he subjected the Great Pyramid and its companions at Giza to the most exacting measurement they had received since the time of their construction. Petrie cared little for social conventions, so in the heat of the day he worked clad only in his pink underwear. This practice "kept the tourist at bay, as the creature seemed to him too queer for inspection."[5] Moreover, since the interior corridors and chambers of the Great Pyramid were too hot and too crowded with tourists during the day, Petrie did much of his measurements in them at night. For this work he was dressed, he later claimed, like

5. W. M. F. Petrie, *Seventy Years in Archaeology* (London: S. Low and Marston, 1931), p. 21.

"the Japanese carpenter who had nothing on but a pair of spectacles, except that I do not need the spectacles."[6] Petrie's results proved the great ability and accuracy of the ancient Egyptian surveyors and engineers. But they also provided the "ugly fact which killed the beautiful theory."[7] Piazzi Smyth's assertions had been based on inaccurate data.

Egypt captivated the young Petrie, and he returned to excavate other sites. However, his interest was information, not museum pieces. So he chose his sites according to their potential for answering questions about the past, not according to their likelihood for yielding artistic treasures. Furthermore, when he applied his precise, methodical mind to archaeological digging, he transformed excavation techniques in Egypt.

Like his contemporary, Pitt Rivers, Petrie insisted on careful digging, emphasizing the importance of all objects, especially those that had been generally ignored in the past: fragments of pottery, weights, beads, and broken or unartistic tools and weapons. Petrie also realized that groupings and associations of materials were important for chronology and for a correct interpretation of cultural development. So, he recorded his finds more precisely and completely than was customary among contemporary Egyptologists. Anything less, he insisted, was not really archaeology:

> The power of conserving material . . . of observing all that can be gleaned; of noticing trifling details which may imply a great deal else; of acquiring and building up a mental picture; of fitting everything into place and not losing or missing any possible clues—all this is the soul of the work, and without it excavating is mere dumb plodding.[8]

Petrie's camp was notoriously Spartan, for he took little interest in his own or his staff's personal comfort. He always assumed that everyone shared his own overriding enthusiasm for the work at hand. A visitor to his camp later recalled that "he served a table so excruciatingly bad that only persons of iron constitutions could survive it."[9] But Petrie's assistants and his hired help learned how to dig. The native

---

6. Quoted in P. Tompkins, *Secrets of the Great Pyramid* (New York: Harper & Row, 1971), p. 101. See also Petrie, *Seventy Years in Archaeology*, p. 21, where he mentions working in the nude inside the Great Pyramid.

7. Petrie, *Seventy Years in Archaeology*, p. 13.

8. W. M. F. Petrie, *Methods and Aims in Archaeology* (London: Macmillan, 1904), p. 5.

9. Charles Breasted, *Pioneer to the Past: The Story of James Henry Breasted* (New York: Charles Scribner's Sons, 1943), p. 75.

Fig. 17. Petrie's typological sequence of wavy-handled jars.

foremen he trained in his excavation methods provided a core of skilled archaeological technicians for many other digs in Egypt. Later, by passing their knowledge on to their children and other fellow country-men Petrie's workers created an archaeological tradition that is still providing well-trained native foremen for modern excavations.

Petrie always published the results of his excavations promptly and, for his time, completely. He published most of his reports within a year after the digs they described. These reports with their pottery drawings and plans of mud-brick walls represented a major advance over most previous publications of archaeological excavations in Egypt.

Petrie also introduced typological sequence dating into Near Eastern archaeology. At Naqada and at Abydos he discovered graves that contained no written material, forcing him to find another way to date them. He kept records of every object from every grave and soon he was able to recognize groupings of objects that were consistently associated with one another. After defining several such contemporaneous assemblages, Petrie constructed typological series for some of the objects within the groups. The most obvious series involved ledge-handled jars (Fig. 17). In one group of graves he found rounded jars with well-made wavy ledge handles to enable the bearer to obtain a better grip. In the assemblage from another group of burials the jars were less rounded and the handles smaller and less functional. In examples from still other groups the handles had disappeared completely to be replaced by a painted wavy line and the jars had become cylindrical. Since the handle-less jars in this series also occurred in datable deposits from the First Dynasty while the ledge-handled jars were not found in assemblages from historical times, the direction of the sequence could be firmly established. Petrie also worked out similar sequences for other objects, and by comparing the overlapping of these typological series he was able to build a relative chronology for the predynastic age in Egypt.

In 1890 Petrie introduced his precise excavation techniques into Palestine when he began excavating at Tell el-Hesi. In later years he also excavated at Tell el-Far'ah (1927–29) and Tell el-'Ajjul (1930–34). At these large mounds formed by one city being built upon the ruins of another, Petrie learned the importance of determining the layer to which building remains belonged. Pottery became his key to understanding stratigraphy and dating, and through comparison of the pottery types and other objects found at each of the sites he dug, Petrie laid the foundations for a pottery chronology for the entire area of Palestine.

An unfortunate aspect of Petrie's career was that he remained active in the field so long that he became an anachronism. It had taken genius to break from the crowd and establish a new path, and Petrie had always been conscious of the inferior capacities of those around him. What he failed to recognize, however, is that once genius had made the breakthrough and shown the way, other men might follow the lead and even improve upon methods they would never have discovered on their own. Petrie never welcomed criticism, even when it was constructive, and he failed to change or further develop his techniques. As a result, during Petrie's old age in the 1930s a new generation of archaeologists tended to be extremely critical of his failings while taking for granted the revolutionary changes he had made in the principles and methods of Egyptian and Palestinian archaeology.

Petrie's careful excavation techniques became widely adopted by Egyptologists by the early years of the twentieth century. The work of two of his disciples, George Reisner and Howard Carter, especially exemplifies the triumph of Petrie's principles and methodology. Reisner, an American, insisted, like Petrie, that every object found, no matter how fragmentary or insignificant, be recorded and, if possible, published. Reisner's patience, meticulous excavation technique, and voluminous recording were shown during his work as leader of the Harvard-Boston Museum of Fine Arts expedition. This expedition spent many seasons between 1904 and 1927 clearing the great mastaba cemetery near the Giza pyramids.

In 1925 Reisner found the carefully hidden and apparently unrobbed tomb of Queen Hetep-heres, the mother of Khufu (or Cheops, as the Greeks called him). The floor of the burial chamber was covered with golden objects, copper tools, fragments of decayed wood, and vessels made of alabaster, copper or pottery. Many of the objects were exquisite museum pieces, but Reisner resisted the temptation to rush in and claim them. Instead, he excavated the chamber inch by inch with the position of every fragment of wood and every piece of inlay carefully noted and photographed.

Two hundred and eighty days, almost two thousand pages of notes and over a thousand photographs later he completed the excavation of the chamber. There followed two more years of work on the objects from the tomb. At the end of that time the queen's carrying chair, bed, arm chair, canopy and jewel box had been completely reconstructed with new wood replacing that which had decayed. This restoration had been possible only because Reisner had insisted on recording the position of every scrap of evidence before removing it. Through such work at Giza and through other excavations at Samaria in Palestine (1908–10) and Kerma in Nubia (1913), Reisner more firmly impelled Egyptian and Palestinian archaeology along the path to maturity that Petrie had blazed.

Howard Carter, a British artist and draftsman, arrived in Egypt in 1892 and worked under several leading Egyptologists, including Petrie. After working for a time for the Egyptian Antiquities Service, Carter became the excavator for the wealthy English aristocrat Lord Carnarvon. While working for Carnarvon in 1922 Carter made the most famous archaeological find of all time, the discovery of the tomb of Tutankhamun.

Carter had systematically but unsuccessfully searched the Valley of the Kings for this tomb since 1917. After five fruitless seasons of digging Carnarvon was ready to give up and relinquish his concession to excavate in the valley. But Carter persuaded him to finance one more season. There was a small area near the tomb of Ramesses VI that Carter had sampled in 1917 but abandoned when he found mud-brick remains of common workmen's huts. This was the only place left to try.

On November 1, 1922, the work began, and once again the diggers uncovered traces of ancient workmen's huts. However, this time Carter had his men remove the huts and dig underneath. They found a step cut into the stone, then eleven more leading downward to a doorway sealed with plaster. Carter examined a small hole in the plaster and saw that the corridor behind it was completely blocked by rubble. The tomb seemed to be intact. The archaeologist filled in the staircase, placed a guard over the excavations, and wired Carnarvon to come to Egypt immediately.

When Carnarvon arrived some three weeks later, the excavations resumed. Soon the stairs and corridor were cleared and another sealed door stood before them. Carter made a small hole, inserted a candle to test for possible foul gases, then looked in.

As my eyes grew accustomed to the light, details of the room within emerged slowly from the mist, strange animals, statues, and gold— everywhere the glint of gold. For the moment—an eternity it must have seemed to the others standing by—I was struck dumb with amazement, and when Lord Carnarvon, unable to stand the suspense

any longer, inquired anxiously, "Can you see anything?" it was all
I could do to get out the words, "Yes, wonderful things."[10]

It soon became evident that robbers had entered the tomb in
antiquity. However, they must have been caught, for it had been only
partially disturbed before being resealed. This was the only sealed tomb
ever found in the Valley of the Kings. Carter, with the help of experts
in photography and other specialties, had to record, restore, and remove
thousands of delicate objects from it. Many of these objects had been
piled on top of one another in the small tomb, requiring the use of
great skill and care if they were to be removed without damage. Carter
purchased a mile of bandages, a mile of wadding, thirty-two bales of
calico, and hundreds of boxes and crates to protect the precious artifacts
for their trip to Cairo. It took some two and a half months to clear
the antechamber and almost three more years of work before the royal
coffin was removed from the burial chamber. The work at the tomb
was not finished until 1928.

Reisner's excavation of the tomb of Hetep-heres and Carter's careful,
methodical excavation of the tomb of Tutankhamun were a far cry
from what had passed for archaeology before Petrie's arrival in Egypt.
Egyptology had at last come of age.

10. H. Carter and A. C. Mace, *The Tomb of Tut.Ankh.Amen*, vol. 1 (London: Cassell, 1923), pp. 95–96.

3

The Rediscovery of
Near Eastern Civilizations

Phase I—Speculation, Antiquarianism, and Early Excavation (1570–1855)

EARLY EXPLORERS IN THE NEAR EAST

Unlike Egypt, few spectacular buildings or monuments survived in Asia Minor, Syria, Palestine, Mesopotamia, or Persia to remind visitors of the splendors of pre-Hellenistic Near Eastern civilizations. A few early explorers from the West wrote accounts of their travels. They include Leonard Rauwolff, a German botanist who traveled to Mesopotamia in the 1570s, and John Eldred, an English merchant who journeyed to Baghdad in 1583. But they could report seeing nothing but great mounds of earth covering sites identified by native traditions as the ancient cities of Babylon and Nineveh. Clearly, biblical prophecies proclaiming the utter desolation of these once great capitals had been amply fulfilled.

Pietro della Valle, a citizen of Rome, brought back a few inscribed bricks from Persepolis in 1626 after traveling through Asia Minor, Egypt, Palestine, Syria, Mesopotamia, and western Persia. And Karsten Niebuhr, a German scholar, made copies of Persian cuneiform inscriptions in 1765 (Fig. 18). These bricks and inscriptions interested a few scholars, but they did not fire the public imagination in the West like reports

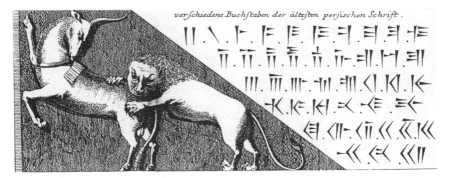

Fig. 18. Niebuhr's drawing of a cuneiform inscription at Persepolis. (From K. Niebuhr, *Reisebeschreibung von Arabien und anderen umliegenden Ländern*, 1774-78.)

of the ruins of Greece, Italy, and Egypt did.

In the early years of the nineteenth century this situation began to change, however. Napoleon's invasion of Egypt and Palestine turned French and English attention to the Near East. Moreover, the contemporaneous scholarly conflict over the accuracy of the Genesis creation accounts and Mosaic chronology seems to have increased popular interest in Palestine and other Bible lands. Western travelers set out for the Near East in greater numbers and several accounts of their journeys became bestsellers.

Edward Daniel Clarke, an English geographer and explorer, arrived in Palestine in 1801 and traveled through Galilee, visiting Nazareth and a shrine marking the supposed birthplace of the Virgin Mary. He then moved southward through Samaria and Judea to Jerusalem. Clarke was disappointed by the questionable antiquity of some of the holy sites he was shown. He even became convinced that the Church of the Holy Sepulcher did not contain within it the remains of an ancient tomb. So, Clarke undertook his own search for genuine biblical sites. His skepticism about the authenticity of traditional sites was a healthy corrective to the unquestioning attitude of most previous visitors to the Holy Land.

Clarke's contribution to knowledge of the Near East did not end in 1817 with the publication of the two volumes describing his travels in the region. He had a strong influence on Jean Louis Burckhardt, one of his students at Cambridge, who became a major figure in Holy Land exploration. Burckhardt was a native of Switzerland who had a deep hatred of revolutionary France. He moved to England and was hired in 1808 by the African Association, a British organization hoping to find a new trade route into Africa from the north. Before setting out, he learned the rudiments of Arabic, medicine, astronomy, and other useful subjects from Clarke and other Cambridge orientalists. It was during the course of these studies that Clarke aroused Burckhardt's interest in the antiquities of the Holy Land.

Burckhardt arrived in Aleppo in 1809 and stayed there for almost three years, perfecting his Arabic and his disguise as a Moslem sheik named Ibrahim ibn Abdulla. Due to Clarke's influence, Burckhardt spent much time exploring ruins (including the ruined city of Palmyra) and copying inscriptions. Then he began his journey southward to Cairo and the interior of Africa.

He chose a route along the eastern side of the Jordan River and the Dead Sea in order to explore little-known territory. This route also avoided the traffic on the main roads, thus protecting his disguise as Sheik Ibrahim. He described scores of ruins (including those of Amman), many of them previously unknown, and identified geographical features mentioned in the Bible. Although he ran the constant risk of attack by bedouin, he continued his explorations, becoming the first European since Roman times to visit the impressive remains of Petra, the "rose-red city half as old as time."[1] This site, located in an out-of-the-way canyon south of the Dead Sea, later became a tourist attraction because of its many monumental tombs carved out of the native red sandstone (Fig. 19).

After reaching Egypt and proceeding into Nubia, Burckhardt also became the first known European to visit Ramesses II's temple at Abu Simbel. However, Burckhardt never discovered the new route into central Africa that he sought. He died of dysentery in Cairo in 1817. Fortunately, however, his journals were published after his death. Their appearance in 1819 and 1822 created even more interest in study of Bible lands.

One of the staunchest defenders of the literal accuracy of the Bible was Edward Robinson, professor of Old Testament at Andover Theological Seminary in Massachusetts and later at Union Theological Seminary in New York. In 1837 he and Eli Smith, a Protestant missionary in Beirut, set out to explore the Holy Land. They hoped to find evidence supporting the Bible's historicity. From Cairo they followed the presumed route of the Israelite Exodus through Sinai to Palestine. In Jerusalem Robinson noticed some oddly projecting stones in the lower portion of the retaining wall around the Haram esh-Sherif, the Moslem sanctuary on the site of the ancient Israelite temple. He recognized these as the base of an arch that once supported a monumental entrance to the temple built by King Herod. These remains are now known as "Robinson's Arch."

---

1. A poetic description by J. W. Burgon.

Fig. 19. El-Khasne ("The Treasury") at Petra. (From David Roberts, *The Holy Land*, vol. 4, 1842.)

More important, though, were the observations Robinson made as he and Smith crisscrossed the Palestinian countryside on their way to Beirut. The biblical scholar was able to recognize in the locations and Arabic names of small towns or abandoned mounds the original places described in the Bible. Bir es-Seba' was Beersheba; Beitin must be Bethel; el-Jib was Gibeon; and so forth. His identifications became

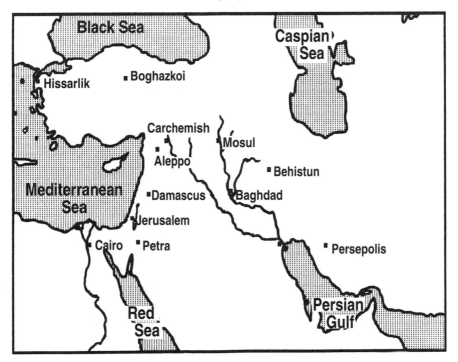

Map 3. Early archaeology in the Near East.

the starting point for all later work in biblical geography and archaeology. Robinson and Smith "had successfully superimposed the map
of ancient Palestine upon the present map of some backward provinces
of the Ottoman Empire, in consequence discovering Palestine's hidden
treasure: the hundreds of Biblical sites scattered all across the desolate
country-side."[2]

However, despite Robinson's hopes, the first evidence clearly sub-
stantiating the historical accuracy of a biblical account was not found
in Palestine. Rather, it was uncovered in Mesopotamia as a result of
French and British rivalry there. In 1783 the British East India Company
had appointed a non-British agent in Baghdad to look after its affairs.
However, when the French Revolution took place and war broke out
between France and England, the company decided to replace the local
representative with a British resident. In 1802 the resident received
consular powers.

_____

2. Neil Asher Silberman, *Digging for God and Country: Exploration, Archaeology,
and the Secret Struggle for the Holy Land, 1799-1917* (New York: Alfred A. Knopf,
1982), p. 45.

Such was the situation in 1808 when Claudius Rich was appointed British resident in Baghdad. At the age of seventeen Rich had enlisted as a cadet in the East India Company. He had a gift for learning languages. Besides classical Greek and Latin and several modern European tongues, the teenager had already learned Turkish, Persian, Arabic, Hebrew, Syriac, and a little Chinese. When officials discovered Rich's linguistic ability they appointed him secretary to the British consul-general for the Mediterranean. Unfortunately, the consul-general died just after Rich's arrival in Malta in 1804, so the young secretary was given permission to travel in the Near East to perfect his languages while awaiting a new assignment. Rich was twenty-one years old when, after serving briefly in a position in Bombay, he received his appointment to Baghdad.

Rich's language studies and travels in the East had awakened within him a curiosity about the ancient cities of Mesopotamia. Thus, at the end of 1811 he took the opportunity to spend a few weeks examining Babil, the site of ancient Babylon. He published his observations on the site in *Memoir on the Ruins of Babylon* (1815). Then, after another visit to the mound in 1817 he added a sequel entitled, naturally, *Second Memoir on the Ruins of Babylon* (1818). Rich's description and plan of Babil (Fig. 20) and his inferences about the buried city's topography were remarkably accurate. He managed to glean virtually all the information about ancient Babylon that could possibly be obtained without excavation. His two books on Babylon were instant best-sellers in Europe, causing widespread curiosity and discussion about the remains of vanished Mesopotamian empires.[3]

In 1821, just before his scheduled departure from Mesopotamia, Rich visited Mosul. While there he was able to survey the neighboring mounds of Kuyunjik and Nebi Yunus, which together formed the traditional site of Nineveh. Soon afterward Rich contracted cholera and died, but his observations on the *tells* that lay across the Tigris from Mosul were published posthumously in his *Narrative of a Residence in Koordistan* (1836).

Claudius Rich's interest in the past had also led him to amass a fine collection of oriental manuscripts and coins along with thirteen

---

3. These books also inspired Lord Byron's satirical comment in *Don Juan* about

... some infidels, who don't
Because they can't, find out the very spot
Of that same Babel, or because they won't
(Though Claudius Rich, Esquire, some bricks has got
And written lately two memoirs upon't).

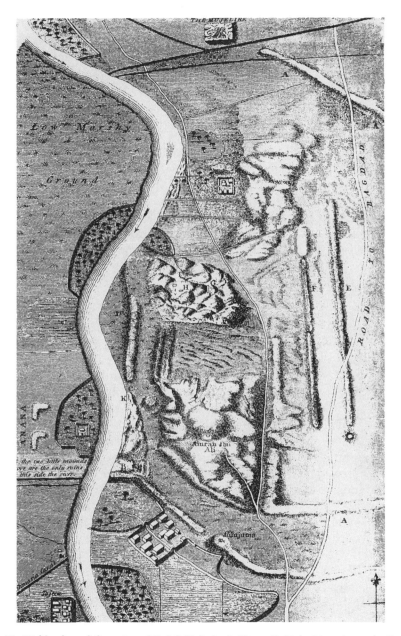

Fig. 20. Rich's plan of the ruins of Babil (Babylon). (From C. Rich, *Memoir on the Ruins of Babylon*, 1815.)

inscribed bricks from Babylon, four inscribed clay cylinders, thirty-two cuneiform tablets and fragments, an inscribed boundary stone, a black memorial stone, and other small antiquities. The British Museum purchased these materials after Rich's death, and they represented the first important display of Mesopotamian antiquities in any European museum. Rich's collection further awakened public interest in the remains of Mesopotamia's past.

The French government was not blind to this British "first" nor slow to realize the possibilities of active archaeological work in Mesopotamia. France had already been considering the appointment of a consul in Mesopotamia so that Britain would not have the area entirely to itself. However, Rich's narratives prompted Julius Mohl, a member of the French Asiatic Society, to insist that the French agent have some experience in archaeology and that he be instructed to collect manuscripts and antiquities for France. Paul Emile Botta was appointed French consul at Mosul in 1840 and the rivalry for Mesopotamian antiquities began.

THE DECIPHERMENT OF CUNEIFORM

The public did not show much interest in Mesopotamian antiquities until after the appearance of Rich's memoirs, but a small number of scholars had long been engaged in the study of Mesopotamian writing. The inscriptions brought to Europe by Valle and Niebuhr consisted of many wedge-shaped characters, so scholars called the writing system "cuneiform" (Latin for "wedge-shaped"). Niebuhr himself had made an important contribution to cuneiform research by pointing out that the inscriptions he had copied in Persia usually occurred in groups of three. The three different sections were in different types of cuneiform characters. Furthermore, the three different types of cuneiform writing always appeared in the same order. Another scholar, Bishop Friedrich Münter of Copenhagen, surmised that the inscriptions dated from the Achaemenian Persian period (circa 550–330 B.C.). Thus, one of the three languages represented in the texts should be similar to the Persian of the Zend Avesta, the sacred book of followers of the ancient Persian prophet Zoroaster (circa 628–551 B.C.). Münter also noted a recurring group of signs that he correctly guessed represented the word for "king."

Using these insights as a starting point, in 1802 Georg Friedrich Grotefend, a twenty-seven-year-old German schoolteacher, made a major advance in cuneiform research. Grotefend selected for detailed investigation two short inscriptions from among those Niebuhr had copied from reliefs above the heads of carved figures, presumably kings.

The occurrence of the group of signs Münter supposed meant "king" in the first line of each inscription supported the assumption that these texts gave the names of two ancient Persian rulers. Grotefend also saw that after an interval of one word the signs for "king" were repeated twice in succession with the addition of four extra signs. He surmised that the "extra" signs represented a genitive ending and that the inscriptions fit the pattern of later Persian designations of a ruler as "So-and-so, Great King, King of Kings, . . . son of So-and-so, Great King, King of Kings." Grotefend noted that the signs that formed the name of the king in the first text occurred in the second as the name of the king's father. The father of the king in the first inscription, however, was not designated as a former king himself.

What Achaemenid Persian rulers mentioned by the ancient Greek authors fit this family tree? Grotefend remembered that Darius I had descended from a subsidiary branch of the Achaemenid royal family. His father Hystaspes had not been ruler of Persia, but Darius' son Xerxes had succeeded him as king. Grotefend applied the letters of the presumed Persian forms of Hystaspes, Darius, and Xerxes to the signs of the three names in the inscriptions and correctly determined the values of twelve of the Persian cuneiform signs.

Unfortunately, the Göttingen Academy of Sciences refused to publish the results of the young schoolteacher's investigations, and Grotefend's theories did not become very widely known. He continued to work on other cuneiform inscriptions, but he was impeded by his limited knowledge of the Persian language and he made no additional discoveries of significance. In fact, some of his later guesses were so obviously wrong to scholars who knew Persian that they tended to ignore the logic of his initial decipherment.

More than thirty years after Grotefend announced his decipherment, Henry Creswicke Rawlinson independently duplicated his results. Rawlinson had become interested in Persian language and history during his first journey to the East as a cadet in the East India Company. In 1835 the twenty-five-year-old cavalry officer was sent to Kermanshah as military advisor to the Persian governor of Kurdistan. Rawlinson's new residence turned out to be only twenty-two miles away from an important ancient monument, the Rock of Behistun. This relief, accompanied by an extensive inscription, was carved some three hundred feet above the ground on the face of an almost sheer cliff (Fig. 21).

Between 1835 and 1837 Rawlinson spent most of his free time visiting Behistun and copying its inscriptions. The twenty-two-mile ride to and from the site was no deterrent to such an excellent horseman. On his first trip, Rawlinson climbed up the side of the peak and

Fig. 21. Rawlinson's drawing of the sculpture and inscriptions on the Behistun rock. These carvings are located about three hundred feet above ground level. (From G. Rawlinson, "The Persian Inscription at Behistun," *Royal Asiatic Society Journal*, 1846.)

carefully made his way over to the smoothed face into which the inscriptions were cut. There he discovered a narrow ledge that ran beneath the carving and he edged out onto it. He was able to stand upright, so he began copying the longest of the inscriptions (which he correctly believed to be Achaemenian Persian), oblivious to the three-hundred-foot drop at his back. On succeeding visits Rawlinson risked his life many times by dangling from ropes or balancing on poorly secured ladders in order to copy more remote portions of the inscriptions. Here is his own account of how he copied the upper parts of the Persian inscription:

> On reaching the recess which contains the Persian text of the record, ladders are indispensable in order to examine the upper portion of the tablet; and even with ladders there is considerable risk, for the foot-ledge is so narrow, about eighteen inches or at most two feet in breadth, that with a ladder long enough to reach the sculptures sufficient slope cannot be given to enable a person to ascend, and, if the ladder be shortened in order to increase the slope, the upper inscription can only be copied by standing on the topmost step of the ladder, with no other support than steadying the body against the rock with the left arm, while the left hand holds the note-book, and the right hand is employed with the pencil. In this position I copied

all the upper inscriptions, and the interest of the occupation entirely
did away with any sense of danger.[4]

On his way to Kermanshah Rawlinson had copied an inscription
at Mount Elvand. Then, by a method similar to that of Grotefend (whose
results he had not yet seen) Rawlinson had succeeded in deciphering
the names of Darius and Xerxes. He also recognized the name of Darius
in the Behistun inscription. Between his trips to Behistun Rawlinson
studied the lines he had thus far copied, adding to the number of cuneiform characters he could read. In 1836 Rawlinson learned of Grotefend's
discoveries, but by then he had progressed so far in his translation
that Grotefend's readings provided no help. Rawlinson had already
independently discovered the values worked out earlier by the German
schoolteacher, and had improved upon the reading of the names identified by Grotefend. In addition, his knowledge of Persian enabled him
to ascertain the values of almost all the signs in the Old Persian
syllabary. By the end of 1837 he had completely copied, transliterated
and translated the first half (two hundred lines) of the Old Persian
section of the Behistun inscriptions. Rawlinson announced his results
in a paper sent to the Royal Asiatic Society. This paper and a sequel
in 1839 support his right to preeminence among those who had labored
to discover the secrets of cuneiform.

The first Afghan War (1839-42) interrupted Rawlinson's philological
research. However, in 1844 he became British resident at Baghdad and
was able to return to his study of the Behistun inscriptions. During
the next three years, with the help of a Kurdish boy, he was able to
complete his copy of all the inscriptions and reliefs at Behistun. His
translation of the entire four hundred lines of the Old Persian text
appeared in the *Journal of the Royal Asiatic Society* in 1846-47.

Rawlinson then turned his attention to the two other inscriptions
on the rock. Transferring the values he had determined for the Persian
cuneiform signs to the same signs in the other inscriptions, Rawlinson
and others began the task of deciphering these writings.[5] Scholars soon
discovered that one of the inscriptions was in a Semitic language related
to Hebrew, Arabic, Aramaic, and other known tongues. Also, this script
and language were identical to those on thousands of Assyrian tablets
and inscriptions uncovered in Mesopotamia from 1842 onward by Botta

---

4. "Notes on Some Paper Casts of Cuneiform Inscriptions upon the Sculptured Rock
at Behistun Exhibited to the Society of Antiquaries," *Archaeologia* 34 (1852): p. 74.

5. We now know that one of these texts was in Elamite, the language of the people
who lived just east of Mesopotamia in antiquity. The other was written in Akkadian,
the language of the ancient Babylonians and Assyrians.

and Layard. With such a wealth of material available for analysis, the decipherment of Assyrian (or Akkadian, as we call it today) proceeded rapidly.

In 1857 the Royal Asiatic Society conducted a test to determine the validity of claims that Akkadian could be read. An unpublished copy of a recently discovered Assyrian inscription was sent to the leading scholars in cuneiform research: Rawlinson, Edward Hinks, Jules Oppert, and W. H. Fox Talbot. The society requested that each man provide an independent translation and return it in a sealed envelope. When the translations were compared, they agreed on the general sense of the text and on all essential points of interpretation and grammar. The Mesopotamian remains could once again speak for themselves after two thousand years of silence.

BOTTA AND LAYARD REDISCOVER THE ASSYRIANS

Paul Emile Botta, the first French consular agent in Mosul, was an ideal choice for the dual diplomatic-archaeological post the French government had decided upon. He was an historian's son who had been educated as a physician and entomologist. However, after becoming a physician in Mohammed Ali's service in Egypt in 1830, Botta had become interested in antiquities. In 1833 France had named him its consul in Alexandria, and while holding this position he had undertaken an expedition into Yemen in Arabia. There he noted the historic remains of this little-visited area. By the time he went to Mosul in 1840 Botta was very knowledgeable in the languages and diplomatic methods necessary for dealing with Arabs and Turks. In addition, he had sufficient antiquarian experience to initiate French archaeological investigations in Mesopotamia.

Soon after his arrival in Mosul Botta began to spend his evenings exploring the countryside on horseback, studying the many mounds. He collected ancient pottery, inscribed bricks, and other antiquities from the natives, always seeking to learn where they had found the relics. In 1842 Botta decided to start digging at Kuyunjik, a large mound across the Tigris River from Mosul. This mound, along with the neighboring tell (mound) of Nebi Yunus, was traditionally the site of Nineveh, capital of the ancient Assyrian empire (Fig. 22). However, after months of excavation all that Botta found were a few inscribed bricks and some badly damaged pieces of stone that may once have been parts of sculptured reliefs or statues.

Thoroughly discouraged, Botta was about to abandon his search for ancient Assyrian remains when a passing Arab from the village

Fig. 22. Nebi Yunus (*left*) and Kuyunjik (*right*) with Mosul in the background. (From A. H. Layard, *Nineveh and Its Remains,* 1849.)

of Khorsabad gave him startling news. The man informed Botta that his settlement was built on a mound that contained sculptured stones and very many inscribed bricks. In fact, he said, his own house and many others in Khorsabad were built almost entirely of bricks dug from the *tell.* Botta was immediately interested, though cautious, for he had followed many false leads in the past. In March 1843 he sent a group of his best workmen to investigate the site. A short time later they sent back their report. The claims were true! Almost immediately after opening their first trench, Botta's crew had encountered walls and stone sculptures.

Botta abruptly shifted his operations to Khorsabad, about fourteen miles north of Kuyunjik, and within days had uncovered rows of stone slabs sculptured in bas-relief. Triumphantly Botta dispatched his now famous message to Julius Mohl in Paris: "I believe myself to be the first who has discovered sculptures which with some reason can be referred to the period when Nineveh was flourishing."[6]

Upon hearing of Botta's discoveries the Académie des Inscriptions et Belles-Lettres requested that the French government grant whatever

6. Seton Lloyd, *Foundations in the Dust,* rev. ed. (London: Thames and Hudson, 1980), p. 97.

funds were necessary to continue the excavations and transport the recovered antiquities to Paris. It was characteristic of the French government's attitude toward cultural endeavors in general and archaeology in particular that it immediately provided three thousand francs to expand the work. In addition, the government dispatched Eugène Flandin, an artist, to draw whatever sculptures Botta found. The French ambassador at Istanbul was instructed to secure a *firman* protecting Botta from interference by local authorities. But this took time, and Flandin did not arrive to deliver the permit to Botta until May 1844. In the meantime, Botta had been forced to close his excavations.

Mohammed Keritli Oglu, the pasha (governor) of Mosul, believed Botta was searching for buried treasure, so he did everything he could to hinder the excavations. He threw some of Botta's workmen into prison in order to force them to confess the Frenchman's plot to steal gold. He attempted to force workers to boycott the excavations. When these actions failed, Oglu ordered the digging stopped on the pretext that Botta was preparing fortifications for use in a plot to seize the country by force.

As if these hindrances weren't enough, Botta also had to contend with the threats that heat, rain, and the villagers of Khorsabad presented to his discoveries. The Assyrian palace he had found had been destroyed by fire in antiquity, causing the limestone reliefs to be extensively cracked and calcined. Often, when Botta uncovered sculptures they crumbled before he could examine them or sketch their scenes. On other occasions, bas-reliefs melted away when Botta was unable to protect them from sudden rainstorms. Because of the fragile condition of the carved slabs, Botta purchased many large beams with which to hold the reliefs in place against the mud-brick walls until they could be drawn and adequately prepared for removal. But since wood was scarce in Mesopotamia and very valuable, at night the local villagers would sneak into the trenches and steal the beams. This caused the collapse and destruction of many reliefs. In frustration Botta finally filled in his trenches and waited for help.

Botta was able to resume digging when Flandin arrived with the *firman,* and in the succeeding months Botta excavated much of the previously unexplored portion of the *tell.* Of course, Botta did not know for sure just what he was digging up, except that it was probably ancient Assyrian. His discoveries convinced him that Khorsabad, rather than the mounds across from Mosul, must be the site of ancient Nineveh. Only later would scholars learn that in antiquity Khorsabad was called Dur-Sharrukin ("City of Sargon") and that the palace Botta found had been constructed by the Assyrian king Sargon II (721–705 B.C.).

As he uncovered new wall reliefs, Botta copied the cuneiform inscriptions while Flandin made careful drawings of the bas-relief figures. Besides the sculptured slabs lining the walls of the palace, Botta found several large stone figures in the form of human-headed winged bulls or lions (Fig. 23). These statues flanked the major entrances to the buried building. Unfortunately, one of the best preserved of these gigantic sculptures had to be abandoned temporarily when the cart carrying it to Mosul broke down under the tremendous weight. Before Botta and Flandin could return to retrieve their statue, local peasants burned the limestone colossus into gypsum for use as mortar and cement. Despite such losses, however, many sculptures were successfully transported by raft down the Tigris to Basra where they were loaded aboard a French naval vessel and carried to France.

The Assyrian monuments arrived in France in December 1846 and were enthusiastically welcomed not only by the French, but by all Europeans. Most major newspapers devoted an unprecedented amount of space to stories about the Mesopotamian sculptures. These remains received greater coverage than any archaeological subject until the discovery of Tutankhamun's tomb in the early 1920s.

The publication of the results of this first excavation in Mesopotamia was as impressive as the display of Assyrian objects at the Louvre. The excavation report, like the excavations themselves, was financed by a generous grant from the French government. The five sumptuous volumes of Botta and Flandin's *Monument de Ninivé* (1849–50) are works of art in their own right. They have remained indispensable for serious study of Assyrian sculpture and architecture.

While he had been unsuccessfully probing the mound of Kuyunjik in 1842 Botta met Austen Henry Layard, a young Englishman on his way to Istanbul. Layard and Botta took to one another immediately, forming a lasting friendship despite the rivalry between their respective nations. Layard was also interested in excavating a Mesopotamian *tell* and had examined several mounds on his journey northward from Baghdad. Without any hesitation, however, he recommended to Botta that if the Frenchman didn't have any luck at Kuyunjik he should open some trenches in Nimrud, the most promising of the sites Layard had visited. For his part, Botta kept Layard informed about his progress. After his great discovery at Khorsabad, since his dispatches had to pass through Istanbul, Botta gave Layard permission to read them before they continued on to France.

Layard had given up a career in law in order to satisfy his longing for travel and adventure in the East. In 1839 the twenty-two-year-old explorer set out with E. L. Mitford on an overland journey through

Fig. 23. Excavating a pair of human-headed winged bulls at Khorsabad. These huge creatures flanked an entrance into the Assyrian palace. It was thought they would keep out demons and other evil spirits. (From P. Botta and M. Flandin, *Monument de Ninevé,* 1849.)

Europe, the Balkans, Asia Minor, Syria, Mesopotamia, Persia, and India with Ceylon as the ultimate objective. When, after many adventures, the two men reached Mesopotamia, they learned that civil war was raging in Persia. This made it unsafe for them to continue their planned itinerary. The two friends could not agree on a common course of action, so they separated. Mitford proceeded to India by ship, while Layard attempted the overland route through the troubled area. After two years of perilous journeys in the territory of the wild Bakhtiyari tribes, many robberies, and countless adventures later, Layard abandoned his attempt to cross Persia. He returned to Mesopotamia, arriving at the Baghdad residency barefoot and in rags.

While Layard was recuperating in Baghdad, news arrived that

Turkey and Persia were on the verge of war over a border dispute. Layard had just spent two years in the area in question, so the resident sent him to Istanbul. There he was to place his knowledge of the region and its people at the disposal of Sir Stratford Canning, British ambassador to the Ottoman Turkish Empire. It was during this trip to Istanbul that Layard met Botta and became his friend.

The British government did not accept Canning's recommendations (based on Layard's information) on the border conflict. But Layard so impressed the ambassador that Canning requested that the Foreign Office appoint him as an attaché to the embassy in Istanbul. Between 1843 and 1845 Layard undertook several important missions for Canning, but no official appointment arrived. Canning was due to return to England for rest and a series of briefings in the fall of 1845. He knew that Layard desired to investigate an Assyrian *tell*, so he personally provided sixty pounds for Layard to begin excavating Nimrud. If Layard uncovered anything of importance, Canning promised to do what he could to persuade the British government to subsidize continued excavation as the French had done with Botta.

Layard hastened to Nimrud, hired six workmen and began to dig. He chose a spot in the southwest portion of the *tell* where part of a limestone slab was visible above the ground. Within a few hours the diggers had cleared a room lined with stone slabs bearing bands of cuneiform inscriptions across their centers. Layard shifted some of his workmen to the northwestern section of the mound and almost immediately they discovered another room with sculptured stone panels along the walls. In less than twelve hours Layard had located two separate palaces!

He increased his work force and cleared additional rooms in each area. He learned some years later that these palaces had belonged to two of the greatest rulers of ancient Assyria, Asshurnasirpal II (883–859 B.C.) and Esarhaddon (680–669 B.C.), respectively.

Mohammed Keritli Oglu, the pasha who had caused Botta so much trouble at Khorsabad, soon learned of Layard's activities. Still convinced that the Europeans were searching for treasure, he sought a pretext to stop the excavations at Nimrud. Oglu informed Layard that he must cease his digging because it was disturbing Moslem graves on the summit of the mound. When Layard investigated, he discovered many headstones near his trenches. So the excavations stopped. Only later did Layard learn why he previously had failed to notice the graves. The captain of the Turkish troops stationed in the area confessed to Layard that on the pasha's orders his men had spent two nights bringing tombstones to Nimrud from surrounding villages. "We have destroyed

Fig. 24. Cutting up a winged bull at Nimrud for easier transportation to England. (From A. H. Layard, Nineveh and Its Remains, 1849.)

more real tombs of the true Believers in making sham ones," he confided, "than you could have defiled between the Zab and Selamiyah."[7]

However, the pasha's triumph was short-lived. Less than a month later he was deposed by the sultan and replaced by a more enlightened governor. Layard resumed his excavation of Nimrud with Hormuzd Rassam, the brother of the British vice-consul in Mosul, as his chief overseer. Rassam hired thirty Nestorian Christians from Salamiyah as the nucleus of the workforce, to minimize future problems that might arise because of Moslem beliefs.

Soon after Oglu's removal Layard received a *firman* from Istanbul protecting him from official interference with his work. Armed with this permit, he decided to dig a trial trench at Kuyunjik. Rich had reported that a stone sculpture had been dug from the *tell*, but Botta had excavated there for months and found nothing. However, Layard's good luck

---

7. A. H. Layard, Nineveh and Its Remains, abridged ed., ed. H. W. F. Saggs (London: Routledge & Kegan Paul, 1970), pp. 88–89.

continued. He was able to find an old stone cutter who claimed that he had been among those who had broken up the carving mentioned by Rich. The old man showed Layard where the pieces had been reburied. Within a short time Layard's workers dug up many pieces of limestone. When Layard pieced together the fragments, they formed the largest pair of winged bulls yet found. Layard could not continue his excavations at Kuyunjik, for his funds had run out. But he had seen enough to become convinced that within that great *tell* palaces and sculptures at least as sensational as those of Khorsabad and Nimrud waited to be found.

In the fall of 1846 the trustees of the British Museum finally responded to Layard and Canning's appeals for funds by awarding Layard two thousand pounds. Considering the magnitude of the discoveries Layard had already made, this grant can only be considered parsimonious. Moreover, this amount was expected to cover not only Layard's personal expenses, the cost of equipment, and salaries of workers for continued excavation, but also the cost of transporting the sculptures to England. Layard abandoned his hopes for systematic excavation and study of the monuments of Nimrud. Instead, his aim became that of obtaining "the largest possible number of well-preserved objects of art at the least possible outlay of time and money."[8] He dug trenches along the faces of walls exposing the sculptured relief slabs, but left the centers of the rooms unexcavated. Thus, many small objects, including inscribed tablets, went undiscovered until the 1950s, when the British systematically reexcavated the site.

Despite the limitations of funds, Layard continued to make spectacular discoveries at Nimrud: winged bulls and lions, bas-relief scenes of hunting and warfare, fragments of frescoes, bronze helmets and bowls, fragile pieces of carved ivory inlay, and a six-and-a-half-foot-tall black marble obelisk with bands of bas-relief depicting conquered kings bringing tribute to an Assyrian monarch. This last object was destined to become the most famous of Layard's finds (Fig. 25). When scholars were able to read the obelisk's inscriptions they found "Jehu, son of Omri (sic), King of Israel" listed among the tribute-bearing vassals of Shalmaneser III. This brief reference to an Israelite king provided the first definite link between an archaeological discovery and biblical history (I Kings 19:16; II Kings 9–10). Although it might seem minor today, this biblical confirmation immediately became a subject of widespread discussion and debate—it arrived at a time when many Victorians felt that adherents of uniformitarian geology were attacking the foundations of their biblical faith.

---

8. Quoted in S. Lloyd, *Foundations in the Dust*, rev. ed., p. 108.

Fig. 25. The black obelisk at Nimrud. (From A. H. Layard, *Nineveh and Its Remains*, 1849.)

Six months of extensive digging at Nimrud virtually exhausted the money provided by the British Museum. Layard reluctantly closed his trenches and used the remaining funds to ship a winged bull and lion, seventy bas-reliefs, the black obelisk, and almost 250 drawings to Basra and thence to England. Then, after a brief pause at Kuyunjik, where he uncovered a few rooms and several sculptures belonging to still another Assyrian king, Layard departed for England and a much-needed rest.

Layard's account of his discoveries, *Nineveh and Its Remains* (for he erroneously believed Nimrud to be part of ancient Nineveh), was published in 1849 and immediately became a bestseller. The London *Times* review was lavish in its praise: "This is, we think, the most extraordinary work of the present age, whether with reference to the wonderful discoveries it describes, its remarkable verification of our early biblical history, or of the talent, courage, and perseverance of its author."⁹ *Nineveh and Its Remains*, the exhibition of the sculptures

---

9. The London *Times*, February 9, 1849.

Fig. 26. Layard drawing sculptures at Kuyunjik. (From A. H. Layard, *Discoveries Among the Ruins of Nineveh and Babylon*, 1853.)

from Nimrud, and newspaper accounts of Layard's work aroused so much popular interest in Mesopotamian archaeology that the trustees of the British Museum offered Layard three thousand pounds to renew his excavations. By late 1849 Layard and Rassam were back at Kuyunjik, on which they had decided to concentrate this expedition's efforts.

By this time Assyrian cuneiform inscriptions could be read well enough for Layard to recognize the name of the Assyrian king Sennacherib (704–681 B.C.) on inscriptions in the palace he had found at Kuyunjik. As he uncovered more rooms of the building complex he came across important new sculptures. Some recorded the building of the palace, including scenes of the carving, transportation and erection of a colossal winged bull like those that Botta and Layard had found so difficult to move. But the most sensational discoveries to the mid-nineteenth-century mind were reliefs showing Sennacherib capturing the city of Lachish in Palestine and an inscription recording his siege of Jerusalem. These Assyrian records were in basic agreement with the biblical accounts of Sennacherib's invasion of Judah in II Kings 18–19.

Not long after these discoveries, Layard's diggers came upon two chambers covered to a depth of more than twelve inches with clay tablets inscribed in cuneiform. These documents had formed part of the Assyrian royal archives. When translated they would reveal much of the history and civilization of ancient Mesopotamia as well as many additional links with biblical narratives (Fig. 26).

Layard's main concern during the expedition of 1849–51 was the work at Kuyunjik, but he also found time to reopen his excavations at Nimrud. He also made soundings (minor exploratory excavations) at several other sites, including Tell Billa, Qal'at Sherqat (ancient Ashur), Niffar (ancient Nippur), and Babil (Babylon). However, except at Nimrud, Layard's excavations at these mounds produced no new discoveries of any significance. These sites represented settlements older than the Assyrian remains excavated by Botta and Layard; stone reliefs did not line the mud-brick walls of their buildings. Their successful excavation would take more money, skill, and patience than Layard possessed.

In 1851 the explorer returned to England to stand for Parliament and to savor the fame and public adulation he had earned. His career as an excavator was over. The results of his last excavations were published two years later in Discoveries in the Ruins of Nineveh and Babylon and The Monuments of Nineveh.

COMPETITION FOR MESOPOTAMIAN ANTIQUITIES

The French government resumed its role in Mesopotamian archaeology in 1851 by instructing Victor Place, the new French consul in Mosul, to reopen the excavations at Khorsabad. From 1851 to 1853 Place systematically explored the areas of the mound Botta had left untouched. Botta had thought that he had found all there was to find at the site, but Place proved him wrong. He uncovered new sections of Sargon's palace, recovering many new sculptured reliefs. Place also produced a ground plan of the entire palace and drawings depicting it as it must have looked in Sargon's time.

The resumption of archaeological activity by the French inaugurated a frantic scramble for antiquities between British and French representatives. Both Victor Place and Hormuzd Rassam (Layard's former assistant and his successor as director of British excavations) tried to claim as many mounds as possible. The Ottoman Empire was not yet regulating archaeological excavations in its territories. So it had become accepted custom that rights to a site belonged to the nation whose representative first excavated it. Thus, Place and Rassam each sent gangs of workmen scurrying around the countryside digging trenches in every mound that seemed promising. These diggers were often left unsupervised for weeks or months at a time. Thus, what finds they did make lost much of their historical value, since the workmen did not keep adequate records of the archaeological contexts in which objects were found.

There was also a constant danger of open conflict between the rival gangs of men. A disaster was only narrowly averted when both excavation parties arrived at the mound of Qal'at Sherqat at the same time and began fighting. The rivalry also led each side to make unsubstantiated accusations against the other. The British claimed that Place had attempted to hire a local sheik to attack some of Rassam's men. On the other hand, the French asserted that the British had bribed the pasha to prevent Place from purchasing a winged bull found by villagers of Nebi Yunus.

The two nations also contested the right to excavate the mound of Kuyunjik (which by that time was known to be the site of ancient Nineveh). Since both Botta and Layard had dug there, France and Britain finally agreed that the mound would be divided into two zones. The French would work in the northern half of the *tell* while the British would continue their excavations in the palace of Sennacherib that Layard had found in the southern portion. However, after a year's digging at Kuyunjik, Rassam was disappointed by his finds, which seemed meager compared to Layard's great discoveries. He coveted the French portion of the mound. So, in December 1853 he decided to do some clandestine digging in Kuyunjik's northern sector. Rassam selected a likely spot for investigation, chose a few trustworthy workmen, and conducted his surreptitious excavations at night so no one would report them to the French. After three nights' digging he found a wall lined with sculptures. This wall led to a group of rooms that were obviously part of a new palace. Rassam now began clearing the chambers in broad daylight, and Place, faced with a *fait accompli,* conceded the area to the British with remarkably good grace.

Around the walls of one of the newly discovered rooms was a series of bas-reliefs depicting the Assyrian king Ashurbanipal (668–626 B.C.) hunting lions and wild asses. These reliefs were in almost perfect condition, and from the first scholars recognized them as the finest examples of Assyrian art yet discovered. In the same room Rassam found a mass of tablets. These texts comprised the remainder of the Assyrian royal library, part of which Layard had unearthed in the palace

Map 4. Early archaeology in Mesopotamia.

of Sennacherib. Together these two palace libraries yielded over twenty thousand tablets dealing with such varied subjects as royal correspondence, chronicles of the reigns of kings, legal contracts, religious rituals, myths, and epics.

In 1854 Hormuzd Rassam was appointed to a diplomatic post in Aden in Arabia. His successor as excavator at Kuyunjik was William Kennett Loftus, who had gained some archaeological experience while on a diplomatic mission in southern Mesopotamia. Loftus had excavated for several weeks at three sites south of Baghdad: Warka (the site of ancient Erech), Senkara (ancient Larsa), and Tell Sifr. His discoveries included a Parthian cemetery containing many slipper-shaped clay coffins, a segment of wall decorated with inlaid terra-cotta cones of different colors, some cuneiform tablets, foundation cylinders of Nebuchadnezzar II, many inscribed bricks, and a large collection of bronze bowls, daggers, axes, mirrors, and other implements.

Assisted by William Boutcher, an artist, Loftus cleared a few more rooms of the palace of Ashurbanipal, uncovering many more slabs carved in bas-relief. He shipped the best-preserved sculptures to the British Museum, where they may still be seen. But much information on the palace and its decoration was lost, partially because of Loftus's failure to keep adequate records of his discoveries, and partially as a result of a catastrophe during the transportation of some of the slabs. Henry Rawlinson, then British resident at Baghdad, had given Place permission to select for the Louvre some of the damaged sculptures from Ashurbanipal's palace. He also set aside several other reliefs for the king of Prussia. These sculptures from Kuyunjik, 148 cases in all, and the entire results of Place's excavations at Khorsabad were lost in 1855. A band of Arab brigands attacked and capsized the rafts carrying the sculptures, sending them to the bottom of the Tigris. To make the disaster complete, Boutcher's drawings of the sunken Kuyunjik reliefs were also lost. They were misplaced in England before being published. It was, as Seton Lloyd has remarked, "a fitting end to the whole unedifying scramble."[10]

Phase II—Near Eastern Archaeology Comes of Age (1855–1926)

THE DISCOVERY OF THE SUMERIANS, THE FLOOD, AND THE HITTITES

The outbreak of the Crimean War in 1855 brought a temporary end to British and French archaeological excavations in Mesopotamia. Scholarly emphasis, therefore, shifted to study of the thousands of tablets and inscriptions uncovered during the previous decade and a half. Akkadian, the Semitic language used by the ancient Babylonians and Assyrians, had begun to yield its secrets by 1855. But among the

---

10. *Foundations in the Dust*, rev. ed., p. 140.

cuneiform tablets from the libraries of Sennacherib and Ashurbanipal were many not written in Akkadian. These texts were in a strange, non-Semitic tongue. In addition, there were bilingual word lists or "dictionaries" giving the Akkadian equivalents for hundreds of words in the unknown language. The identity of the people who spoke this mysterious language was revealed in 1869 by Jules Oppert. In a lecture before the French Society of Numismatics and Archaeology he pointed out that inscriptions showed that early rulers in Mesopotamia had claimed the title "King of Sumer and Akkad." Since the Semitic population of Babylonia and Assyria referred to themselves and their language as Akkadian, the speakers of the non-Semitic language of some of the texts must have been Sumerian.

However, another find among the tablets from Kuyunjik aroused far more public interest than did the discovery of the Sumerians. In 1872 George Smith, an assistant in the Assyrian section of the British Museum, was sorting tablets from Nineveh. He found a broken tablet recording what seemed to be part of a legend or myth and began glancing over its contents. He relates:

> On looking down the third column, my eye caught the statement that the ship rested on the mountains of Nizir, followed by the account of the sending forth of the dove, and its finding no resting-place and returning. I saw at once that I had here discovered a portion at least of the Chaldean [Mesopotamian] account of the Deluge.[11]

Smith searched through the tablets and produced additional parts of the story. However, there was a gap of some seventeen lines near the beginning of the narrative that he could not restore from the tablets and fragments in the museum. Nevertheless, on December 3, 1872, Smith announced his discovery in a paper read before the Society of Biblical Archaeology. Public interest in this find was so great that the London *Daily Telegraph* offered Smith a thousand pounds to equip an expedition to Nineveh to search for the missing section of the narrative. After some delay in obtaining a *firman,* in May 1873 Smith and his expedition arrived at Kuyunjik and began the quest. He began digging through the piles of debris left by previous British excavations at the site. In five days he found over three hundred fragments of tablets that had been overlooked or discarded by earlier excavators. On the evening of the fifth day of excavation:

---

11. Quoted in R. Cambell Thompson and R. W. Hutchinson, *A Century of Exploration at Nineveh* (London: Luzac, 1929), p. 49.

I sat down to examine the store of fragments of cuneiform inscriptions from the day's digging, taking out and brushing off the earth from the fragments to read their contents. On cleaning one of them I found to my surprise and gratification that it contained the greater portion of the seventeen lines of inscription belonging to the first column of the Chaldean account of the Deluge, and fitting into the only place where there was a serious blank in the story.[12]

The Mesopotamian account of the Flood was remarkably similar to the Hebrew story in Genesis. Clearly the two were related in some way. But how? Believers in biblical inerrancy argued that the Mesopotamian story proved that the Flood had really occurred. On the other hand, many scholars became convinced that the Israelites had borrowed the story from Mesopotamia.[13] The debates over this issue heightened public interest in Near Eastern archaeology and initiated a new period of excavation and discovery.

One of the most fruitful of the new expeditions was that of the French under Ernest de Sarzec. Sarzec didn't concentrate his attention on an Assyrian mound in the north as most earlier excavators had done. Instead, he decided to dig at Telloh, one of the most prominent mounds south of Baghdad. Between 1877 and the turn of the century he conducted eleven seasons of excavations at this *tell,* the site of the ancient city of Lagash. At Telloh Sarzec uncovered for the first time sculptured representations of Sumerians. Scholars had recognized the existence of these early inhabitants of southern Mesopotamia only a few years before Sarzec began digging. But now, not only Sumerian statues, but historical stelae and thousands of tablets in Sumerian were found. These materials enabled philologists to make rapid strides in the study of the language and history of these mysterious people.

An American expedition obtained further information on the Sumerians from Niffar (ancient Nippur). This site was extensively excavated by scholars from the University of Pennsylvania. The first season in 1888, under the direction of John Peters, was a disaster. Peters, a clergyman, was unfamiliar with Near Eastern customs. He failed to seek the protection of a local sheik and aroused the enmity of the Arab tribes inhabiting the region. The friction between the excavators and the Arabs became so heated that the natives surrounded the mound. After a skirmish during which the expedition's camp was pillaged and burned, the Americans beat a retreat out of the area.

---

12. Ibid., p. 52.
13. This is the view generally accepted today.

The next year the expedition returned under new leadership. However, the Americans' excavation techniques continued to leave much to be desired until the final season (1899–1900), when Hermann Hilprecht was put in charge. Hilprecht, a German Assyriologist who had become a professor at the University of Pennsylvania in 1886, insisted on orderly, systematic digging. He also made sure that the finds were recorded properly. This had not always been done in previous seasons, which sometimes had lacked an architect, a photographer, and a cuneiform specialist.

Despite these problems, in four seasons of work the excavators found over thirty thousand tablets. Like the texts from Lagash, most of the Nippur tablets proved to be economic, legal, or administrative in nature. But about two thousand of the texts dealt with Sumerian mythology and literature. It soon became apparent that many of the Babylonian and Assyrian compositions (including the famous Flood story) had been based on Sumerian originals. As a result of the excavations at Telloh and Niffar scholars were able to begin reconstructing Sumerian civilization—a civilization whose very existence had been unsuspected only a generation earlier.

While the French and Americans were first bringing to light Sumerian remains in southern Mesopotamia, another unknown civilization was being recovered in Asia Minor. As early as 1812 Jean Louis Burckhardt had noted a strange stone in Hama (ancient Hamath), Syria. It was covered with what appeared to be hieroglyphic writing, though the signs did not resemble those of Egypt. The authors of this inscription were unknown. In 1834 a Frenchman named Charles Felix Marie Texier discovered some monumental city-ruins near the village of Boghazköy in north-central Turkey (Fig. 27). Nearby he found a bas-relief procession of strange god-like figures carved on the stone wall of a cleft in the hills (Fig. 28). Accompanying the figures were hieroglyphic signs like those Burckhardt had seen in Hama. A few other travelers visited Boghazköy in the 1850s and 1860s and described the ruins. Also, similar remains and hieroglyphic writing were noted at Alaca Hüyük and Smyrna in Asia Minor and at Aleppo and Carchemish in Syria. But what ancient people could have left these remains spread over an area from coastal Asia Minor through northern Syria? Until the late 1870s no one knew.

Two British citizens provided an answer to the mystery. In 1878 William Wright, an Irish missionary stationed at Damascus, published an article on the finds from Asia Minor in *British and Foreign Evangelical Review*. In it he suggested that the Hittites, an obscure people mentioned in the Bible, might have created the remains. But Wright

Fig. 27. Ruins of a temple at Boghazköy as drawn by Texier. (From C. F. M. Texier, *Description de l'Asie Mineure, 1839–49.*)

Fig. 28. Texier's drawing of Hittite gods at Yazilikaya near Boghazköy. These figures are carved into the sides of a cleft in the hills. The engraver seems to have restored Texier's drawings, making these weathered and damaged sculptures appear in better condition than they actually are. (From C. F. M. Texier, *Description de l'Asie Mineure,* 1839–49.)

had little evidence to back up his guess, and his article did not attract much attention. Two years later a Welsh Orientalist, Archibald Henry Sayce, made the same inspired guess in a lecture to the Society of Biblical Archaeology. This time, though, the response was different. Sayce's lecture touched off a lively scholarly debate that was followed closely in the popular press.

The debate was still raging in 1884 when Wright published a small book titled *The Empire of the Hittites, with Decipherment of the Hittite Inscriptions by Professor A. H. Sayce.* Wright and Sayce could point to II Kings 7:6, which referred to the Hittites as a great power equivalent to the Egyptians. But they didn't have any "hard" evidence to support their identification until scholars began testing it against Assyrian and Egyptian documents. Assyrian texts frequently referred to a "Land of Hatti" somewhere northwest of Mesopotamia. And Egyptian inscriptions from the New Kingdom (circa 1550–1100 B.C.) mentioned a northern kingdom called *Ht* (Heta or Hatti) that perhaps was the same place.

The Amarna letters, a cache of cuneiform tablets discovered in Egypt in 1887, proved that *Ht* was the Egyptian writing for "Hatti." These tablets turned out to be fourteenth-century B.C. diplomatic correspondence to the Egyptian pharaohs Amenhotep III, Akhenaton, and Tutankhamun. They contained references to and letters from the king of Hatti, who clearly was a major ruler, suggesting that his kingdom was centered in Asia Minor, though his power extended into northern Syria. Wright and Sayce's intuitive hypothesis had been shown to be correct, and another "lost" Near Eastern empire entered the history books.

In 1906 the German Assyriologist Hugo Winckler began excavating the fortress mound at Boghazköy and uncovered an archive of cuneiform tablets. The ones written in Hittite (which turned out to be an Indo-European language) were not deciphered until 1915. However, many of the tablets were written in Akkadian and could be understood immediately. They removed the last doubts that the kingdom of Hatti had been centered in Asia Minor and that in the fourteenth to thirteenth centuries B.C. its power had been equal to that of Egypt and Assyria. These texts also proved that Hattusas, the ancient name for the Boghazköy ruins, had been the capital of the Hittite empire. Furthermore, they provided voluminous material for reconstructing the history of the Hittites, a process that has continued to this day.

STRATIGRAPHIC EXCAVATION COMES TO THE NEAR EAST

The French and American expeditions to Telloh and Niffar in the 1870s and 1880s signaled the start of a new attitude in Near Eastern archaeology. Each of these expeditions chose to concentrate on the extensive investigation of a single site. Moreover, each was adequately funded, equipped, and psychologically prepared for the years of work that such a plan required. Neither group was motivated (as most previous Near Eastern explorers had been) by what Loftus described as "a nervous desire to find important large museum pieces at the least possible outlay of time and money."[14] Nevertheless, the excavation methods used at Telloh and Niffar still left much to be desired.

Emphasis on precise, stratigraphical excavation was introduced into Near Eastern archaeology by Flinders Petrie, Robert Koldewey, and Walter Andrae. Petrie's work was the earliest (1890), but he dug for only one year at Tell el-Hesi in Palestine before returning to his work in Egypt.

However, beginning in 1899 and continuing until 1917 the Deutsche Orient-Gesellschaft (German Oriental Society) excavated the ruins of Babylon. Dr. Robert Koldewey, an architect, art historian, and experienced excavator, directed these excavations. Before becoming director of the Babylonian expedition, Koldewey had dug at Assos in the Aegean, Surgal and el-Hibba in southern Mesopotamia, and other sites in Syria, Italy, and Sicily. At Babylon he trained his workmen to dig slowly and carefully. This enabled them to discern the traces of unbaked mud-brick walls as well as the more easily recognized fired-brick or stone-lined structures. Earlier excavators who dug briefly at Babylon had been looking for bas-relief slabs like those found at Khorsabad and Nimrud. But stone sculptures were extremely rare at Babylon and other southern Mesopotamian sites. Because they had been unable to differentiate the remains of mud-brick buildings from the debris covering them, the early excavators had found very little at Babylon. Koldewey, however, began to reveal the ancient capital in all its splendor.

The first remains he uncovered were portions of the massive city walls. These walls, built by Nebuchadnezzar II (605–562 B.C.), had over-awed the ancient Greek visitors Herodotus and Ctesias. While these writers had exaggerated their circumference, in all other respects the fortifications turned out to be as prodigious as the Greeks had claimed. A twenty-two-foot-wide inner wall of unbaked brick with watchtowers spaced 160 feet apart was surrounded after an interval of thirty-eight feet by a twenty-five-foot-wide wall of baked brick that also had watchtowers spaced along it. In front of this outer wall was a smaller baked-brick rampart twelve feet wide protecting the inner edge of the moat that surrounded the entire citadel. Koldewey determined that the

---

14. Quoted in Seton Lloyd, *Foundations in the Dust*, rev. ed., p. 132.

circuit of the city walls was a little more than eleven miles, making Babylon the largest city in ancient Mesopotamia.

The Germans also uncovered the great stepped tower or *ziggurat* upon which the temple of Marduk once stood. This pyramid-like structure was originally about 295 feet high, and it may have inspired the biblical story of the Tower of Babel. Today only traces of this massive structure remain. After Koldewey and his staff left the site almost all of the surviving bricks of the ziggurat were carried away by natives of the nearby town of Hillah and used to build houses and a dam.

Leading to the temple of Marduk was a wide avenue called the Processional Way. This road was flanked on either side by walls decorated with colorful glazed bricks and reliefs of bulls, lions, and the *sirrush* (the sacred dragon of Marduk). At the wall surrounding the inner city, the Processional Way passed through a monumental fortified gate covered with blue glazed bricks and more bas-relief figures. This entrance was known as the Ishtar Gate in honor of the major goddess of ancient Mesopotamia. The decoration of this great gateway was in a good state of preservation, so Koldewey dismantled it brick by brick. Eventually he shipped the bricks to Germany and reassembled them into a full-size reconstruction of the gate in the Berlin Museum.

Archaeologists from the Deutsche Orient-Gesellschaft also systematically excavated Qal'at Sherqat from 1902 to 1914 under the direction of Dr. Walter Andrae. This mound was the site of ancient Ashur, the first capital of Assyria. Andrae learned that Ashur was much more ancient than most other Assyrian cities. Just as at Babylon and Sumerian sites, unbaked mud-brick structures predominated at Ashur, so great care had to be taken to distinguish walls from the debris covering them. At the site of the temple of Ishtar Andrae found that later temples had been constructed atop the ruins of many predecessors. He excavated them layer by layer, temple after temple, until he reached the earliest sanctuary to be built on that spot. The ruins of each temple were uncovered, completely planned, and photographed before being cleared away so that earlier remains might be studied. This triumph of careful excavation technique set an example for future stratigraphical excavations in Mesopotamia and other parts of the Near East. Furthermore, while not as readable as the accounts of Layard or some of the other pioneers, the German expeditions' reports were as meticulous, detailed, and precise as the excavations themselves.

While Koldewey and Andrae excavated very carefully and observed stratigraphy, they did not recognize the importance of pottery as a dating tool. However, Flinders Petrie's success in developing a prehistoric pottery sequence for Egypt and his emphasis on pottery in his exca-

Fig. 29. The ziggurat at Ur before excavation. (From W. K. Loftus, *Travels and Researches in Chaldea and Susiana*, 1857.)

vations at Tell el-Hesi in Palestine made Near Eastern archaeologists aware of the potential of a stratigraphically based pottery chronology.

Petrie's lead was followed by George Reisner at Samaria in Palestine (1908–10) and Charles Leonard Woolley at Carchemish in Syria (1911–14). Reisner and Woolley not only excavated stratigraphically, but they also kept careful records of the changes in pottery types from one layer to another. Like fossils in geological strata, the pottery sherds in archaeological layers would eventually provide the means to relate the strata and chronologies of many sites over a large area.

After World War I much of the Near East would come under the protection of France or England. Departments of antiquities and local museums were created by the new governments, ending the wholesale plundering of antiquities by Western institutions. Also, stratigraphical excavation and emphasis on pottery and other small finds gradually became the recognized archaeological standard.

The new approach to excavation can be illustrated by Leonard Woolley's excavations at Ur. Here he would uncover an early flood layer[15]

---

15. Woolley thought this layer of silt had been laid down by a great flood that had covered most of Mesopotamia in prehistoric times. He felt that it had given rise to the Mesopotamian flood story which in turn had inspired the biblical Deluge narratives. However, others have shown that the flood at Ur was local and did not even cover all areas of the city let alone most of Mesopotamia.

as well as the great ziggurat of Ur (Fig. 29), palaces, private houses, and the famous royal tombs. These burials, rich in golden objects and beautiful museum pieces, were discovered in 1922, soon after the expedition began its work. However, Woolley immediately stopped digging in that area of the site. He wanted his workmen to gain more experience and come to know and respect him before attempting to excavate such treasure. Also, Woolley felt he first needed to learn more of the history and chronology of the site through excavations in other parts of the mound. Not until 1926 did he feel ready to undertake the painstaking excavation of the cemetery. Between 1922 and 1926 the newspapers were full of reports about the wonderful finds in Tutankhamun's tomb in Egypt. The urge to compete for the spotlight by quickly unearthing his own golden treasures at Ur must have been great, but Wooley successfully resisted temptation and stuck to his plan. Near Eastern archaeology at last deserved to be considered a discipline.

4

The Growth of Aegean Archaeology

Phase I: Speculation, Antiquarianism, and Early Excavation (1500–1870)

REVIVAL OF INTEREST IN GREEK MONUMENTS

In the fifteenth century the Renaissance reawakened European interest in ancient Greek and Roman civilization. However, it did not immediately end the centuries of neglect and destruction to which classical remains had been subjected. The fate of the Parthenon in Athens is an example of the continued deterioration of ancient Greek structures during early modern times. In late antiquity this temple of Athena had become a Christian church. Then, when the Turks conquered Greece in the fifteenth century, they made the Parthenon into a Moslem mosque and added a minaret to it. Despite these changes, it had remained structurally intact. However, in 1687 a fleet of ships from Venice attacked Athens. The Turks decided that the Parthenon, near the center of Athens' Acropolis, was the safest place to store their gunpowder and ammunition. But, as fate would have it, a Venetian shell scored a direct hit on the ancient temple. The blast almost totally destroyed the interior walls and roof of the building. In addition, it knocked down and broke several columns, the sculptured frieze, and many of the statues from the pediments. Before 1687 twenty sculptured figures stood in the west pediment. About twelve of them survived the explosion. By 1800 only four remained.

Fig. 30. The east end of the Parthenon in the mid-eighteenth century. (From J. Stuart and N. Revett, *The Antiquities of Athens*, 1762–1816.)

Fig. 31. Stuart's drawing of himself sketching the Erechtheum. (From J. Stuart and N. Revett, *The Antiquities of Athens*, 1762–1816.)

One organization that brought the plight of ancient Greek structures to public attention was the Society of Dilettanti. This society was founded in London in 1734. It financed an extensive survey of Athenian monuments by artist James Stuart and architect Nicholas Revett between 1751 and 1754. A decade later it sponsored Richard Chandler's similar study of the ruins of Ionia.

The society also published the results of these expeditions, Chandler's *Ionian Antiquities* in 1769, and the volumes of his more detailed *The Antiquities of Ionia* between 1769 and 1797. Stuart and Revett's four-volume work, *The Antiquities of Athens,* began publication in 1762, but the final volume was not published until 1816. The careful measurements and drawings of classical buildings found in these volumes provided much of the inspiration for late eighteenth- and early nineteenth-century architectural classicism. These works were particularly influential in North America, where many private and state buildings utilized Ionic and Doric colonnades, sculptured pediments, and other elements of Greek architecture. Unfortunately, many of the antiquities recorded by Stuart, Revett, and Chandler have since been destroyed, so their publications remain an invaluable source of information on the monuments of classical Greece.

Another landmark in the study of classical antiquities was the publication of Johann J. Winckelmann's *History of Ancient Art* (1764). From the few clues to the chronology of ancient art and architecture in classical writings and by an almost intuitive recognition of stylistic development, Winckelmann (Fig. 32) produced the first systematic chronology for classical remains. Before Winckelmann's book, people had appreciated Greek and Roman antiquities primarily for their esthetic qualities. Now scholars were able to view them also as historically important expressions of changing social and cultural ideals.

EARLY EXCAVATIONS IN GREECE

When Winckelmann wrote, most examples of ancient "Greek" sculpture were, in fact, Roman copies of earlier masterpieces. There had been virtually no archaeological excavations in Greece during the seventeenth and eighteenth centuries. Thus, scholars had no Greek originals against which to compare the Roman copies. That situation changed, however, after the British defeated Napoleon's troops in Egypt. In gratitude the sultan of Turkey gave the British ambassador, Thomas Bruce, seventh earl of Elgin, permission to remove any stones in Athens that might interest him. The British government refused to provide funds for securing Greek sculptures, so Lord Elgin personally bore the expense

Fig. 32. Johann Joachim Winckelmann (1717–68). (From J. J. Winckelmann, *Monumenti Antichi inediti Spiegati ed illustrati,* 1767.)

of the project. Between 1803 and 1812 his workmen removed the Parthenon's surviving metopes, frieze, and pedimental statues. They also took a portion of the frieze and one of the caryatids (columns in the form of draped maidens) from another temple, the Erechtheum. The sculptures were publicly displayed in London for the first time in 1814 and immediately became a focal point for controversy. Some, like Lord Byron, accused the earl of vandalism for removing the sculptures from their original sites. Others, accustomed to the less idealized Hellenistic-Roman style in sculpture, contemptuously dismissed the Elgin Marbles, as they became known, as inferior works of art. After much debate in Parliament, the British Museum purchased the sculptures in 1816, but paid only thirty-five thousand pounds, considerably less than it had cost Lord Elgin to remove the marbles and transport them to England.

At about the same time, English architect C. R. Cockerell and German Baron Haller von Hallerstein uncovered some statues on the island of Aegina. These figures, the most famous of which is a kneeling Heracles drawing a bow, had fallen from the pediment of the Temple of Aphaea. They were slightly older than the Parthenon sculptures but exhibited the same classic idealized naturalism and the same impression of divine aloofness. Prince Ludwig of Bavaria purchased them in 1812. After being extensively restored they were exhibited in 1828 in the Munich Glypothek, where they remain today. These figures and the Elgin Marbles together came to have a strong influence on the artistic taste of the West.

Extensive archaeological work in Greece began during the Greek war of independence against Turkey. In 1829 the French sent forces to aid the Greeks in their fight. With them went a contingent of scholars, who composed the Expédition scientifique de Morée ("The Scientific Expedition of the Peloponnesus"). The scholars explored the Peloponnesus, describing and drawing whatever ancient remains could be found. They also conducted brief excavations at a few sites. At Olympia they uncovered fragments of metopes from the famous Temple of Zeus. At Epidaurus they discovered and excavated a portion of the ancient theater.

Meanwhile, in Athens the Greeks themselves became active in archaeology, combining it with their growing nationalism. During the centuries that the Turks had ruled Greece, they had modified several classical buildings on the Acropolis of Athens. Greek archaeologists now removed all Turkish buildings and renovations from the Acropolis. They also excavated some buried fragments of the Parthenon frieze, and cleared the remains of the Nike Temple, Propylaea steps, and Erechtheum.

The Greek Archaeological Society was founded in 1837 and all excavation in Greece was placed under government regulation. Greek archaeologists now began to play a larger role in the excavation and study of their country's antiquities. But expeditions from other nations did not cease. In 1846 the French established a school of archaeology in Athens to conduct excavations and to foster research into Greece's ancient heritage. Before the end of the nineteenth century the Germans, Americans, British, and Austrians had followed suit. Italian and Swedish schools of archaeology have also been established in Greece in more recent times. These institutions helped provide the necessary financial support and scholarly expertise to bring Aegean archaeology to maturity.

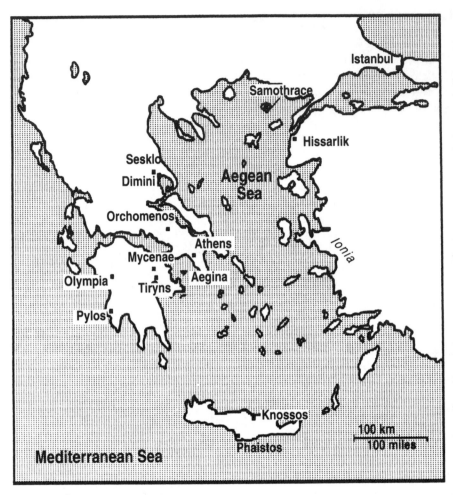

Map 5. Early archaeology in the Aegean area.

Phase II: Aegean Archaeology Comes of Age (1870–1939)

SCHLIEMANN DISCOVERS AEGEAN PREHISTORY

In the spring of 1870 a German businessman began digging into the mound of Hissarlik on the coast of Asia Minor. He found no beautiful sculptures or well-preserved classical temples, but he was destined to be remembered long after the memory of most other excavators in the

Aegean area had faded into obscurity. The man was Heinrich Schliemann, and his discoveries added more than two thousand years to the Aegean area's past.

In later life Schliemann claimed that from his youth he had dreamed of finding the great city of Troy described so vividly in Homer's *Iliad*. His love of the past and his particular fondness for the Homeric epics might have led Schliemann to become a professional classicist. But his father's poverty forced Heinrich to leave school at the age of fourteen. For five years he worked as an apprentice in a grocer's shop in Hamburg. In 1841 he signed up as a cabin boy on a small brig, hoping to improve his health and earn a larger salary. On his first voyage the ship sank in a storm off the Dutch coast, and Schliemann was one of the few crewmen saved. He found himself alone, hungry, and penniless in Amsterdam.

However, Schliemann's fortunes were about to change. Through the recommendation of a friend in Hamburg, Schliemann got a job as an office boy in the firm of an Amsterdam merchant. In his spare time the young German began to teach himself languages. He spent hours memorizing lists, figures, and whole books, until his memory became so good that he never had to look up the meaning of an unknown word twice. It took six months for him to master English, and another six months to learn French. Schliemann's efforts to learn those languages greatly improved his memory and study habits. In the future he was able to learn a new language in only six weeks. He then taught himself to read and write Dutch, Spanish, Portuguese, and Italian. Schliemann soon accepted a new position as bookkeeper and correspondent for another merchant firm in Amsterdam. Since his new employer did a considerable amount of business with Russian merchants, Schliemann decided to learn Russian. Six weeks of intensive study again sufficed for the self-taught linguist to become fluent in speaking and writing his eighth language.

Schliemann's company sent the twenty-four-year-old to St. Petersburg in 1846 as its resident representative. A year later he was able to start his own import-export firm in the Russian capital, becoming wealthy beyond his most optimistic expectations. In less than ten years this German Horatio Alger had transformed himself from a poor, uneducated grocer's clerk into a rich merchant who could conduct business and carry on correspondence in most of the major languages of Europe. This was a feat that even nineteenth-century romantic novelists might have considered too unbelievable for a fiction plot.

Over the next twenty years Schliemann made another fortune in America during the California gold rush, attained American citizenship, and ended by divorce his disastrous marriage to the niece of a Russian business acquaintance. Schliemann also learned nine more languages:

Fig. 33. Hissarlik from the north after the excavations of 1870–73. (From H. Schliemann, *Ilios: The City and Country of the Trojans*, 1880.)

Polish, Slovenian, Danish, Swedish, Norwegian, Arabic, Latin, and both classical and modern Greek. At the age of forty-one he decided to retire from business and devote his full time to realization of a childhood dream—the discovery of Troy.

Schliemann traveled and informally studied archaeology for five years to prepare himself. In 1868 he visited the Troad, the region in northwestern Turkey in which Troy had been located. With *Iliad* in hand he examined the area's mounds searching for a suitable candidate for Troy. Frank Calvert, an American who owned part of the mound of Hissarlik convinced Schliemann that his mound was the most probable site of Homer's Troy. No antiquities had been found at other sites in the area, but Calvert had dug up some interesting artifacts *beneath* classical Greek remains at Hissarlik. Schliemann resolved to excavate there.

However, Schliemann was a lonely man. He desired someone to share his love for the past and his excitement at the prospect of archaeological excavation and discovery. In February 1869 he wrote to an old friend who had become the archbishop of Athens, begging him for help finding a wife who could meet his standards:

Fig 34. Schliemann's great trench through the center of Hissarlik. (From H. Schliemann, *Ilios: The City and Country of the Trojans,* 1880.)

She should be poor, but well educated; she must be enthusiastic about Homer and about the rebirth of my beloved Greece. It does not matter whether she knows foreign languages or not. But she should be of the Greek type, with black hair, and, if possible, beautiful. But my main requirement is a good and loving heart.[1]

It so happened that the archbishop knew a young girl who fit Schliemann's description. Her name was Sophia Engastromenos and she was the sixteen-year-old daughter of an Athenian draper. Schliemann arrived in Athens in August and arranged a series of meetings with Sophia. However, these "dates" resembled examinations more than the normal stages of courtship. (Sample questions: "When did the emperor Hadrian visit Athens?" "Can you recite passages of Homer by heart?") Sophia passed Heinrich's tests and on September 24, 1869, he married her. Soon afterward Schliemann applied for a *firman* from Turkey to excavate at Hissarlik.

In four seasons of digging (1870–73) Schliemann drove several huge trenches through the mound. The largest was about one hundred and

---

1. L. Cottrell, *The Bull of Minos* (New York: Grosset & Dunlap, 1962), p. 28.

thirty feet wide and more than forty-five feet deep (Fig. 34). Superimposed walls and changes in pottery and other artifacts soon led Schliemann to recognize that several cities had been built on this same site over a long period of time. But Schliemann decided that the Troy of the Homeric epics would be found at or near the very bottom of the accumulated debris. As a result, he later admitted that he made little effort to study and record what he found in the upper layers of the site.

> As it was my object to excavate Troy, which I expected to find in one of the lower cities, I was forced to demolish many interesting ruins in the upper strata; as, for example, at a depth of twenty feet below the surface, the ruins of a prehistoric building ten feet high, the walls of which consisted of hewn blocks of limestone perfectly smooth and cemented with clay.[2]

After becoming convinced in 1873 that Priam's Troy was not the lowest city in the mound (Troy I) but the one immediately above it (Troy II), Schliemann made a similar confession.

> In consequence of my former mistaken idea, that Troy was to be found on the primary soil or close above it, I unfortunately, in 1871 and 1872, destroyed a large portion of the [second] city, for I at that time broke down all house-walls in the higher strata which obstructed my way.[3]

Schliemann's switch to Troy II as the city of Homer's epics was due to four factors. First, the objects he uncovered in the first city (the lowest in the mound) were all very primitive. Nothing from that level seemed suited to the mighty city described in the *Iliad*. On the other hand, in Troy II Schliemann discovered a monumental wall, a double gate, and a large building. These remains reminded him of Homer's descriptions of the Trojan fortifications, the Scaean Gate, and the palace of Priam. Furthermore, these structures had been burned as Homer said Troy had been. The first city had not suffered this fate. However, the evidence that was most convincing to Schliemann was his discovery in Troy II of what he came to call "Priam's Treasure."

According to Schliemann's published accounts, he found this treasure on May 31, 1873, only two weeks before that season's excavations were scheduled to end. He claims that he was clearing a portion of the great defensive wall northwest of the "Scaean Gate" when he

---

2. H. Schliemann, *Ilios: The City and Country of the Trojans* (London: John Muray, 1880), p. 23.

3. H. Schliemann, *Troy and Its Remains* (London: John Murray, 1875), p. 348.

Fig. 35. "Priam's Treasure" from Level II at Troy. (From H. Schliemann, *Ilios: The City and Country of the Trojans*, 1880.)

struck a large copper basin and spied behind it the gleam of gold. He quickly ordered Sophia to proclaim a holiday to get rid of his workers. Then he stealthily removed the copper basin, uncovering a large bronze cauldron, a silver jug, a two-spouted gold cup, a golden bottle and goblet, vases of copper and silver (one filled with golden jewelry), and many bronze weapons and tools. As he dug out each object, Heinrich handed it to Sophia, who packed it in her large shawl. They then carried the objects to their house on top of the mound without being observed. Such, at least, was the story told by Schliemann.

However, in recent years scholars have begun to question Schliemann's account.[4] It turns out Sophia was not at Hissarlik when Schliemann claims they dug up the treasure. She was in Athens. We don't know how much of the rest of the account is true. Schliemann may

4. See Donald F. Easton, "Schliemann's Discovery of 'Priam's Treasure': Two Enigmas," *Antiquity* 55 (1981): pp. 179–83, and David A. Traill, "Schliemann's 'Discovery' of Priam's Treasure," *Antiquity* 57 (1983): pp. 181–86.

have found these precious objects over a period of weeks rather than in one hoard. Or they may have come from a Troy III cist tomb dug into the remains of Troy II. But the objects themselves were probably genuine, not faked, as some have claimed.[5] However he found them, the beautiful jewelry and vessels of this "treasure" were worthy of a King Priam or a Helen of Troy. They convinced Schliemann and many others that he had found the city immortalized by Homer.

Under the terms of his permit to excavate Hissarlik, Turkey was to keep half of everything Schliemann found. But, whether from greed or a conviction that the Turks would melt down their share of the treasure for its precious metal content, Schliemann chose to disregard this agreement. "Priam's Treasure" was smuggled out of Turkey and into Greece, where it was divided up and hidden on farms of Sophia's relatives. Once he and the treasure were safely in Greece, Schliemann published accounts of his discovery. Of course, Turkish officials saw these reports and they canceled Schliemann's permit to excavate in Turkey. But despite Turkish protests to Greece and a search of the Schliemanns' home in Athens, the treasure was not recovered.

The discoverer of Troy now wished to continue his vindication of Homer's accuracy by excavating at Mycenae in Greece. According to Homer, Mycenae was the city of Agamemnon, leader of the Greek expedition against Troy. The Greek government, however, was aware of Schliemann's duplicity with the Turks, so at first it refused to grant him a permit to dig. After much negotiation, the Greeks finally agreed that Schliemann could excavate at Mycenae under the watchful eyes of three Greek archaeological inspectors. However, everything he uncovered would belong to Greece and would remain in the country. Schliemann received only the exclusive rights to publish his finds. In August 1876 the quest for Agamemnon began.

Mycenae's location had never been forgotten, and its ruins had been a tourist attraction even in classical times. Schliemann realized that he could not prove very much by simply digging up walls or buildings. So, he set out to uncover the grave of Agamemnon himself. That would prove that Homer's characters were historical and his accounts of the

---

5. We cannot now determine the authenticity of these objects. Schliemann donated them to Germany, and they were put on display in Berlin. However, they disappeared from the city at the end of World War II. Some think they were taken to the Soviet Union where they are still hidden. But, unfortunately, they probably were melted down for their precious metal content. Although the objects themselves cannot now be tested, they are of the right types to belong to Troy II. Other similar objects were found in that layer by Schliemann's workers and by later American excavators. These other artifacts are in a Turkish museum, and they are authentic.

Trojan War not just a myth. The ancient writer Pausanius (late second century A.D.) had stated that the location of Agamemnon's tomb was still known in his time:

> In the ruins of Mycenae is a fountain called Persea; there are also underground chambers of Atreus and his children, in which were stored their treasures. There is the grave of Atreus, along with the graves of such as returned with Agamemnon from Troy, and were murdered by Aegisthus after he had given them a banquet. . . . Clytemnestra and Aegisthus were buried at some little distance from the wall. They were thought unworthy of a place within it, where lay Agamemnon himself and those who were murdered with him.[6]

Schliemann, trusting Pausanius's account, began his excavations on the citadel of Mycenae just inside the Cyclopean fortification wall near the Lion Gate (Fig. 36). The general scholarly opinion of the day held that the graves seen by Pausanius could not have been inside the small citadel, but rather were in the lower city, near a ruined Hellenistic wall. Schliemann disagreed. The wall around the lower city had already been in ruins in Pausanius's time, he argued. Pausanius could only have been referring to the great wall around the citadel. This wall was so massive that the Greeks of classical times thought that the gigantic Cyclopes had built it. Hence, it was called the Cyclopean Wall, and the ages had been unable to destroy it.

As at Troy, Schliemann dug frantically toward his objective, ignoring all other remains. This caused Stamatakis, the chief inspector from the Greek Archaeological Society, to denounce Schliemann's excavation methods repeatedly. In one letter to his superiors the inspector complained:

> A few days ago he found a wall superimposed on another wall, and wanted to pull down the upper one. I forbade it, and he stopped. Next morning, when I was not there, he had the wall pulled down and the lower one exposed. . . . He is eagerly demolishing everything Roman and Greek in sight, in order to lay bare the cyclopean walls. Whenever we find Greek or Roman vases, he looks at them in disgust, and when these fragments are put in his hands, he lets them fall to the ground.[7]

---

6. Pausanius, *Description of Greece* 2. 16. 6–7. The translation is by W. H. S. Jones, *Pausanius*, vol. 1 (Loeb Classical Library, Cambridge, Mass.: Harvard University Press, 1918), pp. 331 and 333.

7. Letter from Stamatakis of August 1876, quoted in E. Ludwig, *Schliemann: The Story of a Gold-seeker* (Boston: Little, Brown, 1932), pp. 167–68.

Fig. 36. The Lion Gate and part of the Cyclopean Wall at Mycenae. Just inside this gate, to the right, Schliemann found a circle of stone slabs within which he excavated five shaft tombs. He believed that these graves belonged to Agamemnon and his companions. In fact, the burials were some three centuries older than the supposed date of the Trojan War. (From H. Schliemann, *Mycenae: A Narrative of Researches and Discoveries at Mycenae and Tiryns*, 1878.)

Schliemann ignored warnings from the Greek authorities. But before the government could make up its mind to take action, he discovered some memorial stelae bearing carvings of warriors in chariots. Soon he uncovered a circular wall of stone slabs and found more carved stelae standing within the circle. Schliemann was confident that the stelae had been erected to mark the sites of tombs cut into the rock below. Finally, at the beginning of December, Schliemann's faith was rewarded. His diggers reached bedrock and discovered five rectangular shaft tombs. (Stamatakis later found a sixth.) The graves contained nineteen bodies and a wealth of burial offerings. There were gold and silver cups, copper cauldrons and tripods, golden breastplates, gold jewelry, and bronze swords and daggers inlaid with gold and silver. Golden headbands adorned the foreheads of the women and golden portrait masks covered the faces of the men. This was an even greater treasure than Schliemann had found at Troy.

The finds in Grave V were especially noteworthy. The tomb contained the bodies of three tall men, one of which was very well preserved. This individual had died in his prime, at about thirty-five years of age. On his chest was a gold breastplate; at his side was a great bronze sword in a gold-plated scabbard; and covering his face was a gold mask depicting a bearded warrior. Slowly, almost reverently, Schliemann removed the mask, kissed it, and stared at the human remains underneath. He believed that he was gazing into the face of Agamemnon.

The great success of the excavations at Mycenae gained Schliemann powerful support for his efforts to return to Hissarlik. Gladstone, the leader of the British Liberal Party, and A. H. Layard, the former excavator of Nimrud and Nineveh who became British ambassador to Turkey in 1877, supported Schliemann's request for a *firman* to renew his exploration of ancient Troy. The Turkish government reluctantly granted the permit to excavate. But it appointed a commissioner to oversee the work and take possession of all finds, and it sent along a body of armed soldiers to keep Schliemann and his workers honest.

In three more campaigns at Troy (1878-79, 1882, and 1890) Schliemann improved his excavation methods and modified many of his earlier conclusions. He was assisted in the last two campaigns by an able architect, Wilhelm Dörpfeld, who had participated in the careful German excavations at Olympia. Dörpfeld did much to make Schliemann's digging more scientific. With Dörpfeld's aid, Schliemann was now able to discern seven successive occupation levels at Hissarlik. In 1890, while digging in an area outside the limits of Level II's walls, Schliemann and Dörpfeld discovered a building belonging to Level VI. Among the pottery sherds in this structure were pieces like those previously uncovered in the palaces at Mycenae and Tiryns (a Greek site where Schliemann and Dörpfeld had dug in 1884).

Reluctantly Schliemann recognized the implications of this discovery. Level VI at Troy, not Level II, was contemporaneous with the Mycenaean culture of Greece. Thus, Level VI must be Homer's Troy. The "late" buildings he had destroyed in 1871-73 in his haste to reach the lowest deposits on the site had been from the age of Priam, Agamemnon, and Achilles (if, indeed, these individuals had ever lived). Furthermore, the great treasure he had found belonged to a period a thousand years earlier than the Trojan War. Schliemann's many illuminations of Homer's descriptions and vocabulary by objects found in Level II all had to be abandoned.

This startling discovery forced Schliemann to consider another campaign at Hissarlik in the following year to uncover more remains from Level VI. But he did not get the chance to return. In December 1890, at the age of sixty-eight, Heinrich Schliemann died. As an archaeologist he had been impetuous and too little concerned with what he considered "late" remains. However, in his later years he had come to recognize the value of careful digging and recording, and he had been willing to learn from younger men like Dörpfeld. He also published his finds promptly, though selectively, usually within a year after excavation. The great nineteenth-century pathologist Rudolf Virchow probably summarized Schliemann's accomplishment best:

> This excavation [of Troy] has opened for the studies of the archaeologist a completely new theatre—like a world by itself. Here begins an entirely new science.[8]

ARTHUR EVANS REVEALS THE MINOAN CIVILIZATON

In the decade following Schliemann's death, great progress was made in the study of the Mycenaean civilization. Dörpfeld returned to Hissarlik for two seasons of excavations (1893–94), during which he discovered two layers of remains previously unrecognized, bringing the number of "cities" at Troy to nine.[9] He was also able to show conclusively the chronological link between Troy VI and the Mycenaean Age in Greece, a synchronism that the finds in 1890 had suggested. Meanwhile, a gifted Greek archaeologist, Christos Tsountas, continued Schliemann's work at Mycenae by uncovering the remains of the Bronze Age palace on the summit of the citadel. A French archaeologist discovered another Mycenaean stronghold and palace at Gla in the neighborhood of Thebes. And various scholars found several large, beehive-shaped tombs (called *tholoi*) in various parts of Greece, some still containing a few precious objects overlooked by ancient grave robbers.

One of the many scholars attracted to the study of the Aegean Bronze Age was Arthur Evans, keeper of the Ashmolean Museum at Oxford. He had previously devoted his attention to European prehistory and to the study of coins and very small seals. As his sister Joan later explained:

> Evans was extremely short-sighted, and a reluctant wearer of glasses. Without them, he could see small things held a few inches from his eyes in extraordinary detail, while everything else was a vague blur.

---

8. From the preface to Heinrich Schliemann's *Ilios: The City and Country of the Trojans* (London: John Murray, 1880), p. xiv.

9. A new German expedition to Hissarlik has recently discovered the remains of a tenth occupation level beneath the "first" city. It seems to date from about 4000–3500 B.C. and has been labeled Troy 0.

Consequently the details he saw with microscopic exactitude, undistracted by the outside world, had a greater significance for him than for other men.[10]

In 1893, while visiting an antiquities shop in Athens, Evans's microscopic vision detected what seemed to be writing on small three- or four-sided stone seals. However, the inscribed signs were not like those of any writing system then known. Evans's curiosity was aroused, and he learned that the seals had come from Crete. The next year he visited that island for the first time. After noting surface indications of preclassical occupation at Knossos, Evans decided that it would be a good place to search for inscribed seals and other antiquities.

War between Greece and Turkey prevented Evans's return to Crete until 1899, but in that year he was able to acquire title to the site of Knossos and draft his plans for excavation. He chose Duncan Mackenzie as his assistant. This capable Scot previously had been the site supervisor of the British School of Archaeology's excavations at Phylakopi on the island of Melos. On March 23, 1900, Evans and Mackenzie commenced digging on the western portion of the mound, and almost immediately they found the remains of a great palace. Some of the walls of the structure were only inches below the surface. In addition to architectural remains Evans uncovered fragments of frescoes and a stucco relief that had decorated the palace walls. He also found many pieces of pottery and numerous oblong clay tablets covered with the same unknown script he had noticed on the seals in Athens. At first Evans called all his finds "Mycenaean." But as he uncovered underlying strata, he came to realize that the inhabitants of Knossos had already attained a high level of cultural development long before the Mycenaean Age. "Evans had come to the site in the hope of finding a seal impression and a clay tablet," recounts Joan Evans, "and Time and Chance had led him to discover a civilization."[11]

Evans had cleared virtually all of the palace by the end of three more campaigns (1901–3) and he had developed the major features of his interpretation of his discoveries. He called the pre-Mycenaean civilization of Crete "Minoan" after the legendary Minos, an early king of Knossos according to Greek legend. Evans was able to discern three major stages of development (the Early, Middle, and Late Minoan Periods) and two different writing systems (designated Linear A and

---

10. Joan Evans, *Time and Chance: The Story of Arthur Evans and His Forebears* (London: Longmans, Green, 1943), pp. 308–9.
11. *Time and Chance,* p. 338.

Linear B). It was clear that the Minoans had strongly influenced the development of the Mycenaean culture on mainland Greece. But Evans became convinced that almost all "Mycenaean" art works had been produced by Minoan artisans. He was equally certain that Crete had received no mainland influences or outside population increments until the end of the Late Minoan Period, when the Dorian Greeks arrived. By the end of 1903 Evans and Mackenzie were also convinced that the last palace at Knossos (to which most of the inscribed tablets and many of the frescoes were attributed) had been destroyed about 1400 B.C. Furthermore, they were sure that the "decadent" Mycenean-type pottery they had found in the upper layers of the site represented only a partial reoccupation of the ruined building by impoverished native squatters. Additional campaigns in 1904 and 1905 and minor clearances and excavations from 1906 to 1914 and again in 1922 added details to the picture of Minoan civilization Evans had formed, but they did not significantly change it.

In addition to excavating the remains of the palace at Knossos, Evans extensively restored them (Fig. 37). He rebuilt walls, replacing the original wooden beams with steel ones painted to look like wood. He also erected cement columns in the holes left by vanished wooden posts. Evans's artists completed the frescoes, of which only scattered fragments usually remained. The excavations and restorations and the publication of the four volumes of The Palace of Minos (all of which cost an estimated quarter of a million pounds) were financed principally by gifts from Evans's father and by Evans's own fortune. Some funds came from other sources, such as the Cretan Exploration Fund, but Evans did not welcome such outside contributions. He explained his feelings in a letter to his father in 1900:

> I am quite resolved not to have the thing [excavation of Knossos] entirely "pooled" for many reasons, but largely because I must have sole control of what I am personally undertaking. With other people it may be different, but I know it is so with me; my way may not be the best but it is the only way I can work.[12]

It is this personal nature of Evans's excavations and restorations that has led to much criticism of his work. At Knossos, more than at any other Cretan site, the visitor is able to form a satisfying mental picture of the appearance of a Minoan palace. But it is a picture seen largely through Arthur Evans's eyes, and it will always be so.

---

12. Time and Chance, p. 335.

Fig 37. The northern entrance passage at Knossos after restoration by Arthur Evans. (Photograph by the author.)

Fig. 38. Large late Minoan pottery jars in basement storerooms of the palace at Knossos. (Photograph by the author.)

Soon after Evans began to dig at Knossos, other excavations in Crete contributed additional evidence for understanding the ancient Bronze Age civilization of Crete. Italian archaeologists led by Luigi Pernier and Frederico Halbherr discovered a palace at Phaistos near the south coast of Crete. The British scholar D. G. Hogarth recovered hundreds of votive offerings from the Dictean Cave, believed by the ancient Greeks to be the birthplace of Zeus. At Gournia, about thirty-five miles to the east of Knossos, Harriet Boyd, an American, uncovered a well-preserved Minoan town. The French also made important discoveries at Mallia and the British at Palaikastro. After lying buried and unknown for over three thousand years, the bulk of Minoan remains known today were brought to light in the first two decades of the twentieth century.

But dominating the field during these years was the intellect and personality of Arthur Evans. He gave Minoan civilization its name. He first established its chronology, and he, more than anyone else, brought the discoveries of Cretan antiquities and their significance to the public's attention. For more than fifty years after the discovery of the palace of Minos at Knossos scholars accepted Evans's views as the "orthodox" interpretation of Aegean prehistory. Despite many revisions necessitated by later discoveries, today they still exercise a strong influence on historians of Bronze Age Crete and Greece.

IMPROVEMENTS IN METHODOLOGY AND CHRONOLOGY

The year Schliemann began gouging his way through Hissarlik, 1870, also saw one of the earliest examples of rigorous excavation in the Aegean area. Alexander Conze, an Austrian scholar, carefully excavated and meticulously recorded classical remains at Samothrace. He produced detailed plans of the material he uncovered and was the first to publish an excavation report illustrated with photographs.

A short time later the German Archaeological Institute initiated its influential work at Olympia. Under Ernst Curtius, the German archaeologists worked from 1875 to 1881 systematically clearing the Altis or sacred precinct of the city. Curtius stressed the need for observing stratigraphy and the findspots of every object uncovered. The Germans spared no expense in this operation even though all of the thousands of fragments of sculpture, bronzes, terra cottas, coins, and inscriptions brought to light (including the group's most famous find, the Hermes of Praxiteles) remained in Greece. The excavations at Olympia provided the training ground in methodical, stratigraphical excavation for Wilhelm Dörpfeld, the systematizer of Schliemann's digs, and served as a model for archaeologists of other nationalities, including the Greeks themselves.

Schliemann's discoveries at Troy, Mycenae, and Tiryns caused many archaeologists to shift their attention from classical remains to prehistoric sites. Careful excavation methods were imperative if the secrets of these mute witnesses to humanity's past were to be successfully revealed. It was also necessary to develop a chronology for artifacts that did not depend on inscriptions or the accounts of ancient classical authors.

Arthur Evans created such a chronology for prehistoric Crete through his finds at Knossos. Evans distinguished many different pottery types and styles of decoration in the successive layers of the palace of Knossos. The presence of datable Egyptian objects in some of these Minoan strata allowed him to provide approximate absolute dates for his entire sequence. The discovery of Minoan pottery in datable contexts in Egypt further strengthened Evans's synchronisms between Egypt and Crete.

Meanwhile, during the early decades of the twentieth century, others were clarifying the sequence of mainland prehistoric pottery types. At Sesklo and Dimini in Thessaly, Christos Tsountas, a Greek archaeologist, uncovered Neolithic strata below layers containing sherds like those of Troy I. By careful association of pottery types with stratified layers of occupation debris, Tsountas established the basic sequence of Neolithic ceramics in Greece.

At about the same time A. J. B. Wace, the director of the British School of Archaeology in Athens, also began excavating Neolithic sites in east central Greece. Like Tsountas, Wace employed the careful, stratigraphical excavation techniques pioneered by the Germans. Also, like his Greek colleague, he paid particular attention to the types of pottery in each stratum. Wace's work proved the basic soundness of Tsountas' pottery sequence while expanding it and making it more detailed.

An American archaeologist, Carl Blegen, further advanced the development of a Greek pottery chronology based on stratigraphical sequences. Blegen conducted his first major excavation in Greece in 1915 at the prehistoric mound of Korakou near Corinth. His succeeding digs were at the equally obscure sites of Gonia, Hagiorgitika, and Zygouries. These mounds had not been the sites of major cities in Mycenaean or classical times, and their ancient names were not known. However, it was this obscurity that made them important sources of information about the cultural development of Greece in prehistoric times. At sites that had been administrative centers during the latter part of the Mycenaean Age or that had been occupied in classical times, archaeologists often found that any early prehistoric strata had been disturbed or almost completely leveled by the elaborate building activities of these later periods. But at these "nameless" sites Blegen was able to carefully study many prehistoric strata and the thousands of sherds of pottery they contained. He developed a fairly complete picture of the sequence of cultures in Greece from the Neolithic period to the end of the Bronze Age (Fig. 39). In 1918 Blegen and Wace brought all this material together in "The Pre-Mycenaean Pottery of the Mainland," an article they co-authored in the *Annual of the British School of Archaeology in Athens*. This article established the foundation for the currently accepted pottery sequence and chronology for the earliest cultures of Greece.

After their success in building a chronology based on unknown mounds, Wace and Blegen each turned to the site of a major excavation of the past. They wanted to see if they could achieve more exact results with their precise methodology. Between 1920 and 1923 Wace excavated some of the undisturbed areas at Mycenae. He dug small areas under the cyclopean walls, in the ramp leading to the Lion Gate, and in the area of the shaft graves. These probes provided evidence for dating the earliest occupation of the site to an early phase of the Early Bronze Age (about 3000 B.C.), and the destruction of the citadel and palace to the end of the Late Bronze Age (1200–1100 B.C.). Wace was also able to show that the shaft graves excavated by Schliemann were much earlier than the remains of Troy VI (which Schliemann had finally accepted as Priam's Troy). The "Mask of Agamemnon" had belonged to a ruler of Mycenae who had lived more than two centuries before the time of the Trojan War.

The most important result of the new excavations at Mycenae, however, was Wace's dating of the *tholos* tombs. Wace arranged the architectural and decorative features of the nine massive tombs near the city into a typological sequence. The evidence suggested that the most advanced tombs were constructed just before the destruction of the citadel at the end of the Bronze Age. But such a date was heresy to those who accepted Evans's view of Aegean prehistory. If Wace was correct, Mycenae was flourishing and building very well-constructed domed tombs at a time when Knossos was in ruins. There could be no question of Minoan architects or artisans. The *tholoi* would have to be regarded as a mainland accomplishment, and one that required engineering skills equal or superior to those of the Minoans. Furthermore, Wace had found some examples of Minoan "palace style" pottery in one of the tombs. He compounded his heresy by insisting that these vases were local products of Mycenaean craftsmen, not imports from Crete. Evans immediately responded with an article denying the validity

Fig. 39. Examples of Mycenaean pottery of the thirteenth century B.C.

of Wace's dating of the Mycenaean *tholoi*. In 1923, as a result of Evans's attacks, Wace's excavations at Mycenae were abruptly terminated and he was removed from the directorship of the British School of Archaeology in Athens.

Carl Blegen followed his work at unknown sites by re-excavating Troy. From 1932 through 1938 he applied his rigorous excavation techniques to parts of Hissarlik left untouched by Schliemann and Dörpfeld. Blegen was able to delineate many sub-strata of the major levels or cities noted by his predecessors. In addition, his stratigraphical study of the excavated pottery made the chronology of the site more precise. He also showed that Mycenaean pottery was present not only in Troy VI, Dörpfeld's choice as the city celebrated in the *Iliad*, but also in the succeeding city, Troy VIIa, Blegen's candidate for Homer's Troy. The question of which occupation layer at Hissarlik represents the Troy described by Homer is still being debated today.

In 1939 Blegen shifted his attention to Ano Englianos in the Greek Peloponnesus. He believed that this site represented the Mycenaean city of Pylos, the capital of King Nestor. The first trench across the top of the mound revealed portions of a Mycenaean palace and uncovered a cache of Linear B tablets. These tablets provided the first evidence that writing had been used on the mainland during the Bronze Age. The Pylos tablets dated to the end of the Mycenaean period, two hundred years after Evans claimed Knossos and its Linear B tablets had been destroyed. This fact led Blegen to begin questioning parts of Evans's reconstruction of Aegean prehistory.

In time, Blegen's discoveries at Pylos also led to the vindication

of his friend Alan Wace. The Pylos tablets made possible the decipherment of Linear B in 1952. To the surprise of most scholars, the language
of these texts proved to be an early form of Greek. This meant that
the records of the last kings at Knossos had been written in *Greek,*
as had the documents of the rulers of Pylos, Mycenae, and other mainland
sites. It has become apparent that Mycenaeans conquered Crete about
1450 B.C. and ruled much of the island from Knossos, probably until
the thirteenth century B.C. As a result, scholars have generally abandoned Evans's theories about the history of the last phases of Knossos.
It is now clear that Wace was right and Evans wrong in their arguments
about the Mycenaean *tholoi.* However, scholars must await the results
of new excavations to solve many of the intriguing problems raised
by past discoveries in the Aegean area.

5

Recovering the Remains of Ancient Italy

Phase I—Speculation, Antiquarianism, and Early Excavation (1450–1860)

THE GRADUAL DESTRUCTION OF ANCIENT ROME

Many monuments in ancient Rome survived catastrophic fires, imperial urban renewal schemes, civil wars, and barbarian invasions only to deteriorate and disappear during the Middle Ages. Abandoned temples, bereft of revenues and worshipers, crumbled into ruins thought to be the haunts of evil spirits. Disastrous floods—frequent occurrences once the ancient practices of dredging the Tiber's bed and maintaining its banks were discontinued—buried many ancient remains under layers of silt. The population and physical extent of the city dwindled to only a fraction of their former size. Thus, some monuments became part of a rural landscape, overgrown with vegetation. In addition, stone-cutters often treated the ruins as quarries for building material. Limestone-burners also consigned marble slabs, statues, and columns to the kilns to be burned into lime.

However, a few buildings survived generally unscathed by remaining in use. Some were converted into Christian churches. Their architecture was altered a bit, and their interior decorations were covered by Christian frescoes or mosaics. But usually it is easy to reconstruct the original forms of these edifices. The Curia (the ancient Roman Senate

143

Fig. 40. Ancient Roman Senate House (on right) in 1575. (From E. Du Pérac, I Vestigi dell' Antichità di Roma, 1680.)

Fig. 41. The Colosseum after being used as a quarry during the Renaissance period. (From G. Piranesi, Vedute di Roma, 1757.)

House) (Fig. 40) and the Pantheon (the greatest of the circular Roman temples) are among the buildings preserved in this way.

Medieval Romans turned some of the most massive ancient structures into castles or forts. The Mausoleum of Hadrian became the major stronghold in a new defensive wall constructed in the middle of the ninth

---

century. Later, various noble families also used the Colosseum, the Arches of Titus and Constantine, the Mausoleum of Augustus, the Baths of Alexander Severus, and Pompey's Theater as fortresses. But the number of monuments that remained in use and thus survived was small.

In the fifteenth century the Renaissance brought renewed appreciation of classical literature and art. Sculptors modeled their work on surviving examples of ancient Roman statues, and architects incorporated classical elements into their designs. The antiquities business became brisk and lucrative as nobles sought ancient works of art to decorate their palaces. Unfortunately, this passion for classical beauty often resulted in the further destruction of ancient monuments. Many Renaissance buildings were constructed with blocks quarried from the ruins, and used columns or decoration stripped from ancient structures. A large marble doorway and some columns of the Temple of Jupiter Capitolinus were still visible in 1447. But these important remains disappeared over the next two centuries. Caesar's Forum, the Baths of Caracalla, the Portico of Octavia, and other famous structures provided materials for the vestibule of St. Peter's Basilica. Additionally, the marble slab benches from the Colosseum provided the covering for St. Peter's steps. Stone from the outer wall of the Colosseum was used to build the Palazzo Venezia and the Palazzo Farnese (Fig. 41).

After observing the pitiable state of the surviving relics of the ancient city, the fifteenth-century humanist Poggio Bracciolini lamented over Rome:

> O mother of illustrious men, emperors and leaders, nurse of all virtues, begetter of just laws, example of every perfection, today thou art but a plaything of fortune. Not only art thou deprived of thy empire, thy majesty, but thou art reduced to the most abject servitude. Stripped of thy beauty, thou hast indeed sunk low, and only when we ponder over thy downfall can we glimpse the grandeur, the glory that once were thine.[1]

THE DISCOVERY OF POMPEII AND HERCULANEUM

Fortunately, at other sites in Italy ancient Roman remains were preserved better than in the capital city. In fact, near Naples three entire cities lay intact under the earth. Mount Vesuvius, a volcano then considered dormant, erupted in A.D. 79, burying the towns of Pompeii, Herculaneum, and Stabiae beneath tons of ash, lava, and mud. Thou-

---

1. Quoted in P. Grimal, In Search of Ancient Italy (London: Evans Brothers, 1964), p. 25.

sands died, and the survivors returned to such devastation that they were forced to abandon all hope of rebuilding their homes or reclaiming their possessions. As the centuries passed only legends kept alive the memory of the buried cities.

However, during the Renaissance scholars rediscovered references to the lost towns in ancient writings. The most important of these sources were two letters written by Pliny the Younger. A seventeen-year-old boy at the time of the eruption, Pliny had been an eyewitness to the disaster. He later described his and his mother's experiences to the historian Tacitus:

> For several days past there had been earth tremors which were not particularly alarming because they are frequent in Campania: but that night the shocks were so violent that everything felt as if it were not only shaken but overturned. . . .
>
> This finally decided us to leave the town. . . . Once beyond the buildings we stopped, and there we had some extraordinary experiences which thoroughly alarmed us. The carriages we had ordered to be brought out began to run in different directions though the ground was quite level, and would not remain stationary even when wedged with stones. We also saw the sea sucked away and apparently forced back by the earthquake: at any rate it receded from the shore so that quantities of sea creatures were left stranded on dry sand. On the landward side a fearful black cloud was rent by forked and quivering bursts of flame, and parted to reveal great tongues of fire, like flashes of lightning magnified in size. . . .
>
> Ashes were already falling, not as yet very thickly. I looked round: a dense black cloud was coming up behind us, spreading over the earth like a flood. "Let us leave the road while we can still see," I said, "or we shall be knocked down and trampled underfoot in the dark by the crowd behind." We had scarcely sat down to rest when darkness fell, not the dark of a moonless or cloudy night, but as if the lamp had been put out in a closed room. You could hear the shrieks of women, the wailing of infants, and the shouting of men; some were calling their parents, others their children or their wives, trying to recognize them by their voices. People bewailed their own fate or that of their relatives, and there were some who prayed for death in their terror of dying. Many besought the aid of the gods, but still more imagined there were no gods left, and that the universe was plunged into eternal darkness for evermore. . . . A gleam of light returned, but we took this to be a warning of the approaching flames rather than daylight. However, the flames remained some distance off; then darkness came on once more and ashes began to fall again, this time in heavy showers. We rose from time to time and shook them off, otherwise

we should have been buried and crushed beneath their weight. . . .

At last the darkness thinned and dispersed into smoke or cloud; then there was genuine daylight, and the sun actually shone out, but yellowish as it is during an eclipse. We were terrified to see everything changed, buried deep in ashes like snowdrifts.[2]

These writings revived interest in the legends of a buried city near Naples and stirred much scholarly debate over the exact locations of the ancient towns. But the eruption had so changed the landscape that topographical hints in the texts proved virtually useless.

In 1594 a Neapolitan nobleman ordered an underground channel dug to divert the water of the Sarno to his villa. As workmen excavated the tunnel they encountered some ruins and antiquities, for, by chance, the channel's course took it directly across the site of Pompeii. The diggers even discovered inscriptions, one of which mentioned a *decurio Pompeiis* (a municipal senator of Pompeii). But neither the workers nor their foreman were scholars. They ignored the remains they found, assuming that they had accidentally stumbled upon a villa of the ancient general Pompey.

The location of Pompeii was still unrecognized in 1709 when the digging of a well shifted attention to an area southwest of Vesuvius. While searching for water, a peasant from Resina (a small town near Naples) struck a layer of marble blocks. Prince D'Elbeuf, an Austrian general who was constructing a villa in the neighborhood, heard of this find and immediately bought the land to secure possession of the marble. He had the well widened and horizontal tunnels dug outward from it in all directions. The excavators found marvelous statues and columns as well as beautiful white and polychrome marble blocks. They didn't realize it, but the well had struck the Theater of Herculaneum, probably the most profusely decorated structure in the ancient town.

Here was one of the greatest archaeological opportunities of all time. No ancient theater had ever been found intact with all its scenery, equipment, stage fittings, and machinery for making gods appear and disappear, as well as its lavish decoration of vases, candelabra, statues, and columns. But Prince D'Elbeuf wanted building material for his villa, not buried history. He never appreciated the true importance of this discovery.

The diggers extracted everything of value without noting the original positions of the finds. They customarily smashed small objects that

2. Pliny the Younger, *Letters* 6. 20. Translation from Betty Radice, *The Letters of Pliny* (Baltimore: Penguin, 2nd edition, 1969), pp. 170–72.

Fig. 42. Eighteenth-century excavations at Herculaneum. (From *Voyages Pittoresques de Naples et de Sicile*, 1782.)

had no architectural or monetary worth. This plunder continued until 1716, when a steady decrease in the number of finds no longer seemed to justify the cost of tunneling. The prince discontinued his excavations and a few years later returned to Austria.

Vesuvius erupted several times between 1717 and 1737, discouraging further investigation of the area around D'Elbeuf's well. There was also a change in political regimes during that time. In 1735 the Spanish Prince Charles of Bourbon drove the Austrians out of southern Italy and became Charles IV, king of Naples and Sicily (he also later became Charles III, king of Spain).

When the new king's young wife saw the antiquities with which D'Elbeuf had decorated his gardens, she begged her husband to search for additional treasures. Vesuvius became quiescent again in 1738, so Charles ordered the excavations reopened. He placed them under the direction of Rocco Gioacchino de Alcubierre, a colonel of engineers in the Neapolitan army. Alcubierre enlarged the old shaft and dug new lateral tunnels. Since the ruins lay under forty to seventy feet of lava and mud, this was the cheapest way to investigate them. Unfortunately, these new excavations were as haphazard and destructive as those of D'Elbeuf's workers. Johann Winckelmann, the eighteenth-century art historian and antiquarian who observed Alcubierre's work, later commented acidly:

> This man, who (to use the Italian proverb) knew as much of antiquities as the moon does of lobsters, has been, through his want of capacity, the occasion of many antiquities being lost. A single fact will be sufficient to prove it. The workmen having discovered a large public inscription, (to what buildings it belonged, I can't say) in letters of brass two palms high; he ordered these letters to be torn from the wall, without first taking a copy of them, and thrown pell mell into a basket; and then presented them in that condition to the king. They were afterwards exposed for many years in the cabinet, where every one was at liberty to put them together as he pleased.[3]

On another occasion Alcubierre uncovered the broken pieces of a bronze statue of a chariot, driver, and four horses. He had the sculptures thrown into a cart, taken to Naples and dumped into a corner of the castle courtyard. Some pieces were stolen and others were melted down and cast into two busts of the king and queen. Eventually one complete horse was patched together from the remaining fragments. But by this time so much had been lost that a few modern pieces were needed to complete even this limited portion of the ancient sculpture.

Alcubierre's tunnels eventually penetrated beyond the theater into the town of Herculaneum itself. He brought to light wall paintings, mosaics, and other treasures. However, his men encountered such finds much less frequently than during the excavation of the theater. The smaller number of art works uncovered in the new tunnels began to discourage Alcubierre.

In March 1748 Alcubierre heard of the discovery of some ancient statues near Torre Annunziata, a site a few miles from Resina. He persuaded the king to allow him to shift his operations to the new area. With twenty-four diggers (twelve of them convicts) the new excavations began. Almost immediately Alcubierre uncovered a wall painting and the ruins of a temple. The city beneath Resina had by this time been identified as ancient Herculaneum on the basis of an inscription found in the theater. But to what town did this newly

---

3. J. Winckelmann, *Critical Account of Herculaneum, Pompeii and Stabia* (London: Carnan & Newberg, 1770), p. 23.

discovered temple belong? Alcubierre thought he had found the remains
of Stabiae. It was not until 1763 that the excavators found inscriptions
proving that these ruins belonged to the most famous of Vesuvius'
victims—Pompeii.

When finds in the temple (which we now know was the Temple
of the Fortuna Augusta) became scarce, Alcubierre shifted to another
spot and dug new shafts. The work was much easier than at Herculaneum. Pompeii was not buried as deeply and its covering consisted
of a crumbly mixture of ash and lapilli (small pieces of volcanic rock)
rather than mud and lava. Alcubierre's workers found and partially
cleared Pompeii's amphitheater, but when no "worthwhile" objects
turned up, they abandoned it. Alcubierre then chanced upon a luxurious
villa that, for some unknown reason, he decided was Cicero's. He
stripped the villa of its frescoes and sculptures, but he found nothing
in neighboring areas. He could not know, of course, that the house
was located on the outskirts of the ancient town with few buildings
nearby. In disgust Alcubierre filled in his shafts and returned to
Herculaneum.

There he was joined by Karl Weber, a Swiss architect appointed
by the king to assist in the excavations. From the start there was friction
between Weber and Alcubierre. Weber believed that the excavators
should make detailed plans of the tunnels and of each building found.
In this way they could eventually produce a map of the underground
city. Alcubierre insisted that such procedures wasted time and had
no value. He took every opportunity to complain to the king of Weber's
"incapacity" and "ignorance." Finally, the dispute became so intense
that Alcubierre had his men remove timber supports from Weber's
tunnels in hopes that they would cave in.

It was Weber, however, who made one of the most important discoveries at Herculaneum. In 1750 a peasant brought word that another
well had uncovered an ancient pavement near the Augustinian Mon-
astery. Weber investigated the site with great care, taking measurements and drawing plans of the ruins he unearthed. He was rewarded
by the discovery of one of the greatest collections of bronzes to survive
antiquity. Among the statues he found were the "Resting Hermes," the
"Sleeping Faun," the "Drunken Silenus," a pair of boy wrestlers, and
two deer—all now the most treasured items in the National Museum
at Naples.

This large villa (more than eight hundred feet long) had obviously
belonged to a person of taste and wealth. More sculpture emerged: busts
of philosophers, portrait busts of famous Romans, copies of Greek works
by Polyclitus, Phidias, and Praxiteles. But Weber uncovered probably

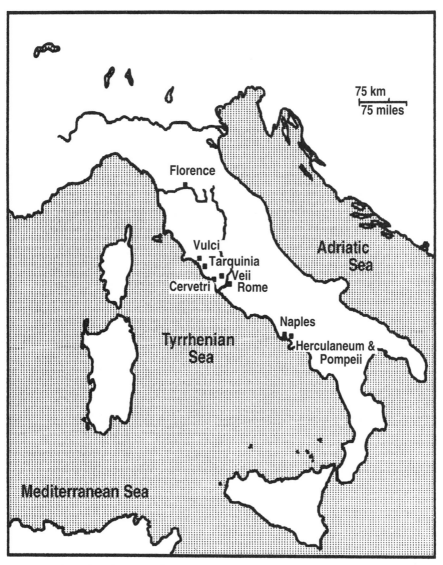

Map 6. Early archaeology in Italy.

the most exciting find in a small room next to what must have been a study. On wooden shelves were stacks of carbonized cylindrical objects that appeared to be charcoal briquettes or logs. These "logs," however, proved to be rolls of papyrus—the first ancient library ever discovered.

When a machine was finally devised to unroll the brittle papyri scholars discovered that the library contained mostly philosophical works. There was what must have been a complete collection of the works of Philodemus, an Epicurean philosopher who lived in Rome at the time of Cicero. There were also treatises by Epicurus and other philosophers. Philodemus was not a particularly popular author, so many scholars believe that the villa belonged to Philodemus's patron, Lucius Calpurnius Piso, father-in-law of Julius Caesar. So far no lost books of Livy's history, unknown Greek plays or poems, or other forgotten literary treasures have turned up in the collection. However, about eight hundred of the library's approximately eighteen hundred scrolls remain unopened, so there is still hope that some presently unknown ancient masterpiece was lying on the shelves in the "Villa of the Papyri" in A.D. 79 and will at last be rescued from oblivion.

The excavations at Torre Annunziata (Pompeii) were resumed in 1754. For the next nine years digging went on at both Resina (Herculaneum) and Torre Annunziata. But when in 1763 scholars learned that Torre Annunziata was ancient Pompeii, all efforts were concentrated on that site.

Heretofore the ruins had been reburied after all art works had been looted. Now it was decided that all buildings excavated at Pompeii should remain uncovered for the benefit of visitors to the site. In the decade following 1763 hundreds of beautiful wall paintings and precious antiquities were removed from the buried city. Several important structures were laid bare, including the Great Theater (1764), the gladiators' barracks (1766), the Temple of Isis (1767), and the Villa of Diomedes (1771).

Soon the reading public of the entire Western world was discussing the incredible discoveries at Pompeii. Publications of the Academy of Herculaneum, Romantic engravings of the ruins, Winckelmann's many accounts of the finds (particularly his *Open Letters* and *Critical Account of Herculaneum, Pompeii and Stabia*), and reports from a steady stream of famous visitors (among whom were Goethe and Thomas Jefferson) whetted the public's interest. The art and architecture of the newly revealed cities helped stimulate the revived classicism of the eighteenth century. Western furniture, china, and clothing, in addition to painting, sculpture, and architecture began to reflect the influence of ancient Pompeiian styles. The impact of the discoveries was especially strong in Britain, where Pompeiian models provided the inspiration for much of the architecture and interior decoration of the Georgian age.

The excavations received fresh impetus when the French seized the throne of the Kingdom of Naples in 1806. Both Joseph Bonaparte (Napoleon's brother) and his successor Murat took a personal interest in the progress of the work. In fact, under Murat the workforce was enlarged from fifty to five hundred and their pay doubled. The diggers were ordered to proceed along a single street, uncovering the houses on both sides, rather than digging here and there as the fancy struck them. In just a few years excavators cleared large sections of Pompeii and restored many of the ancient fountains to working order. At last the treasure hunt was becoming more systematic.

UNEARTHING THE MYSTERIOUS ETRUSCANS

Ancient Roman historians claimed that the Etruscans, a people living to the north of Rome, had once been very powerful. They had even conquered and ruled Rome for a time in its early history. But by the middle of the first century A.D., when the Roman emperor Claudius wrote a book on the Etruscans, knowledge of their language, customs, and early history had been almost completely lost. What remained was mostly myth, legend, and surmise. Unfortunately, even Claudius's history, limited as it was, failed to survive antiquity.

The Renaissance brought renewed interest in the Etruscan past. The discovery and looting of Etruscan tombs was underway by 1489 and collectors began eagerly seeking Etruscan antiquities. However, scholars learned little about Etruscan civilization from the fifteenth- and sixteenth-century tomb-robbing except that the Etruscans had been great artists. Their skill at bronze casting was made evident by the discovery of the "Chimera" and the "Minerva" at Arezzo in 1553–54 and the "Orator" near Lake Trasimene in 1556.

The writings of Sir Thomas Dempster mark the real beginnings of Etruscology. Dempster, a Scottish baronet and scholar, became interested in the Etruscans during his extensive travels in Italy. In 1616–17 he wrote *De Etruria Regali,* a seven-volume work in which he attempted to compile a history of the Etruscans from the information in ancient Greek and Roman texts. Even more important than Dempster's collection of classical textual references, though, were the ninety-three engravings of Etruscan monuments illustrating the book.

This important work remained in manuscript form for over a century. Then, in 1723, Filippo Buonarotti, a Florentine scholar, published it along with his own comments on the plates. To the illustrations Buonarotti added the first reproduction of an Etruscan tomb painting, a scene from the Tartaglia tomb discovered in Corneto in 1699.

Three years after the publication of *De Etruria Regali* twelve scholars of Cortona founded the *Academia Etrusca* (1726). This society dedicated itself to fostering research on the Etruscans and other aspects of Italy's past. Within a short time its membership grew to 140 and included most of the outstanding foreign as well as Italian antiquaries. Twice a month the members of the academy met to hear reports on new discoveries, to examine recently unearthed antiquities, and to discuss the latest scholarly opinions on Etruscan civilization. The society published the communications presented at these meetings in nine large volumes between 1738 and 1795. They provided a great stimulus to the study of Etruscan antiquity.

Another landmark in Etruscology was Antonio Gori's three-volume *Museum Etruscum* (1737–43). This work, illustrated with three hundred plates, described the major Etruscan monuments then known. Gori made many mistakes in the text, often attributing Greek or Roman works to the Etruscans. But scholars could not avoid such errors until they had collected and analyzed a large body of material of definite provenance. The *Museum Etruscum* was an important step towards the formation of a corpus upon which legitimate stylistic comparisons could be based.

Gori was not the only scholar of his time who could not differentiate Etruscan, Roman, and Greek elements in art or architecture. In 1761 Gian Battista Piranesi, an artist famous for his engravings of Roman ruins, wrote a book on the architecture of early Rome. In it he claimed an Etruscan origin for almost every feature of Roman construction and style. He was intent on disproving the commonly held belief that the Romans had learned the art of building from the Greeks. Today we know that many of Piranesi's claims for the Etruscan background of Roman architecture and engineering were correct. But his evidence was faulty. Most of the Roman monuments he used as examples of very early Roman architecture (circa 750–300 B.C.) were really from the period of the Roman Empire (27 B.C. to A.D. 300). They belonged to a time long after Rome had conquered Greece and come under Hellenistic influence. Therefore, they could not provide evidence that the Romans had developed their building skills without help from the Greeks. Also, no Etruscan cities had been excavated at the time Piranesi wrote. So he had to rely on descriptions of Etruscan buildings provided by classical authors (principally Vitruvius), and this was insufficient to establish his case.

Piranesi's conclusions were attacked by Jean-Pierre Mariette, a French classicist, who stoutly defended the view that the Romans had depended on Greek models. Mariette even claimed that the Etruscans themselves were Greek immigrants to Italy:

Signor Piranesi maintains that when the Romans wished to erect massive buildings, the solidity of which astonishes us, they were obliged to enlist the assistance of Etruscan architects who were their neighbors. One might as well say "the assistance of the Greeks," for the Etruscans, who were Greek by origin, were ignorant of the arts and practiced only those of them which had been taught to their fathers in the land of their origin.[4]

Johann Winckelmann also believed that the Etruscans were Greeks. Furthermore, he claimed (correctly, but without adequate proof) that most of the finest vases found in Etruscan tombs had been produced by Greeks of southern Italy or imported from Greece itself. But although he was quick to recognize the Hellenic influence that pervades much Etruscan art, Winckelmann was unable to distinguish the oriental and Italic elements that are also present. Winckelmann tried to determine the correct chronological order for Etruscan antiquities based on stylistic changes. However, his lack of interest in and understanding of the non-Greek character of much of Etruscan civilization doomed him to failure.

The growing movement for the unification of Italy complicated this scholarly debate. Many Italian scholars regarded the Etruscans as the source of Roman and Italian art and culture. Nationalistic impulses led them to become uncompromising in their support of the originality and greatness of Etruscan civilization. Actually, both sides in this debate had recognized a portion of the truth. However, neither the "Etruscophiles" nor the "Graecomanes" realized the complexity of the problem. Careful excavation was needed to establish the correct chronological sequence for Etruscan, Greek, and Roman remains, and to provide an adequate basis for determining the direction and importance of cross-cultural influences.

Meanwhile, Etruscan cemeteries continued to be discovered and plundered. In the latter part of the eighteenth century James Byres, an English painter, sketched several tombs then being uncovered at Tarquinia (Fig. 43). These drawings are important records of the appearance of these monuments at the time of their discovery. They were published in 1842 under the title *Hypogaei, or the Sepulchral Caverns of Tarquinia.*

While most scholars were concentrating their attention on Etruscan art, Abbé Luigi Lanzi became interested in their language. His three-volume *Saggio di lingua Etrusca (Story of the Etruscan Language)*, published in 1789, constituted the first serious attempt to decipher Etruscan writing. Lanzi reproduced about five hundred Etruscan in-

4. Quoted in Raymond Bloch, *The Etruscans* (New York: Praeger, 1956), p. 34.

Fig. 43. Byres's drawing of the Tomb of the Cardinal at Tarquinia. (From J. Byres, *Hypogaei, or the Sepulchral Caverns of Tarquinia,* 1842.)

scriptions along with his translations and commentaries. His interpretations of the texts were almost totally incorrect. He believed that Etruscan was an Italic language like Latin, whereas in reality it is a non-Indo-European tongue. Nonetheless, he advanced scholarship by making available a body of textual material upon which others could base further study.

Lanzi also published a volume on Etruscan pottery in 1806. In this book he proved the correctness of Winckelmann's claim that many vases found in Etruscan tombs were Greek. Lanzi based his conclusions not only on a careful study of style, but also on the Greek inscriptions and signatures that occurred on many pieces of "Etruscan" pottery. Many scholars ignored Lanzi's arguments, however, until the latter half of the nineteenth century, when archaeologists in Greece uncovered vases bearing the same Greek signatures as those discovered in Etruscan tombs.

The early nineteenth century saw the publication of additional illustrated volumes of Etruscan remains. But the most significant advance in Etruscology during this period was the foundation in 1829 of the *Instituto di Correspondenza archaeologica* (which later became the German Archaeological Institute in Rome). With the support of Prince

Fig. 44. Cliff-side Etruscan tombs and part of an inscription. (From G. Dennis, *Cities and Cemeteries of Etruria*, 1848.)

Fig. 45. Etruscan Tomb of the Reliefs at Cervetri. (From G. Dennis, *Cities and Cemeteries of Etruria*, 1848.)

Frederick of Prussia, a young German scholar named Edward Gerhard created this institute to promote international cooperation in the study of Italian antiquity and to coordinate and systematize archaeological study. The institute provided funds for excavations in the Etruscan cemeteries at Corneto, Bomarzo, Chiusi, and Vulci. Furthermore, in *Monumenti inediti,* one of its publications, the institute promptly reproduced drawings of the wall paintings discovered through these excavations. Another of its publications, *Annali dell' Instituto,* printed specialized studies of Etruscan artifacts. The most important of these volumes were Gerhard's still-useful works on Etruscan mirrors.

Many Etruscan remains were located in areas that were still half-wild in the early nineteenth century. George Dennis, a British consul in Italy, journeyed through these hard-to-reach districts of Tuscany observing evidence of the Etruscan past (Figs. 44–45). His detailed descriptions and lively style made the two-volume account of his travels, *The Cities and Cemeteries of Etruria* (1848), an immediate best-seller. The book brought the widespread destruction of Etruscan antiquities to public attention, for Dennis was highly critical of the pillage that passed for archaeology in his time. For example, he described watching workmen at Vulci smashing unfigured pottery and small clay objects:

> In vain we pleaded to save some from destruction; they were *roba di sciocchezza*—"foolish stuff"—the *capo* [foreman] was inexorable; his orders were to destroy immediately whatever was of no pecuniary value, and he could not allow me to carry away one of these relics which he so despised. It is lamentable that excavations should be carried on in such a spirit; with the sole view of gain, and with no regard to the advancement of science.[5]

Dennis's book popularized Etruscology, and many still consider its third edition (1883) an excellent introduction to the subject. It didn't bring about an immediate change in excavation methods, but it helped mobilize opposition to the kind of destruction Dennis had witnessed. Even so, over two decades passed before systematic "scientific" methods began to be employed in the excavation of Etruscan sites.

---

5. G. Dennis *The Cities and Cemeteries of Etruria,* 3rd ed., vol. 1 (London: John Murray, 1883), p. 450.

Fig. 46. The Arch of Septimius Severus (*left foreground*) and the Forum before Fea began his excavations. (From G. Piranesi, *Vedute di Roma*, 1757.)

Phase II: Archaeology in Italy Comes of Age (1860–1920)

CAREFUL EXCAVATION BEGINS IN ITALY

Carlo Fea's work in the Forum of Rome in 1803 and from 1813 to 1820 represents an early attempt at systematic excavation. Fea examined the area near the Arch of Septimius Severus, digging carefully and making detailed notes of whatever he found (Fig. 46). However, he uncovered no major monuments and made no spectacular finds, so his work was generally ignored. His methods were not adopted by most other excavators, whose main interest remained the discovery and removal of ancient artwork.

One scholar who, like Fea, believed that archaeology should seek to provide knowledge about the past rather than just museum pieces was Giuseppe Fiorelli. When Italy was unified under King Victor Emmanuel in 1860, Fiorelli was appointed director of the excavations at Pompeii. He immediately set about imposing order on the operations. One of his first acts was to begin the *Journal of the Excavations of*

Pompeii. Previous record books at Pompeii mainly recorded the visits of prominent people to the site. They included only sketchy accounts of the excavations. Fiorelli's *Journal* contained careful notations of each newly discovered object's location and position, including its relation to observed strata of debris at the moment it was found.

Fiorelli found it necessary to clear the already excavated portions of the city before he could begin excavating new areas. In the past, excavators had not totally removed debris dug from the ruins, but merely shifted it to other spots. There were piles of lapilli and heaps of rubble all over the city, making it difficult for visitors to get an impression of the original plan. The new director put an end to this practice, ordering the complete clearance of the streets and buildings uncovered by his predecessors.

Once he had put the previously excavated areas of the city in order, Fiorelli proceeded to explore the untouched portions of the site. He traced the entire circuit of the town walls, locating the ancient gates. By drawing lines between these gates, Fiorelli had a good idea where the main roads of the city were located. He divided the entire city into nine regions and then systematically excavated one region before proceeding to the next.

Since the early nineteenth century it had been customary for the excavators to dig along a street, entering the houses on either side from street level. This method often caused the collapse of the remains of upper stories as diggers removed the supporting material beneath them. Fiorelli decreed that once a street had been located its approximate course would be marked on the surface, but *not* excavated. Instead, excavations would proceed on either side of the street with the diggers uncovering the houses from top to bottom. Only after excavating the houses on either side would workers begin uncovering the street.

Fiorelli left objects in the places where they had been found whenever this was feasible. Small, easily stolen items, of course, were still removed to the museum in Naples. But wall paintings, statues, altars, fountains, jars, and other large objects remained *in situ.* To protect the newly exposed walls and their paintings and inscriptions from the weather, Fiorelli's workers constructed roofs over the uncovered remains.

In 1864 a group of workers came upon a small cavity in the earth with what appeared to be a skeleton inside it. Fiorelli rushed to the site. After examining the find, he ordered plaster poured down the hole. When the plaster hardened, he carefully removed the earth surrounding it. There in complete detail lay the cast of an ancient Pompeiian! The ashes from the eruption had covered the body and solidified very quickly. After the victim's flesh decayed, the hardened lapilli remained as a solid mold preserving the form of the ancient corpse. Even details of expression

Fig. 47. A street in Pompeii. (Photograph by the author.)

Fig. 48. A street in Herculaneum. In many cases, upper stories of houses and wooden objects were preserved at Herculaneum. The original wooden beams still support the roof of the house in the right foreground. (Photograph by the author.)

and clothing were evident. Earlier excavators had uncovered skeletons at Pompeii. But the full horror of that August day in A.D. 79 became evident only as Fiorelli's workers cleared casts of victim after victim with the fear and agony of death still stamped on their faces.

As a result of the careful excavation methods inaugurated by Fiorelli and followed by his successors, Pompeii has been restored to life (Fig. 47). Through these ruins one can step into the past and see a first-century Roman town and its people with a clarity never before possible. Myriad ordinary objects of daily life—figs, nuts, grain, loaves of bread, and other food items; physicians' implements and carpenters' tools; mirrors, pins, necklaces, and other pieces of jewelry; taverns with their counters designed to hold vats of hot and cold food; the brothel with its many cubicles decorated with amorous paintings and with a different woman's name over each doorway; the baths, theaters, temples, and arena; and above all, on walls throughout the city, graffiti revealing the election slogans, business maxims, proverbs, curses, and love affairs of the common people—all were found as they had been left more than nineteen hundred years ago.

Since 1927 excavators have uncovered Herculaneum in the same way. Digging there is more difficult and slower than at Pompeii because of the depth and hardness of the mud-lava mixture covering the site. Also, much of Herculaneum is still under the modern houses of Resina. Thus, archaeologists have excavated only about one-fourth of Herculaneum, while they have cleared about three-fourths of Pompeii. But at Herculaneum wooden objects and the second stories of some buildings have been preserved much better than at Pompeii. Despite the obstacles, archaeological work has proceeded steadily at the city of Hercules just as at its more famous neighbor (Fig. 48).

At about the same time as Fiorelli's reorganization of the excavations at Pompeii, Pietro Rosa began work on the Palatine Hill in Rome. There, also, excavations had been conducted haphazardly since the sixteenth century. Diggers had unearthed many ruins, but the structures' identifications and the periods of their use remained uncertain. Rosa decided to correct this situation. He carefully distinguished the various levels and building remains in the areas he excavated. This enabled him to reconstruct the original topography of the site and the chronological sequence of its structures.

He came upon a modest-sized house in 1869 and skillfully laid it bare. Both its stratification in the layers of earth and the style of its architecture and well-preserved decoration indicated that it belonged to the first-century B.C. But Rosa discovered that this private dwelling had continued to stand in the first century A.D., even after the Palatine had become the site of the imperial palaces of the Julio-Claudian dynasty. The emperors had built elaborate structures all around it, but they had not demolished the house and replaced it with their palaces. This evidence of the early Roman emperors' respect for this humble dwelling and the evidence for its construction in the first century B.C. were very suggestive. They convinced most scholars that Pietro Rosa's meticulous excavations had restored to us the dwelling of Augustus, advocate of the simple life, champion of the old virtues, and first emperor of Rome.

The first scientific excavation of Etruscan antiquities also took place in 1869. Antonio Zannoni, a municipal engineer, investigated an Etruscan cemetery found by peasants at Certosa, near Bologna. Following the lead of Fea, Fiorelli, and Rosa, Zannoni excavated with care and precision. He made detailed descriptions of each tomb he opened, noting different layers of soil and their relationship to the tomb and the objects within it. Moreover, he carefully cataloged every tomb's contents, describing and preserving even those objects that were unfigured and that had no artistic value.

Such methods became standard in Italian archaeology soon after 1870, when all archaeological sites and excavations were placed under strict government control. The authorities shifted the emphasis of excavation from the collection and study of art objects to the recovery of information about the past. They also recognized that only through the use of orderly, scientific procedures could reliable information be obtained. While a black market in antiquities continued to exist, the days of legalized looting and treasure-hunting in Italy were over.

THE EXCAVATION OF VEII

The new approach in Italian archaeology resulted in more excavations of occupational sites that were rich in history, if not in art. In the years after 1870 archaeologists laid bare sites such as Ostia (the ancient port of Rome), Falerii, Vulci, and Satricum. But perhaps the best example of the new systematic excavation was the work done at ancient Veii.

The search for the ancient Etruscan city of Veii began in earnest shortly before World War I. Scholars knew that the ancient city had been located in the area of Isola Farnese, north of Rome. But although nineteenth-century excavators had found some remains from the time of Augustus and a few Etruscan tombs, they had failed to turn up a trace of the Etruscan city. Even a series of exploratory digs in 1888 and 1889 failed to locate the main settlement.

In 1913 a major campaign to uncover the city got underway. The first trenches uncovered nothing but tombs. However, careful work in the cemetery allowed archaeologists to trace the development of the tombs in chronological sequence from the tenth century to the fourth century B.C. They found a continuous development in burial practices with no signs of sudden change that might signal the arrival of a new population from abroad.

Scholars had been debating the issue of Etruscan origins for a long time. Some supported the view of the fifth-century B.C. Greek historian Herodotus that the Etruscans had moved to Italy from Asia Minor. Others sided with Dionysius of Halicarnassus, who in the first century B.C. claimed that the Etruscans were the aboriginal population of Italy. Still others, like Winckelmann, argued that the Etruscans were immigrants from Greece. Which view was correct?

The excavations in the cemetery at Veii showed that the issue was more complex than most had believed. There was no evidence of massive invasions from the outside. The oriental and Greek elements in Etruscan culture had appeared gradually (and presumably peacefully) over a period of centuries. On the other hand, the early Etruscan burial practices were similar to those found in parts of Italy where languages quite different from Etruscan had been spoken in antiquity. Thus, it was difficult to equate elements of material culture with specific ethnic groups. None of the popular contending theories fit the archaeological evidence very well. Scholars would have to develop newer, more complex hypotheses.

Meanwhile, on a hill near the cemetery, the city of Veii was finally located. In 1913 and 1914 archaeologists were able to delineate a series of successive occupations in which crude huts were succeeded by stone houses. The stratified sequence of pottery sherds they found established a chronology for the site. It also provided a link with the tomb series being developed in the excavations in the cemetery.

One disappointment, however, was that no temples had been located. Nevertheless, the director of the expedition, G. Q. Giglioli, noted that many fragments of tiles and terra cotta statues had been found in one spot at the foot of a hill. In the fall of 1914 Giglioli's trenches located a temple wall halfway up the hill. But before he could clear the site, Italy entered World War I and Giglioli was drafted into the armed forces.

When Giglioli received a period of leave in 1916, he returned to the site, reopened his trenches and uncovered more walls. Near one he discovered a pit containing terra cotta statues removed from the temple in Roman times. Among these broken statues was the life-sized figure of a young god. This statue has become known as the "Apollo of Veii" and it is regarded as one of the greatest masterpieces of Etruscan sculpture. It is fitting that a scientific expedition whose goal was primarily knowledge about the past nevertheless uncovered one of the most spectacular museum pieces produced by the early inhabitants of Italy.

By 1920 archaeology in Italy was in the hands of professionals who utilized careful stratigraphical excavation methods. An archaeological foundation had been completed. Italy was ready for the burst of activity that there, as elsewhere, characterized archaeology in the 1930s.

6

Unearthing the New World's Past

Phase I: Speculation, Antiquarianism, and Early Excavation (1517–1878)

DISCOVERY AND DESTRUCTION OF NEW WORLD CIVILIZATIONS

In 1517 three Spanish ships on a slave-hunting trip in the West Indies were blown off course by a tropical storm. When the weather cleared Francisco Hernández de Córdoba, commander of the expedition, found his vessels near an unknown coast. But a surprise even greater than discovery of a new land awaited Córdoba and his men, for in the distance they could see a walled city with stone pyramids and palace-like structures rising above the trees.

Soon a few Indians wearing cotton clothing and elaborate feathered headdresses appeared on the beach. They made signs inviting the white men ashore. But when the Spaniards landed and began to march toward the city, hundreds of warriors suddenly attacked from ambush. The small band of Europeans were saved from annihilation only by their muskets, which struck terror into the hearts of the natives. The Spaniards fought their way back to their ships and sailed off down the coast.

Fifteen days later they again landed in sight of a city. This time the conquistadors reached a courtyard in the main part of the town before masses of plumed warriors forced them to retreat. For several more weeks the expedition explored the western coast of Yucatan. The Spaniards sighted more cities and had a few more skirmishes with the natives before returning to Cuba.

The survivors of Córdoba's expedition were the first to report the existence of the Maya civilization of Mesoamerica.[1] They told of seeing massive stone temples, elaborate sculptures, and colorful wall paintings. But more important to their fellow Spaniards were descriptions of ornaments and effigies of copper, gold, and jade. Some members of the expedition had even brought back a few examples.

Visions of untold wealth soon inspired others to attempt the conquest of this new land. Two hundred and forty conquistadors set out for Yucatan the following year. They obtained some gold jewelry from a few Maya by trade. But they learned that the Maya's gold came from a place to the northwest, a land the Indians called "Méjico." So they sailed up the Mexican coast to a point near present-day Veracruz. There they were met by Aztec messengers who brought large quantities of gold as a gift. Ironically, this "peace offering" ensured the destruction of Aztec power.

In 1519 Hernando Cortés landed in Mexico with a well-equipped army. He found flourishing cities and civilized Indian tribes organized into an empire ruled by the Aztecs. However, with the aid of vassal tribes anxious to be free of the Aztec yoke, Cortés seized the Aztec capital, Tenochtitlán (now Mexico City), captured the Emperor Montezuma, and destroyed the Aztec empire. He sent back to Spain a fortune in gold, silver, and jade that he took from the Indians.

Driven by a lust for adventure, gold, and power, as well as a desire to spread the true faith among the heathen, conquistadors embarked on additional conquests. Spanish armies subjugated the Maya in Mesoamerica (1527–46) and destroyed the Inca empire in Peru (1532–72). The Indians were enslaved and often transplanted from their villages to the estates of the new Spanish landowners. Ancient cities and temples were abandoned. Vegetation gradually covered the stone monuments, and even the Indians forgot the locations and former functions of most of their once-teeming cities.

Accompanying the conquistadors were Franciscan and Dominican missionaries. In their zeal to convert the red men, the friars usually did everything they could to destroy native cultures and traditions. They smashed altars and images of the ancient gods and imposed harsh pen-

---

1. In 1502, near Honduras, Columbus had met some Indians in a canoe who said they came from Maia. But Columbus turned east and never saw the mainland or Maya cities.

alties on Indians caught practicing their former religions. They also publicly burned Maya hieroglyphic manuscripts. In the opinion of the missionaries these books "contained nothing in which there was not to be seen superstition and lies of the devil."[2] Religious myths and ceremonials, astronomical observations and calculations, literature, and perhaps historical records of centuries of civilization were lost forever.[3]

One of the most zealous agents of this destruction was a Franciscan friar named Diego de Landa. He arrived in Yucatan in 1549 and immediately began studying the Maya language and culture in preparation for his mission among them. For fifteen years he crusaded against native traditions, burning books and beating anyone who persisted in worshiping heathen deities. However, through his writings he also provided modern scholars with the means to reconstruct many aspects of late Maya society and history.

About 1566 Landa wrote a history of Yucatan entitled *Relación de las Cosas de Yucatán* (*An Account of the Affairs of Yucatan*). In this small book he described what he had learned of Maya life—their history, calendar, diet, tribal customs, folklore, and religion. It is no substitute for the Maya books he consigned to the flames. But without Landa's account our knowledge of Maya culture at the time of the conquest would be considerably poorer.

Other early reports also provide valuable information on the Maya, Aztec, and Inca civilizations. Especially noteworthy are *A General History of the Affairs of New Spain,* a late-sixteenth-century account of Aztec life by Fray Bernardino de Sahagún, and *The Royal Commentaries of the Incas* (1609) by Garcilaso de la Vega. Such manuscripts were usually sent back to Spain to enlighten the royal court. But there they were deposited in the archives and "lost" for hundreds of years. Thus, few Europeans got to read these descriptions of Indian civilizations written by soldiers and priests who had observed them first hand.

Though lacking detailed information, many scholars were willing to speculate on the origins of the civilizations found in Middle and South America. As early as 1530 a poet named Giralamo Fracastoro suggested that the New World civilizations were remnants of Atlantis, the lost continent described by the ancient philosopher Plato. Other sixteenth-century Spanish authors agreed, including the historian Fran-

---

2. Diego de Landa, as quoted in Charles Gallenkamp, *Maya: The Riddle and Rediscovery of a Lost Civilization* (New York: Viking Penguin, 3rd revised edition, 1985), p. 12.

3. The Maya were the only American people to independently develop writing. Their books (called codices) were made of strips of bark joined at their sides and fan-folded to lie flat. Only four of these codices are known to exist today.

cisco Lopez de Gomara, who repeated the idea in his *General History of the Indies* (1553). Sir Francis Bacon used this theory as the basis of his unfinished utopia, *The New Atlantis* (1627), and in the next century the Atlantis-in-America idea was supported by leading scholars such as Georges Buffon, Jacob Krüger, and Alexander von Humboldt.

The true origins of the stone cities in the Americas were soon forgotten by most Spaniards and Indians alike. When Diego Garcia de Palacio stumbled upon the ruins of Copán in 1576 he was unable to determine what people had once lived there.[4] Palacio's report was also buried in the archives and forgotten (it was not published until 1840). Over the next two centuries knowledge of the very existence of great pre-Columbian cities in America gradually faded. When remains of New World civilizations were rediscovered at the end of the eighteenth and beginning of the nineteenth centuries, the news came as a shock to many people.

THE MYSTERIOUS MOUND-BUILDERS

Early European explorers and settlers of the eastern coast of North America found no stone cities or highly developed Indian civilizations. They did, however, notice many large earthen mounds that obviously had been erected by human hands. Colonists encountered these "tumuli" or "barrows," as they called them, even more frequently as they moved inland towards the Mississippi River. Most of the mounds were shaped like large round hillocks; some were shaped like truncated pyramids; still others had the forms of animals or birds. Moreover, there were large trees growing atop many of them, attesting to their great age (Fig. 49). Who had constructed these strange monuments and what was their purpose?

Some of the circular mounds had clearly been used for burials, for they contained bones. But what customs governed the burials? How had the mounds developed? Some said that the mounds contained the bones of warriors killed in battle. Each mound would have been erected soon after a battle to bury the dead and commemorate the event. Others thought that the mounds had grown through periodic collection and reburial of the bones of a community's dead. Still others agreed that each mound was the general burial place for a nearby town, but argued

---

4. Many Maya centers, especially those in the Petén region (in what is now Guatemala), had been abandoned centuries before the arrival of the Spaniards. However, their continuity with northern Yucatan's cities would have been apparent if the campaign against native traditions had not been so thorough.

Fig. 49. The large Grave Creek Mound in West Virginia. (From E. G. Squier and E. H. Davis, *Ancient Monuments of the Mississippi Valley*, 1848.)

Fig. 50. A conical burial mound at Marietta, Ohio. (From E. G. Squier and E. H. Davis, *Ancient Monuments of the Mississippi Valley*, 1848.)

that the first person who died in the town was placed erect with earth heaped about him to cover and support him. When others died their bodies would be leaned against the first and covered with earth. In this way the mound would grow larger and larger.

The first person to scientifically investigate these issues was Thomas Jefferson. Around 1780 the statesman-archaeologist excavated a mound in the Rivanna River Valley in Virginia near his home, Monticello. The circular barrow had a diameter of forty feet at its base and was seven and a half feet high. Jefferson estimated, however, that before plowing had reduced its elevation the mound must have been about twelve feet high.

At first Jefferson dug "superficially" in several parts of the mound and found collections of human bones buried at different depths below the surface. He then decided to dig a trench through the middle of the barrow so that he could see how it had been created. This "perpendicular cut" as he called it "was opened to the former surface of the earth, and was wide enough for a man to walk through and examine its sides."[5]

Here is Jefferson's description of the stratigraphy, written about 1781:

> At the bottom, that is, on the level of the circumjacent plain, I found bones; above these a few stones, brought from a cliff a quarter of a mile off, and from the river one-eighth of a mile off; then a large interval of earth, then a stratum of bones, and so on. At one end of the section were four strata of bones plainly distinguishable; at the other, three; the strata in one part not ranging with those in another.[6]

Jefferson noted the bones and teeth of children in the mound. He also found that none of the bones had holes or damage caused by bullets, arrows, or other weapons. He therefore concluded that the mound was not the grave of warriors killed in battle. It was also clear that the barrow was not covering bodies buried upright against one another.

Furthermore, Jefferson observed that the bones nearest the surface were not decayed as much as those further down. He thus concluded that the mound had grown from the customary collection and deposition of bones over a long period of time. He reasoned that "the first collection had been deposited on the common surface of the earth, a few stones put over it, and then a covering of earth, that the second had been

---

5. T. Jefferson, *Notes on the State of Virginia*, ed. William Peden (Chapel Hill: University of North Carolina, 1955), p. 99.
6. Ibid.

laid on this, had covered more or less of it in proportion to the number of bones, and was then covered with earth, and so on."[7] This conclusion was supported by the number and condition of the bones and their positions in different strata separated by layers of stones and earth.

Thomas Jefferson thus became the first person known to have used the principles of stratigraphy to interpret archaeological finds.[8] His work, therefore, deserves the title of "the first scientific excavation in the history of archaeology."[9] As another writer observed, it "anticipates the fundamental approach and the methods of modern archaeology by about a full century."[10]

The future president attributed the mound he had excavated and others found in various parts of the United States to the American Indians. He also noted the resemblance between Indians and the peoples of eastern Asia and speculated that the Indians had come to America across the Bering Strait.[11] Jefferson was right on both points. But over a century passed before most Americans would agree that Indians had built the mounds.

Two other early investigators of North American mounds were Gen. Rufus Putnam and the Rev. Manasseh Cutler. In 1787–88 they founded Marietta, Ohio, in an area containing hundreds of these earthen monuments (Fig. 50). Putnam surveyed the region, mapping the mounds and noting the many differences between them. Cutler was also intrigued by the mounds. In 1798 he hit upon the idea of dating a huge Marietta mound by examining one of the large trees growing on its summit. He cut down a tree, counted its tree-rings, and discovered that the mound was at least 463 years old at that time.

Many of the mounds in the Ohio Valley are immense. The Great Serpent Effigy Mound in Adams County, Ohio, has a total length of 1,330 feet (Fig. 51). The 78-foot-high mound near Miamisburg, Ohio, contains approximately 311,000 cubic feet of earth. The Cahokia Mound in Illinois is over 100 feet high, 710 feet wide and 1,080 feet long. Its base is almost 200,000 square feet larger than that of the Great Pyramid of Giza, Egypt. Could Indians have produced these gigantic earthworks,

---

7. *Notes on the State of Virginia*, p. 100.

8. As mentioned in chapter 1, about seventeen years after Jefferson's excavation John Frere in England also used stratigraphy to interpret his finds.

9. Mortimer Wheeler, *Archaeology from the Earth* (Baltimore: Penguin, 1956), p. 20.

10. K. Lehmann-Hartleben, "Thomas Jefferson, Archaeologist," *American Journal of Archaeology* 47 (1943): p. 163.

11. As early as 1648 Thomas Gage had argued that Indians had come to the New World from Asia by means of the Bering Strait. By Jefferson's time this view was widely accepted by scholars.

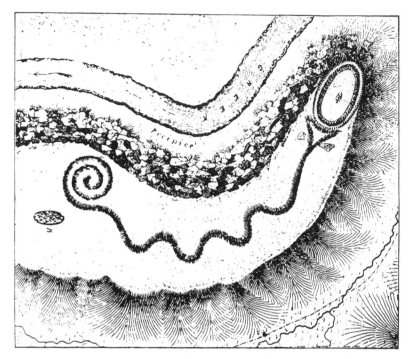

Fig. 51. Squier and Davis's plan of the Great Serpent Effigy Mound in Ohio. The mound forming the snake's body is four to five feet high and averages twenty feet in width. (From E. G. Squier and E. H. Davis, *Ancient Monuments of the Mississippi Valley*, 1848.)

whose construction must have required the organized expenditure of untold hours of labor?

Many educated people, disagreeing with Jefferson, thought not. In 1783, after receiving some information about the huge Ohio mounds, Ezra Stiles, then president of Yale College, argued that the mounds as well as the civilizations of Mexico and Peru were the work of Canaanites who had been driven out of Palestine by Joshua. Benjamin Franklin, a friend of Stiles, was a bit more cautious. His suggestion, accepted also by Noah Webster in 1787, was that the Ohio earthworks had been erected by the Spanish explorer De Soto during his wanderings. Another work published in 1787 claimed that the mounds were built by Danes who eventually migrated to Mexico where they became known as "Toltecs."

However, one of the most popular theories credited American antiquities to the "Lost Tribes of Israel." After King Solomon's death (circa 922 B.C.) the Hebrew people had split into two nations. Israel, located in the north of Palestine, contained ten of the twelve original Hebrew tribes. Judah, the southern kingdom, had only two tribes. When the kingdom of Israel fell to the Assyrians in the eighth century B.C., the upper classes were carried off into captivity, settled in other Assyrian territories, and lost to history. They thus became the "ten lost tribes" of later historical speculation. While some sixteenth-century scholars accepted the New World cultures as offshoots of Atlantis, others declared them to be products of the "lost tribes." These Israelite tribes were thought to have arrived in America either by migrating across Asia and the Bering Strait or by crossing the Atlantic in Phoenician ships.

Some of the early Lost Tribes advocates believed the Indians themselves to be descendants of the Israelites. Such well-known figures as Roger Williams, founder of Rhode Island, and William Penn, founder of Pennsylvania, accepted this view. Another of the theory's supporters was James Adair, who lived among Indian tribes for forty years before writing *The History of the American Indians* in 1775. Adair saw Jewish parallels to virtually every Indian custom or ceremony and derived many Indian words from Hebrew.

However, many other late eighteenth- and early nineteenth-century theorists placed the Mound-Builders in a totally separate category from the Indians. While the Mound-Builders might have been descendants of the Lost Tribes, these writers felt sure that the Indians were not.[12] In an 1805 article the Rev. Thaddeus M. Harris of Massachusetts concluded that it was impossible for the relatively small and poorly organized North American Indian tribes to construct the large mounds noted in Ohio. Thus, the idea of a "lost race" of Mound-Builders— variously identified as Israelites, Danes, Phoenicians, Egyptians, or other Old World peoples—became widely accepted.

William Henry Harrison, later to become the ninth president of the United States, was one who romanticized the lost Mound-Builders. He believed that they had been driven from their midwestern homes and replaced by more savage tribes. But where had they gone? In a study titled *Discourse on the Aborigines of the Valley of the Ohio* (1838) Harrison noted that the Aztecs were said to have arrived in Mexico about the middle of the seventh century.[13] He concluded that they were the fleeing Mound-Builders:

---

12. In fact, some Protestants who denied that the Indians were descendants of the Lost Tribes felt that native Americans weren't even human. Since Indians were not mentioned in the Bible, some people argued that they were not descendants of Adam and Eve. A papal bull of Pope Paul III in 1537 had declared that the Indians *were* human beings, but Protestants did not accept papal decrees.

13. Today archaeologists date the arrival of the Aztecs in central Mexico to the thirteenth century.

> An American author, the Rt. Rev. Bishop Madison of Virginia, having with much labor investigated this subject, declares his conviction that these Astecks are one and the same people with those who once inhabited the valley of the Ohio. The probabilities are certainly in favor of this opinion. . . . There is every reason to believe, that they were the founders of a great empire, and that ages before they assumed the more modern and distinguished name of Mexicans, the Astecks had lost in the more mild and uniform climate of Anhuac, all remembrance of the banks of the Ohio.[14]

This view came close to modern scholarly opinion, which also sees cultural connections between various groups of Mound-Builders and some of the inhabitants of Mexico. But even more in keeping with recent archaeological thinking were some of the ideas of Albert Gallatin, secretary of the treasury under Thomas Jefferson and founder of the American Ethnological Society. In *A Synopsis of the Indian Tribes Within the United States East of the Rocky Mountains and in the British and Russian Possessions in North America* (1836), Gallatin briefly discussed the mounds. Like Harrison and others, he noted similarities between the flat-topped rectangular mounds in the United States and the temple pyramids of Mexico. But he didn't conclude that Aztecs or Toltecs had migrated south from Ohio. Instead, like modern scholars, he posited a gradual diffusion of agriculture and pyramid building northwards from Mexico to the United States. However, he could not explain what had happened to the mound-building agriculturalists of early Ohio.

There were some, though, who agreed with Jefferson in rejecting the idea of a vanished race of mound-builders. Dr. James H. McCulloh dug into a few mounds in Ohio in 1812 and noted that the skeletons he found were no different from those of Indians. His conclusions were supported in 1839 by Dr. Samuel G. Morton of Philadelphia. Morton, often termed "the father of American physical anthropology," systematically studied hundreds of skulls of all races. He discovered that an individual's racial identity could almost always be determined on the basis of ten skull measurements—longitudinal diameter, facial angle, horizontal periphery, and so forth. When he compared the measurements of Mound-Builder skulls with those of modern Indians he found no significant differences.

Despite the evidence cited by McCulloh and Morton, the belief that

---

14. W. H. Harrison, *Discourse on the Aborigines of the Valley of the Ohio* (1838), as quoted in E. G. Squier and E. H. Davis, *Ancient Monuments of the Mississippi Valley* (Washington, D.C.: Smithsonian Institution, 1848), p. 306.

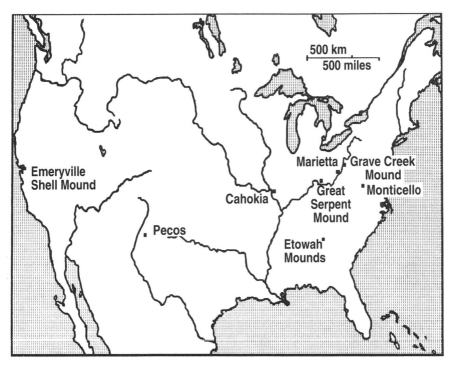

Map 7. Early archaeology in the United States.

the Mound-Builders had been Indians remained a minority opinion. Theories about the mysterious disappearance of an unknown people were far more appealing to the public. When, in 1833, a writer named Josiah Priest published a work supporting the vanished Mound-Builder hypothesis, it sold over twenty-two thousand copies in only three months, making it a runaway bestseller in that day.

There were probably some deep-seated psychological reasons why the myth of the Mound-Builder race caught the national fancy and held it for so long, as Robert Silverberg has noted:

> The dream of a lost prehistoric race in the American heartland was profoundly satisfying; and if the vanished ones had been giants, or white men, or Israelites, or Danes, or Toltecs, or giant white Jewish Toltec Vikings, so much the better. The people of the United States were then engaged in undeclared war against the Indians who blocked their path to expansion, transporting, imprisoning, or simply massacring them; and as this century-long campaign of genocide proceeded, it may have been expedient to conjure up a previous race whom the

Indians had displaced in the same way. Conscience might ache a bit over the uprooting of the Indians, but not if it could be shown that the Indians, far from being long-established settlers in the land, were themselves mere intruders who had wantonly shattered the glorious Mound Builder civilization of old.[15]

Whatever the reason for their acceptance, myths about the lost Mound-Builders remained popular until the 1930s and are still accepted by some people today.

One of the most important contributions to the study of the mounds was made in the late 1840s by two amateur archaeologists from Chillicothe, Ohio. Ephraim George Squier, editor of a Chillicothe newspaper, and Dr. Edwin H. Davis, a physician, were brought together by their deep interest in antiquities, particularly in the remains of the Mound-Builders. For more than two years, Squier and Davis traveled throughout the valleys of the Ohio and Mississippi rivers surveying and mapping mound sites (Figs. 49–52). They dug test shafts into more than two hundred mounds, collected artifacts, noted evidence of stratification, and hypothesized about the original purposes of the mounds. In 1848 the young Smithsonian Institution (founded in 1846) published Squier and Davis's survey as the first volume of the "Smithsonian Contributions to Knowledge" series. This work, *Ancient Monuments of the Mississippi Valley* (1848), is regarded as a classic in North American archaeology. It laid the foundations for a systematic approach to the riddles of the mounds.

Squier and Davis worked out a classification system for the different types of mounds they observed. They distinguished mounds from earthwork enclosures. Furthermore, within the mound classification they recognized the differences between conical burial mounds like the one Thomas Jefferson had excavated, temple mounds (flat-topped, pyramidlike structures that served as platforms for temples or chieftains' houses), and effigy mounds constructed in the forms of bears, snakes, birds, turtles, and other animals, including men. They noted that some mounds stood in isolation while others were built in groups surrounded by earthen embankments. Long causeways or raised earthwork avenues often linked mound groups or enclosures to one another.

Squier and Davis believed that most of the mounds had been built by a vanished non-Indian race. But the differences in the form, contents, and uses of the mounds led them to conclude correctly that at least

---

15. R. Silverberg, *Mound Builders of Ancient America: The Archaeology of a Myth* (Greenwich, Conn.: New York Graphic Society, 1968), pp. 57–58.

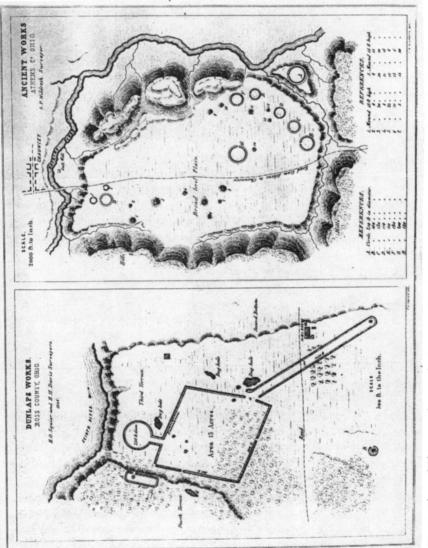

Fig. 52. Plans of Ohio mound groups by Squier and Davis. (From E. G. Squier and E. H. Davis, *Ancient Monuments of the Mississippi Valley*, 1848.)

some of the mounds had been erected either by different peoples or at different times, or both. However, Squier and Davis's attempts to identify the peoples responsible for the mounds were far off the mark.

Meanwhile, antiquities dealers and collectors were also becoming aware of the great diversity of relics hidden within the mounds. Some burial mounds contained beautifully carved stone pipes in the shapes of animals, birds, or people, and beaten copper tools, weapons, breast-plates, and jewelry. In temple mounds diggers found well-made pottery vessels in human or animal forms, circular discs of shell engraved with designs of humans with severed heads, woodpeckers, eagles, toads, and skulls. By the time of the Civil War antiquities dealers were making a considerable amount of money from the sale of objects plundered from the mounds.

Some collectors, though, preferred organizing their own excavations rather than securing relics from dealers. One such collector was an eccentric (and very wealthy) cotton trader named Cyrus Moore. Every summer for many years Moore and a crew of diggers drifted down the Ohio and Mississippi rivers on a specially built houseboat. Whenever he spotted an interesting-looking mound among the thousands visible from the rivers, Moore stopped the boat and sent his men ashore to excavate. Each fall the floating museum arrived in New Orleans loaded with Mound-Builder artifacts for Moore's collection.

Another well-known collector was Gerard Fowke, a former Union cavalry officer. During the Civil War, Fowke vowed that when the war was over he would never again ride a horse. True to his word, after 1865 Fowke did all his traveling on foot. Trudging along the dusty roads from Georgia to Michigan, he examined and tabulated the collections of hundreds of private individuals and museums. He also surveyed and excavated many mounds himself. Like Squier and Davis, Fowke came to recognize that there must have been more than one group of Mound-Builders. But he was unable to successfully distinguish the various cultures on the basis of their artifacts. The identity of the Mound-Builders remained a mystery.

THE REDISCOVERY OF MAYAN CIVILIZATION

In the late eighteenth century Spanish officials in Guatemala heard reports of strange ruins in the jungle. They tried to secure more information on these ruins, but failed. So, in 1786, the authorities dispatched Antonio del Rio, a captain in the Spanish army, to investigate the stories. Del Rio and an artist named Ricardo Almendáriz spent months hacking their way through extremely dense jungle undergrowth before they came upon several stone buildings almost completely hidden by vegetation. They had found the ruins of Palenque (Fig. 53).

Copies of del Rio's brief report on the remains and a few sketches by Almendáriz were deposited in the archives in Guatemala City and in Spain, where they were ignored for a generation. However, during the Latin American revolutions against Spain in the early nineteenth century, a manuscript of the report fell into the hands of a man named McQuy, who took it to England. In 1822 he had it translated and published as *Description of the Ruins of an Ancient City, Discovered Near Palenque.*

In the meantime another expedition had investigated the ruins. Guillermo Dupaix and José Luciano Castañeda, his artist, arrived at Palenque in 1808 after spending three years examining many pre-Hispanic remains in Mexico. Dupaix prepared detailed descriptions of Palenque's major monuments, such as "the Palace" and "the Temple of the Cross." Meanwhile, Castañeda made several very accurate drawings. The report and illustrations were filed with the Cabinet of Natural History in Mexico City. Years later they were published by H. Baradère in his *Antiquités Mexicaines* (1827) and by Lord Kingsborough as part of his eight-volume *Antiquities of Mexico* (1830–48).

Others also visited Maya sites during the early part of the nineteenth century. Among the most notable of these explorers were Juan Galindo, a political adventurer who visited Palenque and Copán, and Jean Frédéric Waldeck, an artist who produced drawings and descriptions of ruins at Copán, Palenque, Uxmal, and Chichén Itzá. But the accounts of these men were often published in limited and expensive editions, and they did not attract much attention.

Credit for making most educated Americans and Europeans aware that a great civilization once flourished in Central America belongs to John Lloyd Stephens. This New York lawyer became interested in antiquities during a two-year journey through Europe, Turkey, Palestine, Sinai, and Egypt. At the end of his tour in 1836, Stephens passed through London, where he met Frederick Catherwood, an architect and artist who had also traveled in the eastern Mediterranean. The two men immediately became friends. Catherwood had made a number of excellent drawings of the archaeological remains of Egypt and the Holy Land. Catherwood showed these to Stephens, and during their discussion of antiquities he told his new friend about del Rio's account of a forgotten city near Santo Domingo de Palenque.

Stephens returned to New York and busied himself with politics and his legal practice. But his thoughts occasionally wandered to images of ruins in the American tropics. One day, the owner of a bookstore

Fig. 53. The "Palace" at Palenque. (From J. L. Stephens, *Incidents of Travel in Central America, Chipas, and Yucatan*, vol. 2, 1841.)

Fig. 54. The "Nunnery" and "House of the Dwarf" at Uxmal. (From J. L. Stephens, *Incidents of Travel in Central America, Chipas, and Yucatan*, vol. 2, 1841.)

called Stephens's attention to Waldeck's recently published volume and its engravings of ruined cities in southern Mexico and Yucatan. Stephens immediately began seeking more information. He secured copies of the works of del Rio, Dupaix, and Galindo. Their accounts confirmed the truth of Waldeck's statements about the mysterious stone cities. His imagination inflamed by these writings, Stephens made arrangements to go to Central America to see for himself the marvels they described.

Meanwhile, Catherwood had moved from London to New York.

Stephens had little trouble persuading his friend to close his Wall Street office and accompany him on his expedition. Shortly before the two men were scheduled to depart, Stephens was appointed U.S. ambassador to the Central American Confederation. This position gave the explorers at least a small measure of protection during their journeys through the strife-ridden republics south of Mexico. In October 1839 the new ambassador and his artist-companion set sail for Belize.

Stephens and Catherwood had decided to search for Copán, the most inaccessible of the cities described by earlier explorers. First they sailed down the coast from Belize to Livingston and down the Rio Dulce to Lake Izabal. Then they struck out overland across extremely difficult terrain. Heavy rains had made the mountain trails virtually impassable. But after several minor accidents and an "arrest" by a band of irregular soldiers, the explorers reached the village of Copán.

The next day, after cutting their way through a few more miles of jungle, Stephens and Catherwood had their first view of the ruins. On the far bank of the Rio Copán was a high wall almost entirely covered with vines and trees. They crossed the river and ascended a stairway to the top of a terrace so overgrown by the forest that they could not discern its form or limits. As they began clearing some of the jungle growth, they uncovered stone stelae and portions of pyramids even more wonderful than they had imagined. Stephens later described his thoughts at that moment:

> America, say historians, was peopled by savages; but savages never reared these structures, savages never carved these stones. We asked the Indians who made them, and their dull answer was "*Quien sabe?*" "Who knows?"
>
> There were no associations connected with this place, none of those stirring recollections which hallow Rome, Athens, and "The world's great mistress on the Egyptian plain." But architecture, sculpture, and painting, all the arts which embellish life, had flourished in this overgrown forest; orators, warriors, and statesmen, beauty, ambition, and glory had lived and passed away, and none knew that such things had been, or could tell of their past existence. Books, the records of knowledge, are silent on this theme.[16]

Stephens hired workers to clear away more of the vegetation while Catherwood began to draw the remains they uncovered. At first Catherwood found his job very difficult, for the heavy foliage did not admit

---

16. J. L. Stephens, *Incidents of Travel in Central America, Chipas and Yucatan,* 12th ed., vol. 1 (New York: Harper and Brothers, 1856), pp. 104–5.

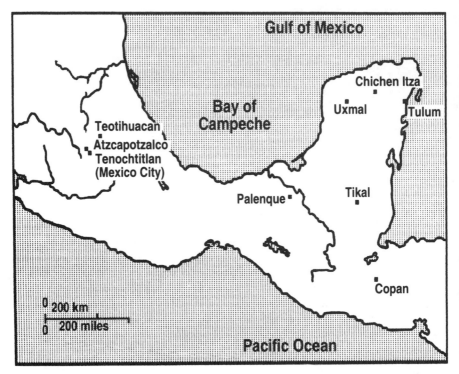

Map 8. Early archaeology in Mesoamerica.

enough light to bring out the figures carved in high relief. Moreover, the images and designs were so different from anything he had ever seen that he initially could not depict them accurately. After a number of attempts, however, the artist was at last able to produce drawings that met his perfectionist standards (Fig 55).

There were other problems as well. The mayor of the village of Copán suspected the motives of the strangers from North America, and he became angry when some of his workers left his employ to work for Stephens. The man who owned the land containing the ruins was also angry over what he considered a violation of his property rights. To avoid problems, Stephens offered to buy the land. But although the landowner was quite willing to rid himself of unproductive land cluttered with carved stones and ruined buildings, he was reluctant to deal with the strangers. He feared the sale would get him into trouble with the government. Stephens displayed his credentials and letters of recommendation from officials in Guatemala, but suspicions lingered. Finally, he hit upon the idea of putting on his full dress diplomatic

Fig. 55. Catherwood's drawing of stele "N" at Copán. (From J. L. Stephens, *Incidents of Travel in Central America, Chipas, and Yucatan*, vol. 1, 1841.)

coat with its profusion of gold braid, medals, and brass buttons. The villagers were at last convinced that an important personage was in their midst. The landowner hastily signed the deed giving Stephens ownership of the ruins for the grand sum of fifty dollars.

Catherwood remained at Copán exploring and drawing the ruins while Stephens traveled to Guatemala City to fulfill his diplomatic obligations. Early in the spring of 1840 the two men set out on another difficult journey, to Palenque in southern Mexico. They noted many carved stelae and ruined pyramids on the way. But none were as wonderful as the stucco reliefs and reasonably well-preserved structures at Palenque.

From Palenque they made their way to Yucatan, where they examined the ruins of Uxmal (Fig. 54). Their stay at this site was cut short, however. Soon after their arrival, Catherwood collapsed and became delirious from malaria. As soon as he was well enough to travel, the two explorers returned to New York.

Fig. 56. Catherwood's drawing of a temple at Tulum. (From J. L. Stephens, *Incidents of Travel in Central America, Chipas, and Yucatan*, vol. 1, 1841.)

Incidents of Travel in Central America, Chipas and Yucatan, Stephens's two-volume account of their adventures illustrated with Catherwood's engravings, appeared in September 1841. It was an immediate bestseller. *Incidents of Travel in Central America* and its sequel, *Incidents of Travel in Yucatan* (1843), which describes Stephens and Catherwood's 1841–42 return trip to Uxmal and their visit to Chichén Itzá and Tulum (Fig. 56), made the ruined cities of Mesoamerica common topics of conversation. They prompted the study that was to become Maya archaeology.

EARLY ARCHAEOLOGY IN SOUTH AMERICA

After looting the Inca treasures and destroying the Inca empire in the sixteenth century, the Spanish paid little attention to the remains of the pre-Columbian cultures of Peru and Bolivia. Spain didn't allow her colonies to trade with other nations, and few outsiders were given permission to visit her New World possessions. As a result, European and North American scholars generally disregarded the early Spanish reports about Inca civilization, considering them to be legends or exaggerations.

The world rediscovered the existence of Peruvian civilizations through the works of the famous German naturalist Alexander von Humboldt. Between 1799 and 1804 Humboldt toured the Spanish colonies in America by special permission of the Spanish king, Charles IV. He carefully observed the flora, fauna, geography, and other natural features of the areas he visited. But he also noted archaeological remains. Humboldt's vivid descriptions and sketches of Inca roads and buildings were published in 1810 as *Vues des Cordillères et Monuments des Peuples Indigenes de l'Amerique* (*Survey of the Cordilleras and the Monuments of the Indigenous People of America*). This work aroused extensive scholarly interest in pre-Hispanic Peruvian history.

One young man on whom Humboldt's narratives had a profound influence was a Boston historian named William H. Prescott. Inspired by Humboldt's accounts of Peruvian and Mexican antiquities, Prescott began studying the early Spanish records of the conquest. His research led him to write two masterful books on the destruction of native American empires. *History of the Conquest of Mexico* appeared in 1843 on the heels of Stephens's descriptions of the ruins of Central America and Yucatan. Four years later Prescott's *History of the Conquest of Peru* revealed the splendor of the Inca civilization at the time of the white man's arrival.

Sir Clements Markham provided additional information on the remains of Inca civilization. Markham was a British geographer who traveled through the Andes between 1852 and 1854. He described many pre-Columbian monuments in his book, *Cuzco: A Journey to the Ancient Capital of Peru* (1856). In later years he also located and translated several early Spanish chronicles that had been unknown to Prescott.

Archaeological excavation in Peru began with the arrival of Ephraim George Squier, the man who, with Dr. E. H. Davis, had surveyed the mounds of the Mississippi Valley. In 1849 Squier abandoned his study of the North American mounds to take the position of United States chargé d'affaires in Central America. He naturally took advantage of this opportunity to examine the monuments described by Stephens and Catherwood. Then, in 1862, President Lincoln sent him to Lima to represent the United States in settling an economic and legal dispute with Peru.

After completing his diplomatic mission, Squier toured Peru and Bolivia for eighteen months, surveying, drawing, photographing, and digging at a number of pre-Columbian sites (Figs. 57–58). He achieved his most important results at the coastal site of Moche. There his excavations led Squier to conclude that, "There were originally several detached and distinct civilizations in Peru, . . . [and] some of them antedated the Incas." Squier published his discoveries in 1877 in *Peru: Incidents of Travel and Exploration in the Land of the Incas.* This work remained the most reliable handbook on Peruvian antiquities for over a generation.

CONTINUED SPECULATIONS ABOUT ORIGINS

The works of Stephens and Catherwood, Prescott, and others convinced the public that highly developed pre-Columbian civilizations had flourished in America. But how had those civilizations begun? When Stephens first saw Copán he had conceded that the identity of its builders might never be known. However, after visiting other sites and doing some research, Stephens's views changed.

He noted that the American monuments were quite different from those of India, China, Japan, Egypt, and other Old World civilizations. He also pointed out that early accounts of the conquest indicated that some of the cities were still occupied by Indians when the Spanish first arrived, and that a comparison of the hieroglyphs at Copán and Palenque with copies of those in the surviving Maya books revealed remarkable similarities. These facts led him to state,

> As yet we perhaps stand alone in these views, but I repeat my opinion that we are not warranted in going back to any ancient nation of the Old World for the builders of these cities: that they are not the work of people who have passed away and whose history is lost, but that there are strong reasons to believe them the creations of the same races who inhabited the country at the time of the Spanish conquest, or of some not very distant progenitors.[17]

Prescott's research also supported this conclusion. Many years passed, however, before this opinion became the generally accepted view. The different groups that were suggested as the builders of the North American mounds—the Lost Tribes of Israel, Egyptians, Phoenicians, Chinese, and others—were also put forward as the creators of the Middle and South American cities. However, one of the earliest, most popular, and most persistent theories traced both the New and Old World civilizations back to a common source, supposedly a lost super-civilization known variously as Atlantis or Mu.

Abbé Charles-Étienne Brasseur de Bourbourg, a Flemish scholar, became an ardent supporter of the Atlantis hypothesis. For years he

---

17. J. L. Stephens, *Incidents of Travel in Central America, Chipas and Yucatan,* 12th ed., vol. 2 (New York: Harper and Brothers, 1856), p. 455.

Fig. 57. Inca ruins of Ollantaytambo, Peru. (From E. G. Squier, *Peru: Incidents of Travel and Exploration in the Land of the Incas,* 1877.)

Fig. 58. "Gateway of the Sun" at Tiahuanaco, Bolivia. (From E. G. Squier, *Peru: Incidents of Travel and Exploration in the Land of the Incas,* 1877.)

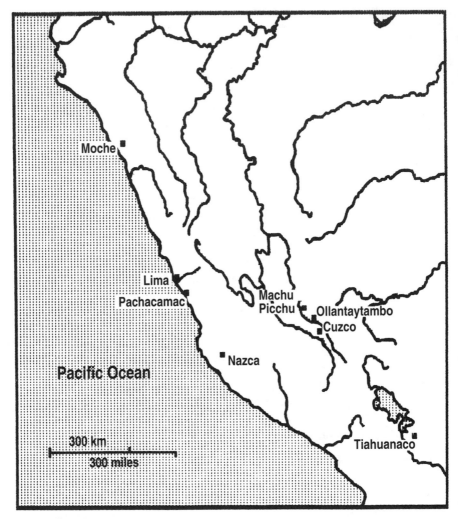

Map 9. Early archaeology in Peru.

traveled in the Americas, searching out old documents and learning Indian languages in order to understand the origins and history of the American civilizations. Then, in 1864, he discovered in Madrid an abridged copy of Diego de Landa's description of Maya culture. In addition to discussions of customs and ceremonies, Landa provided what he thought was a key for reading Maya hieroglyphic writing (Fig. 59). His interpretation of the signs for the days and months of the Maya calendar proved to be accurate and provided the key for reading

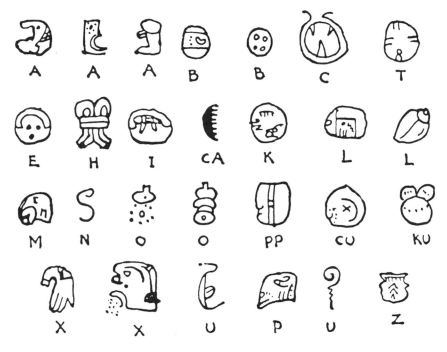

Fig. 59. Diego de Landa's Maya "alphabet." Some scholars used this faulty "key" to Mayan writing to find references to Atlantis or Mu in Maya inscriptions. (From D. de Landa, *Relación de las Cosas de Yucatán*, written in 1566 but published with a French translation and commentary by Brasseur de Bourbourg in 1864.)

dates on Maya monuments. However, Landa mistakenly assumed that the rest of the writing system was alphabetic, like European writing. In reality, it seems to consist of a complex combination of ideographs (signs representing individual words) and syllabic signs denoting sounds. The readings he gave for the Maya "alphabet" have since been shown to be incorrect.[18]

Of course, Brasseur de Bourbourg was unaware of Landa's error. He used the supposedly alphabetic signs and a lot of imagination to "read" one of the four surviving Maya books. Brasseur interpreted it as an account of a great cataclysm that had engulfed a large island

---

18. Maya writing has recently been deciphered based on intensive research during the last twenty-five to thirty years. See Linda Schele and David Freidel, *A Forest of Kings: The Untold Story of the Ancient Maya* (New York: Willam Morrow, 1990), pp. 46–55, and Michael D. Coe, *Breaking the Maya Code* (New York: Thames and Hudson, 1992) for accounts of the decipherment and descriptions of the Maya writing system.

in the Atlantic in the year 9937 B.C. According to Brasseur the Indian name for this lost continent was Mu, but he argued that it was obviously the same island that Plato had called Atlantis.[19]

Brasseur's ideas about Mu/Atlantis were developed further in the 1880s and 1890s by an eccentric Frenchman named Augustus Le Plongeon. This amateur archaeologist visited many sites in Yucatan and conducted excavations at Chichén Itzá, the first true excavations at a Maya site. Le Plongeon claimed to be able to decipher Maya inscriptions, interpreting several of them as records of the destruction of Mu. He also claimed that certain Maya texts recounted the story of a princess named Moo who became queen of Yucatan. She was driven from her throne and tried to find refuge on the island of Mu, her ancestral home.[20] However, she found that the island had been destroyed. Therefore, she continued on to the Muvian colony in Egypt where she built the Sphinx and came to be worshiped as the goddess Isis.

Ignatius Donnelly, a contemporary of Le Plongeon, also made use of Brasseur's translations. However, Donnelly's book, *Atlantis: The Antediluvian World* (1882), became more famous than any of the works of Le Plongeon or of Brasseur himself. This perennially popular work has gone through many editions, some still available today. Donnelly claimed that Atlantis "became, in the course of ages, a populous and mighty nation, from whose overflowings the shores of the Gulf of Mexico, the Mississippi River, the Amazon, the Pacific coast of South America, the Mediterranean, the west coast of Europe and Africa, the Baltic, the Black Sea, and the Caspian were populated by civilized nations."[21] Donnelly supported this statement by a variety of arguments, including many supposed similarities between the civilizations of the Old and New Worlds. He also asserted that the sinking of Atlantis over eleven thousand years ago gave rise to the biblical story of the Deluge and to other flood stories around the world.

At the time that the Atlantis hypothesis was reaching its height

19. Other scholars' attempts to use Landa's "key" to read Mayan texts soon proved that the "alphabet" was incorrect and that Abbé Brasseur's translation of the Madrid Codex was invalid. In fact, Brasseur compounded Landa's errors by reading the codex backwards. It is now generally recognized that this codex is really an astrological treatise, not an account of Atlantis.

20. Both Brasseur and Le Plongeon claimed that Mu was the Maya name for Atlantis. But some people came to regard it as a shortened form of Lemuria, a hypothetical lost continent in the Pacific. Thus, some popular books came to trace all civilization (even that of Atlantis) to the Pacific continent of Mu.

21. I. Donnelly, *Atlantis: The Antediluvian World*, modern rev. ed., ed. Egerton Sykes (New York: Gramercy, 1949), p. 1.

during the 1880s and 1890s, the groundwork was being laid for a more scholarly understanding of American civilization's origins. By the early decades of the twentieth century developments in philology, anthropology, and archaeology made it clear that the New World civilizations were indigenous products of various groups of Indians. Nevertheless, theories tracing these civilizations to Atlantis, Mu, Egypt, Phoenicia, or other sources outside of America remained popular into the twentieth century. Some people continue to believe them today.

Phase II: New World Archaeology Comes of Age (1878–1930)

THE COMING OF ORDER AND STRATIGRAPHIC EXCAVATION: NORTH AMERICA

Method and system became an integral part of the study of the North American mounds in the 1880s. In 1878 the Smithsonian Institution established the Bureau of American Ethnology to scientifically investigate problems relating to the Mound-Builders. Under the direction of Cyrus Thomas the archaeological division of the bureau undertook a program of professional archaeological exploration, mapping, and excavation during the 1880s. Before beginning this work, Thomas had supported the idea of a lost race of mound-builders. However, as his assistants brought forth more and more data from the mounds, Thomas was forced to change his mind. He became convinced that the mounds were the work of Indians. Moreover, he was equally sure that different tribal groups had built different types of mounds in different eras.

Thomas published his conclusions about the mounds in 1894 in the twelfth *Annual Report of the Bureau of American Ethnology*. This work, regarded as a classic in American archaeology, presented the evidence gathered by the bureau very effectively. It demonstrated the connections between Indians and the mounds and demolished the idea of a vanished mound-builder race. Professionals, at least, became convinced that the mystery of the mounds had been solved.

The Bureau of American Ethnology's work on the mounds was supplemented by the efforts of Frederick Ward Putnam, curator of Harvard's Peabody Museum from 1874 to 1909. Putnam and his associates at the museum undertook several important mound excavations, including that of the Great Serpent Mound in Ohio. These excavations were models of careful, scientific surveying, digging, and recording of finds.

During the final decades of the nineteenth century North American archaeology became increasingly professionalized. College- and university-based researchers like Putnam replaced the amateur scholars of earlier times. Leading universities, museums (especially the New York State Museum and the American Museum of Natural History), and professional societies (such as the Archaeological Institute of America and the American Anthropological Association) became the principle sponsors of archaeological work. Additionally, new journals such as the *American Antiquarian* (founded 1878) and the *American Anthropologist* (founded 1888) reflected the trend and helped to promote it.

As the discerning reader will have noted from the preceding paragraphs, as archaeology in the Americas became more professional it also became more directly linked to anthropology. By contrast, most European archaeologists tended to think of their developing discipline as a branch of history. Even the prehistoric European Bronze and Iron Age societies had been in contact with ancient Near Eastern or Mediterranean civilizations that had written history. But the New World did not have a long written history to which archaeological remains could be related. To understand their finds American archaeologists had to turn to ethnology and note parallels with recent native societies. Thus, in most American universities archaeology joined ethnology and linguistics as a subdiscipline of anthropology.

The last quarter of the nineteenth century also saw a revival of stratigraphical excavation methods and their use in chronological interpretation. Not much stratigraphical work had been done in North America since the time of Thomas Jefferson. However, in the 1870s a naturalist named William Dall excavated several caves and shell-mounds in Alaska, carefully recording the existence of various strata and noting the locations and relationships of objects found within them. Unfortunately, Dall's publications seem to have had little influence on the archaeologists of his time.

Friedrich Max Uhle, an archaeologist trained in his native Germany, also championed stratigraphical digging. Uhle became a professor at the University of Pennsylvania, then at the University of California. As will be described below, he first applied the stratigraphical method in his excavations in Peru. However, in the first years of the twentieth century he also excavated the Emeryville shell-mound near San Francisco Bay layer by layer. He noted changes in the artifacts from stratum to stratum and recognized these changes as evidence of cultural development through time.

Max Uhle's work, like Dall's, did not have an immediate broad impact. But it did influence a young man named Nels C. Nelson. Nelson first experienced stratigraphic digging while working under Uhle on California shell-mounds. In 1913 he visited Europe and observed archaeologists excavating caves in Spain and France layer by layer. When Nelson returned to the United States, he began using the stratigraphic method in his excavation of southwestern sites. Like Flinders Petrie, Nelson arbitrarily removed a fixed amount of earth in each layer (usually twelve inches). But he kept the potsherds from each of these levels separated, and noted changes in style and frequency from one stratum to the next. His 1916 article, "Chronology of the Tano Ruins, New Mexico" in *American Anthropologist* described his method and demonstrated its value.

Nelson's contemporary Alfred V. Kidder also promoted the stratigraphic method. Kidder, a Harvard graduate, had taken a course in field methods under George Reisner, the great Egyptologist discussed in an earlier chapter. Reisner was one of the most meticulous stratigraphic excavators of the early twentieth century, and he seems to have had a strong influence on Kidder. When Kidder began excavating in the American Southwest, he also used the stratigraphic method. However, like Reisner, Kidder followed the natural stratigraphy of his sites while digging rather than removing arbitrary levels of soil at a time. Despite this difference in method, Kidder's pottery sequence from the Pajarito Plateau and at the Pecos site in New Mexico confirmed that of Nelson.

The publications of Nelson and Kidder had more influence on their contemporaries than had the work of Dall and Uhle. Other archaeologists began excavating stratigraphically in Alaska and the eastern United States as well as in the Southwest. By 1930 the stratigraphical method and the use of stratigraphically based artifact sequences were well-established in North American archaeology.

THE COMING OF ORDER AND STRATIGRAPHIC EXCAVATION:
MIDDLE AND SOUTH AMERICA

Precise, scientific study of Maya sites began in 1883 with the work of the English scholar Alfred P. Maudslay. He recorded and mapped many previously unknown ruins, made plaster casts of sculptures, and carefully copied hieroglyphic inscriptions. He was also one of the first to use photography to record the appearance of Maya monuments. Maudslay's publications were as accurate and thorough as his work in the field. In eleven years of labor he provided a body of factual information on the Maya ruins upon which scholarly hypotheses and future research programs could be based.

The first careful, stratigraphical excavation in Mesoamerica or South America began in 1896. In that year Max Uhle started excavating Pachacamac, a Peruvian coastal site just south of Lima. Uhle had become interested in Peruvian civilization while curator of the Dresden Museum in Germany. However, his excavations at Pachacamac were sponsored by the University Museum of the University of Pennsylvania. Uhle was already familiar with Inca pottery and the presumably earlier wares found at Tiahuanaco. So, when he uncovered a third style of pottery in graves at Pachacamac, he argued that it must be intermediate in date. His careful excavation techniques produced evidence of several distinct occupation layers at the site and proved the legitimacy of the pottery sequence he had proposed (Fig. 60).

As we have seen, Uhle later conducted excavations in California. However, he remains best known for his work in Peru and Bolivia in the last decade of the nineteenth and the first decade of the twentieth centuries. His careful excavations there established the existence of what are now known as the Mochica and Nazca cultures, proving the correctness of E. G. Squier's view that there had been several pre-Inca civilizations in Peru.

From the public's point of view, the most spectacular discovery in Peru occurred in 1911. In that year Hiram Bingham, an American explorer and mountaineer, led a Yale University–sponsored expedition into the Andes. He was looking for Vilcabamba, the last stronghold of the Incas, lost since the time of the conquest. Following clues from some conquest accounts, Bingham and his companions searched peaks alongside the Urubamba and Vilcabamba River valleys. They finally came across an almost inaccessible site on a ridge below a peak called Machu Picchu. This, Bingham felt, was the lost city of the Incas.

Bingham returned to do some excavation at this site the following year. It was extremely well-preserved with many of its buildings almost intact. However, a text discovered since Bingham's time proves that Machu Picchu was not Vilcabamba. Nevertheless, Bingham's accounts of its discovery and excavation aroused great public interest. Machu Picchu became the best-known site in Peru and a tourist mecca.

Meanwhile, Mexico had also yielded clues to the existence of civilizations earlier than the ones found by the Spanish. Scholars had noted a Teotihuacan pottery style different from Aztec wares. Then, at Atzcapotzalco in the Valley of Mexico, sherds of a third style were found on the surface along with Aztec and Teotihuacan pieces. What was the chronological relationship between these three types of pottery?

In 1911 Manuel Gamio, a student of the famous anthropologist Franz

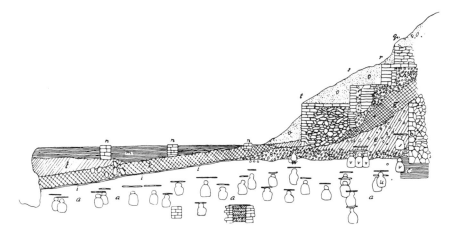

Fig. 60. Uhle's cross-section showing the stratigraphic relationship between architectural remains and tombs at Pachacamac. (From M. Uhle, *Pachacamac*, 1903.)

Boas, undertook stratigraphic excavations to solve the problem. He removed the earth in arbitrarily determined layers, but also noted evidence of natural stratification at the site. He was particularly careful to keep the pottery and artifacts from each stratum separate. Gamio found Aztec pottery in levels near the surface. Teotihuacan wares were in layers below the Aztec material, and the third pottery style was found in the deepest layers. At first called "Archaic," this pottery is now known as "Preclassic" or "Formative." Gamio also noted transitional types of figurines and mixtures of the Formative and Teotihuacan pottery in levels between those containing the pure types. Thus, Gamio's excavation not only proved the sequence of cultures in the Valley of Mexico, but also indicated that Teotihuacan culture probably had developed gradually out of the earlier Formative one.

George Vaillant, a student who had worked under Alfred Kidder at Pecos, began even more thorough stratigraphic excavations in Mexico in 1930. He generally confirmed Gamio's results. However, he provided more detail on the preclassic cultures of the area and extended their origins still further back in time. Archaeology in the New World was finally the equal of that being practiced in the Old.

7

Archaeology in the Far East and Sub-Saharan Africa

Phase I—Speculation, Antiquarianism, and Early Excavation (1500–1880)

THE WONDERS OF THE ANCIENT EAST

Until recently the East was mysterious and unfamiliar to Westerners. The ancient Greeks and Romans had at least a dim perception of the Indian and Chinese civilizations with which they traded. And at the end of the thirteenth century Marco Polo described some of the marvels of China, Java, Sumatra, Siam, Burma, Ceylon, the Zanzibar coast, Madagascar, and Abyssinia. He also gave a hearsay report about Japan, although he didn't visit it. However, many people did not believe his narrative. Though it inspired some to pioneer new routes to the East, it did not really enter the public consciousness. East Asia, the "Indies," remained almost totally unknown territory to Europeans until the fifteenth-century voyages of discovery.

Even then, national rivalries promoted secrecy that allowed little information to leak out to ordinary citizens. The Portuguese, for example, had an official compiler of chronicles in the East. His name was Diogo do Cuoto and he lived in the Portuguese colony of Goa in India. In his chronicles Diogo included reports about India and other Eastern civilizations along with narratives of Portuguese activities. He

199

seems to have become the first European to write about Angkor Wat and Angkor Thom in Cambodia, probably based on a verbal account by Antonio de Magdalena, a Capuchin friar who visited Angkor around 1585. However, Diogo's narratives did not get wide circulation in Europe. Only a few other seventeenth-century Portuguese and Spanish chroniclers seem to have read his work (which was not published until 1953), and their writings also had a very limited distribution.

One of the earliest popular accounts of an exotic Eastern civilization appeared in London in 1681. It was a narrative by a seaman named Robert Knox describing his almost twenty years of detention in Ceylon (now known as Sri Lanka). As a fourteen-year-old boy, Robert had gone to sea with his father, a ship owner also named Robert Knox. Some four years later, in 1659, their ship was badly damaged in a storm off the coast of southern India. They put into port at Cottiar, Ceylon, to buy a new mast and make repairs. However, Rajah Singho, the Singhalese ruler of the island, took the father, son, and sixteen members of the crew prisoner. The elder Robert Knox died in captivity, and his son was not able to escape until 1679.

Arabs had long traded with the island they called Serendip. The first modern Europeans to arrive, however, were the Portuguese, who established trading posts on the coast of Ceylon early in the sixteenth century. But these settlements were destroyed and the Portuguese driven out by the Dutch in 1658, a year before Knox's ship limped in for repairs. However, like the Portuguese, the Dutch did not make other Europeans aware of Ceylon's civilization or of its ruined jungle cities. In fact, Dutch desire to keep other merchants out of the area probably contributed to Knox's long detention at Rajah Singho's court.

Knox's narrative, written after his return to London, describes the government, religion, and customs of Ceylon, and records information about the principal cities of the island, including Kandy, the capital of Rajah Singho. He also mentions several "ruinous places" in the jungle where earlier kings once reigned. One of these ruined cities, Anuradhapura, was located in the northern part of the island. Knox states that Anuradhapura was an ancient capital from which ninety kings had reigned in succession. It contained many wonderful temples, pillars, and statues, and, he records, was still considered sacred to the Singhalese people of Ceylon.

Knox had no way of knowing that Anuradhapura had been founded in the fourth century B.C., during the lifetime of Alexander the Great, and that it had continued to flourish until the eighth century A.D. It covers over 250 square miles, and some of its mounds of masonry with shrines atop them are more than three hundred feet high. But while Knox did not learn of all of the wonders of this ruined city, he did know that it was very old. He made his readers aware that civilization had flourished in the jungles of Ceylon long before the Europeans had arrived.

The British gained control of India's coast and of Ceylon in the latter half of the eighteenth century. Over the next century they would gradually extend their rule over the entire Indian subcontinent. In the process, not only the British, but all Westerners became more cognizant of the East's antiquities. In 1784 the Asiatic Society of Bengal was founded in Calcutta to study the history, antiquities, literature, arts, and sciences of Asia. The society began publishing its *Archaeological Researches* in 1788.

One of the first discoveries brought to public attention by the Asiatic Society occurred in 1790. A peasant plowing a field near Nellore north of Madras in India struck some bricks. He began digging, and soon uncovered the remains of a small Hindu temple. But a greater surprise lay in store. Within the ruins of the temple the farmer found a small pot filled with second-century A.D. Roman coins and medals. The antiquity of the site was thus demonstrated.

However, this excavation, rudimentary as it was, was unusual. Most of the early archaeology in the area consisted of exploration and description of temples and monuments still visible. Many of these structures clearly were the equal of ancient Egyptian, Greek, and Roman monuments being brought to public attention in the early nineteenth century. Some viewers, in fact, thought them superior.

> It is my humble opinion that no monuments of antiquity in the known world are comparable to the Caves of Elora .... whether we consider their unknown origin, their stupendous size, the beauty of their architectural ornaments, or the vast number of statues and emblems, all hewn and fashioned out of the solid rock![1]

This quotation comes from the account of John Seely, a young British officer stationed just north of Bombay. Seely was more sensitive to native culture than many of his fellow countrymen. He complained about Europeans who visited a Hindu cave temple on Elephanta Island near Bombay and deliberately damaged the carved figures. These vandals also had disfigured many of the deities by drawing indecent appendages on them. Seely felt such actions by supposed "gentlemen" were disgusting.

---

1. J. B. Seely, *The Wonders of Elora* (London, G. & W. B. Whittaker, 1824), quoted in Bruce Norman, *Footsteps* (Topsfield, Mass.: Salem House, 1988), pp. 75–76.

Fig. 61. The Kailasa Temple at Ellora from the southwest. (From J. Wales, *Hindoo Excavations in the Mountain of Ellora, Near Aurungabad in the Decan*, 1803-04.)

In 1810 he undertook a difficult three-hundred-mile journey to see the cave temples of Ellora. These monuments had been "discovered" by Europeans only a short time before, for they were located outside of British-controlled territory. In Seely's day British power in India extended only a little over a hundred miles inland from the coast. Beyond were unfriendly rulers and bandits, not to mention tigers, snakes, and other dangerous animals. So the trip to Ellora through jungle and over mountains was hazardous as well as physically difficult.

The spectacular carved temples of Ellora were first brought to the attention of European readers through the descriptions and drawings of an Englishman named James Wales. He published the two volumes of his *Hindoo Excavations in the Mountain of Ellora, Near Aurungabad in the Decan* in 1803 and 1804. Seeley does not seem to have read this work. But he had heard of the site and wanted to see it for himself.

For protection Seeley traveled with five servants, three bullock drivers, three porters, and seven armed native soldiers. Ten days and many adventures later, the Englishman and his party arrived at Ellora. With growing feelings of admiration and awe Seely gazed upon the more than thirty Buddhist, Hindu, and Jain temples at the site. All but two of these monuments consisted of chambers and tunnels cut into the sides of the mountain. This was an amazing feat in itself, especially when one considers the many elaborate sculptures, columns, and other decorative features adorning these artificial caves.

However, the other two temples were even more awe-inspiring. They had been created by cutting away the entire mountain around them, leaving them as free-standing structures in the center of the excavation. The larger of the two, the Kailasa Temple, is "so large, so complex and so profusely decorated that it must rank as the largest and most sophisticated piece of sculpture in the world."[2] This temple of the Hindu god Siva was begun in the first half of the eighth century A.D. It required the excavation of a pit 276 feet long, 154 feet wide and 100 feet deep. Within this pit are bridges, large free-standing columns, elephant statues, shrines, porches, and a great columned central hall. All have been hewn directly out of the volcanic rock. Still other galleries and chapels have been excavated into the rock faces around the sides of the pit. Most of the surfaces of these structures are elaborately decorated with sculptured scenes from Hindu mythology (Fig. 61).

Seely marveled at these works and tried to convey to his readers the vast amount of labor and dedication required to create them. He also urged that these amazing temples be protected and preserved. His account, The Wonders of Elora, was published in 1824. This work, along with Wales's book and a later volume by James Fergusson,[3] helped make educated Europeans realize that India had antiquities to rival the more familiar ones being uncovered in Mediterranean lands.

The first scholarly study of the art and culture of ancient Java (now part of Indonesia) also appeared in 1824. It was one of the results of work initiated by the Leyden Museum, a Dutch research center on the island. This institution, founded in 1817, was the first European research establishment dedicated to Southeast Asian studies.

The early decades of the nineteenth century also saw important advances made in our understanding of ancient Eastern texts and inscriptions. James Prinsep, assay master of the mint in Calcutta, became the first to decipher the Brahmi script, the earliest of several used to write ancient Sanskrit. Prinsep's work made it possible for other scholars to begin gleaning information about Indian history and civilization from early Sanskrit literature.

2. Bruce Norman, Footsteps: Nine Archaeological Journeys of Romance and Discovery (Topsfield, Mass.: Salem House, 1988), p. 90.

3. James Fergusson, Illustrations of the Rock-cut Temples of India (London: N.P., 1845).

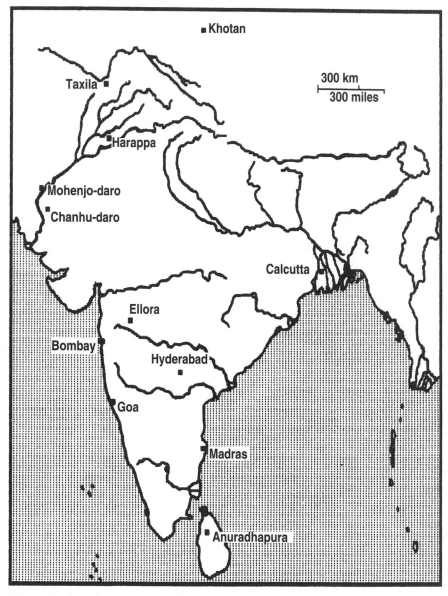

Map 10. Early archaeology in southern Asia.

In 1861 Gen. Alexander Cunningham retired from the army and became the first surveyor general of the newly created Archaeological Survey of India. During the 1860s, 1870s, and early 1880s Cunningham and his assistants located, explored, and mapped hundreds of sites in northern and central India.[4] Their discoveries were reported annually in the *Archaeological Survey of India Report*.

The Archaeological Survey of India concentrated on historical sites, but other scholars began revealing India's prehistory. In 1842 a British doctor uncovered a group of stone knives and arrowheads while digging in his garden in the Raichur district. And during the 1850s Col. Meadows Taylor excavated and published many megalithic graves in the Hyderabad region using techniques that were quite advanced for his time. He recorded the exact find-spots of artifacts and noted evidence of stratigraphy.

The title "Father of Indian Prehistory," however, has been awarded to geologist Robert Bruce Foote. In 1863 he found a Paleolithic artifact near Madras. This was the first object from the Old Stone Age to be excavated in India. During the following decades Foote discovered many other prehistoric sites throughout India. Wherever his geological studies took him, Foote also searched for and found Stone Age remains.

Meanwhile, the growth of French influence and power in Indochina led to Western awareness of major Cambodian monuments. From the late seventeenth through the mid-nineteenth centuries several French missionaries wrote descriptions of Angkor and other important sites, but few people seem to have read them. However, this situation changed in 1864. In that year a posthumously published account of Angkor by French botanist Henri Mouhot caught the public's interest. Soon many Western travelers were making their way to the site.

Mouhot's descriptions were quickly supplemented by visual records of the ruins. In 1867 J. Thompson, a British photographer, published the first photographs of Angkor in his book, *The Antiquities of Cambodia*. Shortly afterward, the French explorer-artist Louis Delaporte made detailed drawings of Angkor and other sites (Figs. 62–63). These engravings appeared in Francis Garnier's *Voyage d'exploration en Indo-Chine* (1870) and in Delaporte's own *Voyage au Cambodge* (1880).

Thus, by the last decades of the nineteenth century Westerners were able to read about and see illustrations of many of Asia's greatest monuments. The wonders of the East had taken their rightful place alongside the masterpieces of ancient Egypt, Greece, and Rome.

---

4. Among the important sites discovered were Taxila and Harappa, two centers of early civilization in the region. Both these sites are now located in Pakistan, which split off from India in 1947.

Fig. 62. Delaporte's drawing of the Bayon at Angkor Thom. (From L. Delaporte, *Voyage au Cambodge*, 1880.)

Fig. 63. The south gate in the outer wall of Angkor Thom. (From L. Delaporte, *Voyage au Cambodge*, 1880.)

DISCOVERING "LOST CITIES" IN AFRICA

The cultures of the northern coast of Africa and those of Europe had maintained contact with one another since antiquity. But starting in the fifth century B.C. the classical Greeks and Romans had also become aware of a black civilization just south of Egypt. The ancient Egyptians had called this area Kush, but the Greeks called it Ethiopia. Successive empires would arise in this region, with the cities of Napata, Meroë, and Axum as their capitals.

During the last centuries of the Roman Empire, Christianity spread up the Nile and strengthened the area's links with the Mediterranean cultures. But those contacts were severed when Islam spread across North Africa in the seventh and early eighth centuries. The Muslim rulers of North Africa sought to maintain a monopoly on commerce with black Africa to the south. So, they would not allow European Christians access to the interior. In the following centuries, despite Christian Ethiopia's staunch resistance, Islam spread throughout the Sudan.

It wasn't until the fifteenth century that European explorers and merchants (mostly Portuguese) began venturing down the coast of Africa below Morocco. In 1497–99 Vasco da Gama succeeded in sailing around the southern tip of Africa to India. This opened the floodgates for Portuguese merchants to exploit the coasts of Africa as well as the East. They soon heard stories of fabulous kingdoms and great cities in the interior of Africa.

These stories were confirmed by Leo Africanus, a Spanish Muslim who was captured and converted to Christianity. Leo (or Hassan ibn Mohammed el-Wazzan ez-Zayyati, as he was called before his capture) had traveled extensively in Africa. In 1526 he wrote an account of Africa for Pope Leo X. This work was published and made generally available in 1563. In it Leo described the trade and wealth of Gao and other places he had visited south of the Sahara, particularly noting the abundance of gold.

From medieval Arab writers and archaeological evidence we now know that during the Middle Ages there were cities and cultures in sub-Saharan Africa as advanced as those of Europe. A number of large, well-organized kingdoms had developed from the ninth century onward. Learning and Islamic theology, as well as trade and commerce, had flourished at Timbuktu, Gao, Djenne, Jebel Uri, and other cities. However, the only whites to visit these places were Muslim Arabs or Berbers.

By the time Europe rediscovered black Africa, the cultural levels of the two areas had become very different. During the Renaissance and the seventeenth-century scientific revolution, European civilization made great advances, especially militarily. But during that same era the kingdoms and wealth of the Sudan were in decline. This development obscured the cultural similarities that had existed between Europe and Africa during ancient and medieval times.

In the latter part of the sixteenth century the Moroccan sultan, seeking the source of the Sudan's gold, sent his armies southward against the Kingdom of Songhay. Though outnumbered, the invaders were armed with new matchlock firearms. These weapons enabled them to capture and loot Timbuktu and Gao. The sultan's general brought back to Marrakesh thirty camel-loads of unrefined gold and 120 camel-loads of other valuable commodities. However, he was unable to discover where the gold had come from. While it did not accomplish its purpose, this expedition destroyed the administrative organization of Songhay. It also caused a great decrease in the volume of trade within the Sudan and between the Sudan and North Africa.

The overseas slave trade also took its toll. African kingdoms had long enslaved prisoners of war. And some slaves had been sold to Arabs or to other black African kingdoms. But the demand for black slaves increased dramatically in the sixteenth century when Europeans began using them as laborers in the New World. Some coastal African kingdoms and tribes became middlemen, supplying slaves from the interior to the Portuguese and other Europeans. The insatiable demand for slaves caused severe population decline in some areas, increased warfare between African groups, and had a destructive influence on African societies and governments. Thus, only small, debased vestiges of the former kingdoms remained by the eighteenth and nineteenth centuries, when European states began to spread their power inland from the African coasts or southward from Egypt.

Despite the earlier accounts, Europeans became convinced that black Africans had never risen more than slightly above the level of beasts. The image of primitive, simple people with no arts and no sciences seemed to justify European imperialism. Just as in the Americas and the Far East, white Europeans thought that they were "saving" the poor benighted natives. They felt they were performing a service by bringing civilization and Christianity to "savage" and "heathen" lands.

This attitude had already become widespread by 1772, when a Scotsman named James Bruce ventured into black Africa. He journeyed up the Blue Nile hoping to discover the source of the Nile. To his great surprise, he found an organized kingdom whose ruler commanded well-trained cavalry forces. These black horsemen wore steel shirts of chain-mail and copper headpieces. Each carried a small oval shield and was armed with a lance and a large broadsword. This "black horse of Sennar"

Fig. 64. A pyramid tomb at Meroë in the Sudan. (From F. Cailliaud, *Voyage à Méroé*, 1826.)

made a great impression on Bruce. But his account, published in 1790, was not given much credence in Britain. The belief in primitive blacks with no history or culture was already too strong.

Strangely enough, Westerners accepted the fact that there had been an ancient civilization in the same area. Herodotus and other ancient historians had described the "Ethiopian" civilization south of Egypt. In 1821 Mohammed Ali, ruler of Egypt, conquered the Muslim Kingdom of Sennar described by Bruce, and several European adventurers followed his army southward to the city of Meroë. One of these explorers, Frédéric Cailliaud, published an illustrated four-volume account of the antiquities and monuments of Nubia in 1826 (Fig. 64). Other travelers and scholars followed, including Champollion and Rosellini in 1828–29 and Karl Richard Lepsius in 1842–45, as discussed in an earlier chapter. But the monuments around Meroë were generally of Egyptian type. There were pyramids, Egyptian-style temples, and Egyptian-looking reliefs. Thus, this civilization could be dismissed as an offshoot of ancient Egypt. It was not seen as a black African civilization in its own right, nor were its links with modern cultures in the area generally recognized.

If Europeans found it difficult to accept the existence of the Arabized Muslim kingdoms of the Sudan, they were even less prepared to believe that the Negroes of southern Africa could have produced any monuments of substance. But as early as 1506 a Portuguese explorer informed the king of Portugal that inland from Sofala there was a large walled city where the ruler of the area resided. And in 1552 another Portuguese writer mentioned this site in connection with the gold mines in the area:

> These mines are the most ancient known in the country, and they are all in the plain, in the midst of which is a square fortress, of masonry within and without, built of stones of marvelous size, and there appears to be no mortar joining them. . . .This edifice is surrounded by hills, upon which are others resembling it in the fashioning of the stones and the absence of mortar, and one of them is a tower more than 12 fathoms [72 feet] high.[5]

This author went on to point out that all of these structures were called "Symbaoe" (or, as we write the word today, Zimbabwe).

Even earlier than these Portuguese accounts, medieval Arab writers had commented on the rich trade in gold, ivory, animal skins, and iron in Malindi, Kilwa, Sofala, and other large cities along the East African coast. Such stories led some scholars to identify Southeast Africa with the biblical land of Ophir.[6] Several biblical verses mention Ophir as a source of gold and other precious commodities or as a symbol for wealth and opulence.[7] But the best-known passages were those that told of King Solomon sending a fleet to Ophir from which he obtained 420 talents of gold and unspecified amounts of silver, ivory, almug trees, precious stones, and exotic animals.[8] Thus, writers also often referred to eastern or southern Africa as the location of "King Solomon's mines."

The Arab and early Portuguese writers had indicated that the prosperous, cultured, urban East African merchants and artisans were *black*. But according to Genesis 10:29 the people of Ophir were descendants of Shem, like the Israelites and other Semites. So, when signs

---

5. Joao de Barros, as quoted in Bruce Norman, *Footsteps*, p. 133.

6. Among those who accepted this identification was the poet Milton. In *Paradise Lost* (published in 1667) Milton places Ophir "in the realm of Congo, and Angola farthest south."

7. See I Chronicles 29:4, Job 22:24 and 28:16, Psalms 45:9, and Isaiah 13:12.

8. I Kings 9:26-28, 10:11, and 10:22, and repeated in II Chronicles 8:17-18, 9:10, and 9:21. The animals mentioned are probably two different kinds of monkeys, although some think the Hebrew terms refer to apes and peacocks.

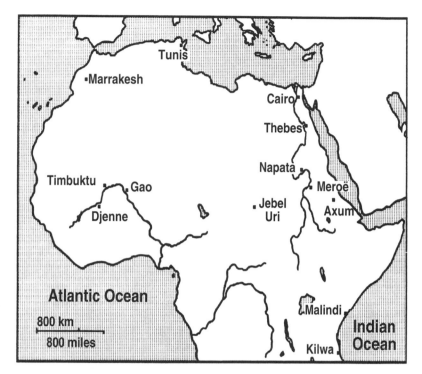

Map 11. Important ancient and medieval sites in North Africa.

of earlier civilization began to be found in Southeast Africa, Europeans tended to credit them to a supposed *white* population that had vanished or been destroyed.

In 1865 a German explorer and adventurer named Karl Mauch landed on the east coast of southern Africa. He became one of the first white men to discover gold in the area, but he chose not to become a miner. He wanted to continue his search for ruins that he had heard were located in the interior, ruins he thought might belong to ancient Ophir.

Thus, in 1871 Mauch set out to explore the region between the Limpopo and Zambezi rivers. After two months of contending with difficult terrain, wild animals, hostile natives, and untrustworthy porters, Mauch arrived at the village of Chief Pika. Nearby there lived a fellow German named Adam Render who had married two African women. Mauch disapproved of Render's marriages and non-European lifestyle. However, Render proved very helpful to Mauch, especially in dealing with the local tribesmen.

Mauch wound up staying with Chief Pika for nine months, for

Fig. 65. Mauch's drawing of Great Zimbabwe. The Citadel is at the top of the hill and the Great Enclosure is at the lower right. (From F. Garcia Ayuso, *Viajes de Mauch y Baines al Africa del Sur redactados con sujeccion á sus memorias y relaciones*, 1877.)

not far away, he was told, were large stone ruins. Chief Pika's tribe had moved into that region only fifty years before, so they claimed no connection with the ruins. They also did not know the origin of a piece of iron that some tribesmen had found. Mauch investigated further and found iron slag near the village. These discoveries convinced him that white men had once lived in the area. He was unaware of the earlier Arab reports that blacks in the region had owned and worked iron mines and had traded in wrought iron.

During several excursions from the village in 1871 and 1872 Mauch finally got to explore the stone ruins about which he had heard so much. At the foot of a high hill he found a great circular enclosure with granite walls about twenty feet high. Inside were lower, partially crumbled walls and a conical tower about thirty feet high. All were constructed of stones about twice the size of bricks that had been fit together without mortar. On the hill were more ruins protected by a strong fortification wall that varied from six to twelve feet in thickness. These massive structures, as well as many smaller ones between the Citadel and the Great Enclosure, were overgrown with trees and vegetation. Mauch had found the site now called Great Zimbabwe (Fig. 65).

The German explorer sketched the remains and speculated on their origins. Convinced that the carefully constructed walls could not be the work of black Africans, Mauch saw fancied resemblances to Phoenician and Israelite architecture:

I believe that I do not err when I suppose that the ruin on the mountain is an imitation of the Solomonic Temple on Mount Moria, the ruin on the plain a copy of that palace in which the Queen of Sheba dwelled during her visit to Solomon.[9]

Mauch's belief that Great Zimbabwe was linked to King Solomon, the Queen of Sheba, and Ophir became widespread in Europe and America. When similar remains were found elsewhere in southern Africa, they also were credited to ancient Semitic colonists from Arabia or Palestine. Unfortunately, many continue to hold this mistaken view today.

Phase II—Archaeology in the Far East and Africa Comes of Age (1880–1939)

FAR EASTERN ARCHAEOLOGY BECOMES MORE SYSTEMATIC

So far, no mention has been made of early archaeological discoveries or excavations in Japan. That is because after the Portuguese made initial contacts in the sixteenth century, Japan largely closed itself to Westerners. American Commodore Matthew Perry forcibly opened Japan to the West in 1842, and after 1868 the Japanese adopted an official policy of westernization. A little later Professor Edward S. Morse initiated the first true archaeological research in Japan. When Morse arrived in the islands, he immediately noticed signs of Neolithic habitation. So, in 1877, he excavated some shell-mounds at Omori, a town on the railway line between Tokyo and Yokohama. He uncovered evidence of a Neolithic culture that flourished in what is now called the Joman Period in Japan.

However, just a little later a Dutch anatomist named Eugene Dubois found something much more ancient in Java. Dubois went to Sumatra as a military doctor in 1887 in hopes of finding "ape-man" fossils. He knew that large anthropoid apes lived in only two areas, Central Africa and the East Indies. So, he reasoned, the ancestral links between apes and humans probably would be found in those regions also. Gradually, various clues led him to focus his attention on deposits in the Solo river bed in central Java. In 1891 and 1892 he finally uncovered two teeth, a femur, and a skull cap of a large primate. The brain capacity of this creature was much greater than that of the anthropoid apes,

9. Quoted in Bruce Norman, *Footsteps*, p. 153.

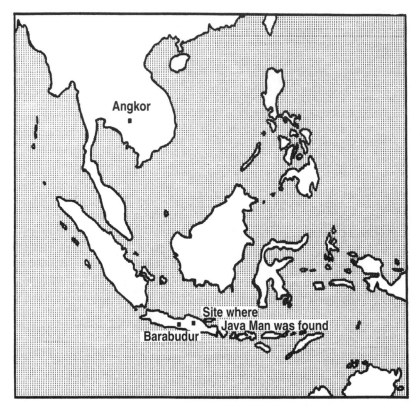

Map 12. Early archaeology in Southeast Asia.

but smaller than that of modern man. When he published his finds in 1894 he named his discovery *Pithecanthropus erectus* ("erect ape-man"). However, it soon became popularly known as Java Man. The East had revealed a human prehistory even more ancient than that of Europe.[10]

The turn of the century saw the creation of several institutions to foster and systematize archaeological research in the East. In Indochina the French placed all archaeological remains under their control. To explore, excavate, study, and restore sites in this region they established the École Française d'Extreme-Orient (the French School of the Far East).

10. However, in 1907 the jawbone and teeth of a member of the same species was found at Heidelberg in Germany. At that time it was designated *Homo heidelbergensis*, Heidelberg Man. Of course, now even older human ancestors have been uncovered in Africa. Currently it is thought that human beings probably originated in Africa some two million years ago.

The scholars of this institution undertook many important projects, and some of their publications are still valuable today.[11]

In 1901 the British reorganized the Archaeological Survey of India and placed it under the direction of Sir John Marshall. Marshall initiated a program of excavation and restoration at many historical sites and began a new series of annual reports. The survey's excavations greatly expanded knowledge of early India and provided many exhibits for India's museums. Marshall also appointed Indians as members of the survey's archaeological staff for the first time.

Among the projects sponsored by the Archaeological Survey during Marshall's tenure were the expeditions of Sir Aurel Stein, a Hungarian who became a naturalized British citizen. Stein undertook four campaigns of exploration and excavation in central Asia (1900–01, 1906–08, 1913–16, and 1930). He located many of the ancient towns on the trade routes from Iran and India to China. And although his excavations were generally brief, Stein uncovered many ancient manuscripts, some of which were in heretofore unknown scripts and languages.

Stein's most important discovery took place in 1907, during his second expedition. In one of the "Caves of the Thousand Buddhas" at Ch'ien Fo Tung on the western border of China he found an entire library of early Chinese texts. Many of the manuscripts were of lost or unknown works. But the most treasured work in the library turned out to be a Chinese copy of a well-known Buddhist text. What makes it so precious is that this work, made in 868 A.D., was *block-printed!* It is the earliest printed book known.

Indonesia's first official commission for archaeological research was also established in 1901. Twelve years later the Dutch rulers reconstituted it as the Archaeological Service. It undertook the repair and restoration of many monuments, including the beautiful Barabudur temple in Java (1907–11).

China, like Japan, was forced to open itself to the West during the second half of the nineteenth century. But traditional Chinese antiquarian studies continued to dominate China's perception of its past until the 1920s. In 1920 the Chinese government hired J. Gunnar Andersson, a Swedish geologist, to undertake research on prehistoric sites. His excavations at Yang-shao in 1921 resulted in the discovery of a Neolithic culture that has been named after the site. This discovery aroused scholarly interest in Chinese prehistory. Universities and research institutes established departments of archaeology and anthro-

---

11. For example, E. Lunet de Lajonquière's *Inventaire descriptif des monuments du Cambodge* (Paris, 1902–11).

pology on Western models, and more excavations were undertaken. Thus, during the next decade excavators uncovered many more Neolithic remains, some predating the Yang-shao culture.

Andersson had noticed some cave deposits rich in fossil bones in 1920. The following year he returned to the site near the village of Chou-kou-tien, about twenty-five miles south of Beijing (or Peking, as it was then spelled), and began excavating. Along with many fossils of extinct species of mammals, Andersson found a molar belonging to an extinct anthropoid. It was similar to an upper molar a doctor had purchased from a Chinese apothecary in 1899. But scholars could not agree whether these teeth belonged to apes or humans.

In 1926, closer study of the Chou-kou-tien molars (a second one had been found in the interim) indicated that they were human. Andersson then turned the teeth over to Dr. Davidson Black, a Canadian anatomist who was the head of Peking Union Medical College. Excited by the finds, Black convinced the Rockefeller Foundation to finance a large-scale excavation of the Chou-kou-tien site, and in 1927 he turned up another well-preserved molar. Without further ado, he audaciously proclaimed the discovery of a new prehistoric human genus, *Sinanthropus pekinensis*.

In 1928 the excavators dug up a clearly human jaw bone, so Black's faith in Peking Man was vindicated. The following year Dr. C. W. Pei, a Chinese paleontologist who had been working with Black, found a primitive human skull cap in the cave. Pei also uncovered chipped stone implements and evidence of fires, clear proof that *Sinanthropus* was human.

Subsequent excavations up to 1939 unearthed the remains of some thirty-seven additional individuals at the site. It was soon evident that Peking Man closely resembled the earlier finds of Java Man and Heidelberg Man. Today it is agreed that these remains all belong to the same species, *Homo erectus*. Unfortunately, the remains of Peking Man disappeared in 1941, when Beijing was under Japanese occupation.[12] However, casts had been made, so the evidence was not totally lost.

The Academia Sinica (Chinese Academy) established the archaeological section of its Institute of History and Philology in 1928. Its first fellow and head was Li Chi, who had received his Ph.D. in anthropology from Harvard University five years earlier. Under Li Chi's guidance

---

12. Exactly what happened to the fossils is not certain. One account claims that they were stored in the Peking Union Medical College until later in the war. Then the Japanese decided to move the remains to Japan, but the ship carrying them was sunk by an American submarine. For more information on this mystery see H. L. Shapiro, *Peking Man: The Discovery, Disappearance and Mystery of a Priceless Scientific Treasure* (New York: Simon and Schuster, 1974).

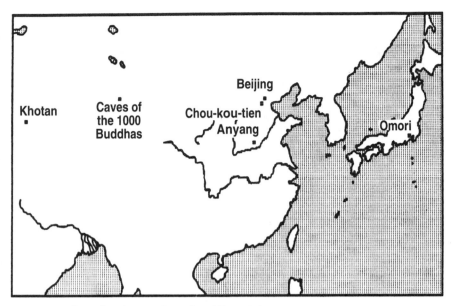

Map 13. Early archaeology in Central and East Asia.

the archaeological division of the Academia Sinica took the lead in sponsoring excavations and publishing scholarly works on Chinese archaeology throughout the 1930s.

THE DISCOVERY OF FAR EASTERN BRONZE AGES

India and China had textual evidence and archaeological monuments of great antiquity. By 1921 Stone Age remains had also been found in both countries. However, there was a great chronological gap between the Indian and Chinese Neolithic cultures and their complex empires of classical antiquity. Hints of early civilizations had turned up in both areas. But scholars had uncovered no protohistoric Bronze Age cultures in the East like those of early Mesopotamia or Egypt.

This situation changed dramatically during the 1920s. In 1921 and 1922 Sir John Marshall and the Archaeological Survey of India initiated excavations at the mounds of Harappa and Mohenjo-daro in the Indus River valley (both sites are in present-day Pakistan). At both mounds the excavations continued into the early 1930s. However, it did not take long for the initial field directors, Daya Ram Sahni at Harappa and R. D. Banerji at Mohenjo-daro, to recognize the protohistoric nature of these sites.

Fig. 66. Indus seals from Mohenjo-daro. The writing on these seals is still undeciphered. (Drawn from a photograph in Sir Mortimer Wheeler, *Civilizations of the Indus Valley and Beyond*, New York: McGraw-Hill, 1966, p. 38.)

When Gen. Alexander Cunningham had discovered Harappa some two generations earlier, he had picked up a seal inscribed in an unknown script. More of these seals were found when excavations got underway at Harappa, and the unreadable written characters became known as the Harappan script.[13] However, when the digging at Mohenjo-daro, four hundred miles to the south, got below a few buildings of the historical period, the excavators found similar seals and other Harappan-style artifacts (Fig. 66). Clearly Harappa and Mohenjo-daro both had been centers of an unknown civilization that had flourished in the Indus Valley in very early times.

While the excavations at Harappa and Mohenjo-daro were still taking place, Aurel Stein and others discovered Chanhu-daro and many other sites of what became known as the Harappan or Indus civilization. It is now clear that these ancient settlements were spread throughout the valley of the Indus and its major tributaries and along the coast from the Iranian border to the Gulf of Cambay. The Indus civilization thus occupied an area greater than that of either the Mesopotamian or Egyptian civilizations.

---

13. Unfortunately we still cannot read this script. The inscriptions are all very brief, and probably most represent personal names. This fact and the lack of a bilingual inscription make it likely that unless some dramatic new evidence is found, Indus Valley writing will remain undeciphered.

Finds of Indus-style seals and artifacts in the Persian Gulf region and in southern Mesopotamia showed that the Indus people had engaged in wide-ranging trade. Connections with Mesopotamia also indicated that the Indus Bronze Age had begun in the third millennium B.C. However, before the advent of radiocarbon dating it was difficult to establish precise dates for the beginning and end of this newly discovered civilization.[14]

The results of the excavations by Marshall and his colleagues were historic, but technically they left much to be desired. Compared to contemporaneous excavations in the Near East or Europe, the work of the Archaeological Survey of India was primitive. At Harappa and Mohenjo-daro the archaeologists took levels for principal finds, but they did not recognize the natural stratigraphy of the sites. As Glyn Daniel has commented,

> It is a good example of archaeologists not looking back at the history of their subject: had Marshall and Mackay [Marshall's principle successor as excavator at Mohenjo-daro] never heard of Worsaae, Fiorelli and Pitt-Rivers, not to mention Thomas Jefferson? Apparently not.[15]

True stratigraphical excavation would not come to India until Mortimer Wheeler became director-general of antiquities in 1943.

Meanwhile, clues to the existence of another early civilization had turned up in China. Late in the nineteenth century farmers plowing fields near Anyang had unearthed some inscribed animal bones and pieces of tortoise shell. However, they were sold to apothecaries as "dragon bones" and ground up to be used in various potions. They continued to turn up, though, and in 1899 an antique dealer spotted some of them and brought them to the attention of scholars. The Chinese characters on these bones were very archaic. But after much scholarly work in the early years of this century, paleographers and philologists deciphered the inscriptions. The objects turned out to be oracle bones—devices used to answer questions about the future (Fig. 67).

Oracle bones were made from flattened tortoise shells or the shoulder blades of cattle. A question to the spirits would be inscribed on the face of the bone or shell. Then the diviner applied a heated bronze point to a small circular pit on the other side. The pattern of the cracks that appeared on the face of the oracle bone would indicate the answer to the question.

---

14. The evidence now indicates that the Indus Valley civilization began around 2500 B.C. and ended about 1500 B.C.

15. G. Daniel, *A Short History of Archaeology* (London: Thames and Hudson, 1981), p. 175.

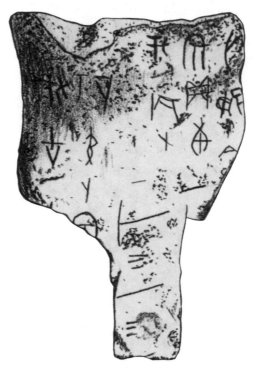

Fig. 67. An oracle bone from Anyang. (Drawn from a photograph in Glyn Daniel, *A Short History of Archaeology*, p. 174.)

Because the writing on the bones was clearly very ancient, scholarly interest in these oracular devices continued to grow. This led the National Research Institute of History and Philology of the Academia Sinica and the Smithsonian Institution to undertake joint excavations at Anyang in 1928. With Li Chi as director, fifteen excavation campaigns were conducted during the next nine years until the Japanese invasion forced a halt to the work in 1937.

The first three campaigns were trial digs that located a number of archaeological sites on both sides of the River Huan northwest of Anyang. The most important of these sites, and the one on which most of the later work was concentrated, was Hsiao-t'un. This proved to be the location of "Great Shang," the capital city during the latter part of the Shang Dynasty, the first known to have ruled China.

From the fourth campaign on, the work at the Anyang sites became more systematic. Eventually, four strata were noted at Hsiao-t'un with the third (counting from the bottom) belonging to the Late Shang period (circa 1400–1100 B.C.). This was the era from which most of the oracle bones came. The archaeologists also uncovered many tombs of kings and nobles in the area, as well as graves of sacrificial victims interred beneath the foundations of buildings and gates. These various burials produced a wealth of pottery, many bronze vessels and weapons, remains of chariots, and other artifacts of stone, jade, and ivory. They also showed that during the Shang era not only were individuals killed as part of foundation rituals, but many servants and animals were also buried with their master when he died.[16]

Before 1921 textbooks usually stated that India's history began with the Vedic period (circa 1200–500 B.C.) and that China had no history before the eighth century B.C. But within little more than a decade archaeology discovered a lost civilization in India and largely substantiated early Chinese written accounts of the Shang Dynasty. These two great centers of Eastern culture had regained their Bronze Age roots and knowledge of the first stages in the development of their civilizations.

SOLVING GREAT ZIMBABWE'S MYSTERIES

In the generation after Mauch's discovery of Great Zimbabwe the theory connecting it with Ophir and "King Solomon's mines" had disastrous consequences. Many visitors, concerned only with finding gold, wreaked havoc on the ruins. One of the first of these treasure hunters was Willi Posselt, who reached Great Zimbabwe in 1889. He used vines that were growing over the Great Enclosure to climb the wall and go down into the interior. To his great disappointment, he found no gold or artifacts. But he had more success on the citadel. There he discovered some carved soapstone birds, a feature that Mauch had failed to notice. Even after Posselt cut some of the birds off of their five-foot-high stone pedestals, they were too heavy to carry. So he took one with him and hid the rest, hoping to return for them later.

Two years later Theodore Bent, at the bidding of the Royal Geo-

---

16. These excavations set the stage for the 1974 discovery of the spectacular third century B.C. imperial tomb of Ch'in Shi Huang Ti (also written Qin Shi Huang Di). Ongoing Chinese excavations of this tomb near the city of Xian are unearthing a huge army of life-size terra cotta figures meant to accompany and protect the dead Ch'in Dynasty emperor. (See Audrey Topping, "China's Incredible Find," *National Geographic,* April 1978, pp. 440–59.) Archaeologists have also located nearby many royal tombs of the early Han Dynasty (206 B.C. to A.D. 6). Recent excavation of one of these tombs has revealed another terra cotta army, though the figures are only two feet high instead of life-size. (See O. Louis Mazzatenta, "A Chinese Emperor's Army for Eternity," *National Geographic,* August 1992, pp. 114–30.)

graphical Society in London, arrived to examine Great Zimbabwe and other ruins in the area. Bent, an antiquarian, brought with him his wife, who took photographs of the ruins, and R. M. W. Swan, who surveyed the site and made a plan. Bent found the carved birds Posselt had hidden and discovered a few more on the citadel. He also cleared some of the undergrowth from the Great Enclosure and dug a trench around the base of the conical tower. He was trying to get information about how the tower was constructed, but he learned nothing. Instead, he destroyed the stratigraphy around the tower that later archaeologists would need to determine its date.

Bent's digging turned up a few Arab or Persian beads and glass fragments among many, many native African artifacts of clay, stone, and metal. But despite these finds, he and Swan remained convinced that Zimbabwe had been constructed by a lost white race. Swan thought the ruins had an astronomical purpose and could by dated around 1100 B.C. Bent thought they had been erected by a prehistoric race like the builders of Stonehenge. But neither seems to have thought of connecting the builders with the makers of the African artifacts found at the site.

The greatest damage to Great Zimbabwe and well over a hundred similar ruins occurred between 1895 and 1900. During that brief period the Ancient Ruins Company had a concession from the British South Africa Company to exploit all ancient ruins south of the Zambezi. W. G. Neal, a prospector and the head of the Ancient Ruins Company, led the pillage of the monuments. The company itself recovered only about five hundred ounces of gold, but other prospectors were active at the sites as well. We will never know how many golden artifacts were found and melted down, but the number must have been considerable. In addition, the gold hunters caused substantial damage to many of the stone walls and buildings at the sites while searching for gold.

In 1902 the new Legislative Council of Southern Rhodesia passed a law protecting Great Zimbabwe and other ruins. Soon afterward, R. M. Hall, co-author with Neal of The Ancient Ruins of Rhodesia (1902), became curator of the ruins. Hall finished clearing creepers and underbrush from the site and excavated around some of the buildings. He uncovered some gold, but, more importantly, he found layer after layer of earth filled with what he recognized were native African artifacts. Like Bent he came across a few bits of Persian and Arab porcelain and beads. These objects, however, were clearly outweighed by the large amount of local pottery, soapstone dishes, iron nails, tools, weapons, and stone phalli. Unfortunately, also like Bent, Hall disregarded the material he himself had excavated, thinking it later native

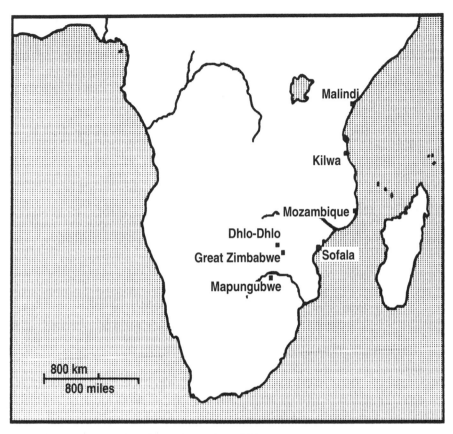

Map 14. Important medieval sites in southern Africa.

rubbish. He continued to argue that the architectural style of the ruins supported a South Arabian and Phoenician origin.

Hall's conclusions were soon disputed, however, by the first true archaeologist to investigate Great Zimbabwe. David Randall-MacIver, an Egyptologist and a student of Petrie, examined the stone ruins of Rhodesia in 1905 under the sponsorship of the British Association. Randall-MacIver dug a trial trench through a floor in the Great Enclosure all the way to bedrock. Beneath the floor he found the same types of African pottery and other artifacts that he had found above it. Most of the materials were like those still being used by the modern Makalanga (Shona) people in the area. This showed that the enclosure had been built by people whose material culture was virtually identical with that of the *black Africans* still living nearby. Furthermore, the few

Arab and Persian imported objects in the deposits showed that the
structure dated from the Middle Ages, not the ancient period of King
Solomon, the Phoenicians, or the Queen of Sheba. Randall-MacIver also
recognized that the architecture at Great Zimbabwe showed no traces
of Near Eastern or European styles from any period. He concluded
that Great Zimbabwe had been constructed in the fourteenth or fifteenth century by black Africans with no outside help.

This conclusion was greeted with a storm of protest by white Rho-
desians and other supporters of the Ophir/Solomon/Sheba theory of
origins. The controversy led other archaeologists to investigate the ruins,
and their evidence harmonized with Randall-MacIver's. In 1926 J. F.
Schofield studied the building methods at the site and concluded that
they were of native African type. In 1929 Gertrude Caton-Thompson
undertook more excavations for the British Association. She showed
that the short winding walls within the Great Enclosure had originally
connected huts built in typical native style. Her published report, *The
Zimbabwe Culture: Ruins and Reactions* (1931), stated that she could
find no evidence that contradicted a native African origin or medieval
date for the ruins.[17]

Further, on the last day of 1932 a farmer named van Graan found
a hidden way to climb to the top of Mapungubwe. This hill, taboo
to the natives, was just south of the Limpopo River and about two
hundred miles southwest of Great Zimbabwe. Its summit was littered
with fragments of pottery, beads, and bits of copper and iron. But in
one eroded area van Graan found something much more exciting—a
piece of gold! A little digging soon uncovered a buried skeleton accompanied by gold beads, fragments of gold jewelry, and pieces of plate
gold that had been shaped into small rhinoceroses.

The farmer planned to keep his discovery secret, but his son, a
past student at the University of Pretoria, revealed the find to a former
professor. The government of South Africa quickly acquired the site
and entrusted the University of Pretoria with its study. Archaeologists
began excavating in 1934 and continued until 1940. They uncovered
many more burials, most containing gold bangles and other artifacts.

---

17. Studies since Caton-Thompson's time have confirmed her claims. There seems
to have been some occupation on the site in the early centuries of the Christian era,
but the walls and tower are much later. Radiocarbon testing showed that the earliest
construction could not predate A.D. 700. However, the test dated the time when part
of a tree used in construction had been alive. Construction of the building using the
wooden beam could actually have occurred centuries later. Analysis of the development
of building styles has indicated that the earliest structures were built around A.D. 1100
and that the latest (the wall of the Great Enclosure) dates from about 1450.

Mapungubwe proved to be the first royal burial ground from pre-European times uncovered in southern Africa.

The site clearly had links with the Zimbabwe culture to the north, but the exact relationship has not yet been determined. The pottery from Mapungubwe is similar to that found in the early remains at Great Zimbabwe. And the gold jewelry and ornaments in the graves are similar to those looted earlier from a burial at Dhlo-Dhlo by an agent of the Ancient Ruins Company. The Mapungubwe horde provides us with a partial idea of what must have been destroyed at Great Zimbabwe and other sites in the years before 1902.

Archaeology has now solved many of the mysteries of Zimbabwe. Perhaps in dispersing images of the Queen of Sheba or King Solomon's envoys walking through the ruins it also destroyed some of the romantic lure that had drawn Westerners to the area in the past. But truth is almost always less romantic than myth. Archaeology has restored Great Zimbabwe and other Iron Age sites in southern Africa to their true builders, thus returning to black Africans an important part of their heritage.

8

Reclaiming Sunken History

Phase I—Speculation, Antiquarianism, and Early Excavation (1446–1952)

THE DAWN OF UNDERWATER EXPLORATION

People have always lived in intimate contact with rivers, lakes, and seas. They have drawn physical sustenance from them, relied on them for a degree of protection from enemies, and used them as avenues for trade and population movements. But until very recently humans have been strangers to the world below the water's surface. The alien underwater environment jealously guarded the treasures committed to it. It has kept its secrets about man's past long after burial mounds, desert *tells*, or jungle-covered cities have been forced to yield theirs. It is only within the past forty years that scholars have been able to develop precise, systematic methods for recovering and recording underwater remains. Thus, archaeology under water was the last field of archaeological research to attain respectability as an academic discipline.

Nevertheless, this discipline's roots stretch as far into the past as most other fields of archaeology. The earliest known attempt at underwater archaeology occurred in the mid-fifteenth century. Cardinal Colonna, an avid collector of ancient Greek and Roman art, heard stories about sunken ships near Rome. Two ancient vessels supposedly were lying on the bottom of Lake Nemi, seventeen miles southeast of the city. The cardinal commissioned the famous architect Leon Battista Alberti to search for the ships, and in 1446 Alberti's hired swimmers located two large vessels. They were on the floor of the lake at a depth of ten fathoms (sixty feet). From a float he had constructed, Alberti attached ropes to one of the ships, then attempted to raise it or pull it ashore. However, the ropes would not hold. All he succeeded in raising were a few planks and the torso of a large Roman statue.

Repeated attempts to salvage the ships followed. In 1535 Francesco Demarchi, inventor of a primitive diving suit, descended into Lake Nemi and measured the ships. One was 234 feet long and 66 feet wide while the other was 230 feet long by 78 feet wide. Demarchi noted the ships' precious decorations, but he could find no way to remove the vessels from their watery grave.

Nearly three hundred years later, in 1827, another expedition used a diving bell large enough to hold eight people. But still only fragments of wood, nails, mosaics, columns, porphyry, and marble were brought to the surface. The efforts in 1895 of Eliseo Borghi, a Roman antiquities dealer, were no more successful. While further damaging the hulls of the two vessels, Borghi's divers and grappling irons retrieved only a jumble of tantalizing pieces of the ships and their decoration. The recovered objects included hundreds of feet of wooden planks (which dried out and crumbled on the shore), copper nails, sections of lead water pipe, bronze lion and wolf heads with rings in their teeth, a large piece of mosaic decking, terra cotta tiles, sheets of copper, and fragments of stone sculptures.

These early essays into the field of underwater archaeology ended in failure, for there was as yet no suitable means for excavating the ships while they remained under water. Moreover, the vessels' wooden hulls were too weak to allow them to be raised out of the lake by conventional methods. But if the ships could not be removed from the lake, might not the solution be to remove the lake from atop the ships? This idea was suggested by a professor named Emilio Gluria after the fiasco of the 1895 expedition. However, draining the lake was far too expensive an enterprise for anyone to attempt until 1928, when Mussolini ordered the project undertaken by the Italian government.

When the ships were finally exposed in 1932, they were carefully excavated, studied, and preserved. They proved to be barge-like floating palaces from the first century A.D., probably built during the reign of the emperor Caligula (A.D. 37–41). The salvage efforts over the centuries had destroyed most of the elaborately decorated structures

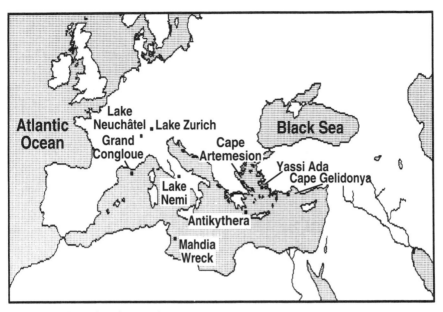

Map 15. Early archaeology under water.

above the deck. But the hulls were well preserved, providing much evidence on Roman ship-building techniques.

Unfortunately, today we have only photographs, plans, and models of the Lake Nemi ships. In 1944 retreating German troops burned these ancient relics, whose recovery had cost so much money, time, and labor.

Switzerland was also the scene of pioneering efforts to retrieve underwater remains. As early as 1472 groups of what were thought to be tree stumps had been noted on the bottoms of Swiss lakes. However, their significance escaped the observers. In 1853-54 an exceptionally cold, dry winter caused the lake waters to drop to their lowest levels in centuries. Farmers anxious to reclaim as much of the newly uncovered land as possible began building walls along the new shorelines. Mud was dredged from beneath the shallow waters of the lakes and used to fill in the area between the walls and the old shorelines. While undertaking such a reclamation project, the inhabitants of Obermeilen on the north side of Lake Zurich found their efforts hampered by many pilings under the water just beyond their new retaining wall. Moreover, their dredging operations brought up a number of stone and bronze implements. The local schoolteacher recognized the importance of these finds and immediately notified Ferdinand Keller, president of the Zurich Antiquarian Society.

Keller and some members of the Antiquarian Society studied the maze of pilings through the clear waters of the lake. Using mechanical "grabs" on poles, they picked up anything that seemed interesting. They also combed through the mud already excavated by the local farmers, recovering many objects overlooked during the initial dredging operation. The scholars collected bronze axes, bracelets, and chisels as well as flint knives, axes, and scrapers. They also found wooden handles for knives, fragments of baskets, reed mats, cloth, netting, and bones of sheep, goats, pigs, cattle, dogs, deer, and fox. However, the fact that the site was under water, even though the water was shallow, precluded careful excavation and recording of the remains. Thus, the antiquarians could not determine the historical contexts of the materials they found.

Keller theorized that the posts had been the foundations for an ancient stilt-village built over the lake for protection. This idea was influenced by accounts of South Pacific dwellings that were still being constructed that way in the nineteenth century. The report on the Obermeilen finds led to the examination of other Swiss lakes. Within a short time more than two dozen other pile-dwelling sites were discovered.

Keller's conception of Bronze Age villages above the shallow waters of the Swiss lakes was very persuasive. It has continued to appear in popular works on archaeology and even in some textbooks. However, more recent excavations have shown that the ancient villages actually stood on the lakes' shores and not over their waters. The pilings were for support in the marshy earth around the lakes. The sites are now under water because the water level in the lakes has risen as glaciers have melted over the millennia since the villages were last occupied.

In 1857-58, four years after Keller's report on the stilt-village at Obermeilen, another group of pilings was found. This time the site was on dry land, a silted-up river mouth near the edge of Lake Pfaffikon. Because of this, the remains could be studied more thoroughly. Jacob Messikommer, an amateur antiquarian, systematically excavated the site by digging small, six-by-three-yard sections at a time. He proceeded downward inch by inch, noting virtually everything he found. He discovered that the tops of the pilings stood at two or three different levels and that portions of the debris were separated by layers of burned material. These finds indicated that three successive villages had stood on the site, each destroyed by fire. Many of the objects Messikommer found were like those from Obermeilen. However, since he kept the objects belonging to each layer separate, he was able to note that the bronze artifacts came from a different stratum than most of the stone ones. This evidence constituted one of the earliest stratigraphical demonstrations of the validity of the "Three Age" system of chronology introduced more than a generation earlier by Scandinavian antiquarians.

At the same time as Messikommer's discovery, a Swiss gentleman-archaeologist named Friedrich Schwab found an interesting site in Lake Neuchâtel. Schwab was searching for evidence of stilt-villages in the lake when one of his assistants noticed a mound under three feet of water at the eastern end of the lake covered with stones and metal implements. When Schwab's men brought up and cleaned a few of the artifacts they saw that they were weapons—swords (some with their scabbards), spearheads, and lances. Surprisingly, they were made of iron rather than bronze.

Schwab began "excavating" this mound, which he learned was called La Tène by the local inhabitants. He used a specially designed boat that allowed him to see the bottom of the lake. He also developed long-handled tongs, shovels, and grabs that could reach the site from the lake's surface. With these tools he recovered hundreds of iron weapons in an excellent state of preservation. Schwab's work produced the largest collection of objects characteristic of the Iron Age culture that archaeologists later named La Tène. But when compared with Messikommer's precise stratigraphical work, the deficiencies of Schwab's "excavation" are evident. Until scholars were able to work under water for a reasonable length of time, study of submerged sites could consist of little more than the salvaging of artifacts.

ANCIENT MASTERPIECES FROM BENEATH THE SEA

Diving suits were developed in the 1850s. By the end of the nineteenth century they were almost identical to the suits in use today. The diver wore a metal helmet containing a small glass window in front and an air hose to supply compressed air from the surface. A watertight suit covered his entire body except for his hands. Heavy lead weights were attached to his chest, back, and feet to keep him upright under water and prevent him from floating to the surface.

At first it was thought that such an apparatus would allow a person to work underwater for an unlimited amount of time. However, experience proved otherwise. Divers who stayed underwater for long periods of time or who rose too swiftly to the surface often died in excruciating pain. Those who survived were frequently crippled for life. They were suffering from "the bends," caused by underwater pressure.

As a diver descends and the water pressure increases, the pressure of the air he breathes must also increase. Otherwise his lungs, ears, and nasal passages would collapse. The compressed air (which is 80 percent nitrogen, just as on the surface) enters the diver's bloodstream. If the pressure on his body is suddenly reduced by a rapid rise to the surface, the nitrogen quickly expands. Bubbles form in the diver's blood, blocking arteries and causing death or paralysis.

The only way to prevent the bends is to rise slowly to the surface, stopping for a time at various depths. This procedure gives the body a chance to gradually adapt to the lower pressure and rid itself of the pressurized nitrogen. By the early part of the twentieth century scientists had created tables indicating the length of time a diver could safely work at various depths. These tables also showed the amount of time he should spend in decompression stops during the return to the surface. Unfortunately, most of the users of diving suits were (and still are) Greek and Turkish sponge fishermen. Most of them knew nothing of the scientific explanation for the bends nor of the existence of decompression tables. Even today, the bends remain an occupational hazard for divers.

In the autumn of 1900 a group of Greek sponge fishermen were sailing for home when they got caught in a storm. They decided to ride out the squall in the sheltered waters behind the island of Antikythera. Making the best of the unscheduled stop, the captain sent a diver below to look for sponges. The man had no sooner reached the bottom at thirty fathoms (180 feet) than he returned to the surface. He was clearly frightened and kept babbling about horses, men, and naked women on the sea floor. The captain, a seasoned diver named Dimitrios Kondos, donned his gear and went down himself to investigate. A short time later he returned to the boat laughing and clutching a bronze arm. The "sea creatures" were marble and bronze statues, the cargo of an ancient ship.

The wreck and its cargo were scattered over a 150-foot-long area on the sea bottom. The captain carefully noted the site, apparently intending to return later to loot the remains. However, on reaching their home island of Syme, one of the sailors let the story of their discovery slip out. The news spread so rapidly that the captain had no choice but to notify the government as required by law.

When he heard of the find, the Greek minister of culture secured the use of a naval supply ship possessing the hoists and tackle needed to raise the statues. By the end of November 1900 the sponge fishermen were back at Antikythera, this time in the employ of the Greek government. One of the first objects to be brought up was the bronze head of a bearded man, probably a third-century B.C. statue of a philosopher. In the days that followed the divers recovered other fragments of bronze and marble sculptures, but no complete statues.

Frequent storms and poor visibility on the sea bed hindered the work. The cumbersome diving suits made it difficult for the sponge fishermen to move freely on the bottom. Moreover, the depth of the wreck limited each diver to two five-minute periods of work a day. Nevertheless, the salvage operation continued.

Finally a complete sculpture was found. It was a fourth-century B.C. bronze statue of a god or an athlete by the Greek sculptor Lysippus. The Greek archaeologist aboard the salvage ship could hardly control his excitement, for the importance of the find was inestimable. In his time, Lysippus had been as famous as his contemporary, Praxiteles. It was known that he had been a prodigious worker who had created over five hundred statues. Yet not one piece of his work was known to have survived until the bronze figure was recovered at Antikythera.

The divers resumed their work with renewed enthusiasm. However, they soon reported that the bulk of the cargo was buried under several huge stones. Before the search for statues could continue the boulders had to be moved. The divers fastened cables around one of the large stones, the ship lifted it slightly, and then towed it a short distance to deeper water. The process was repeated for days, when suddenly it occurred to the expedition's archaeologist that the "boulders" might actually be large statues that the divers could not see clearly on the murky sea bottom. He ordered that they raise the next block to the surface. The winches strained and the ship listed alarmingly, but finally the stone was brought up. As it broke the surface the crew could clearly see that it was a monumental statue of Hercules.

The salvagers now realized that they had plunged several statues into depths from which they might never be recovered. Additional discoveries could only partially alleviate the dejection they felt. The new finds included a few more fragmentary bronze and marble statues, a number of glass vessels, a bronze bed decorated with animals' heads, a gold brooch studded with pearls, ceramic roof tiles, and many pieces of pottery.

Then tragedy struck. One diver died of the bends and two others were partially paralyzed. At the end of the summer the search had to be halted. When the fragments of sculpture were cleaned, sorted, and pieced together, they filled an entire gallery of the National Museum in Athens. In terms of museum pieces this proved to be the second most productive archaeological discovery in Greece, exceeded only by Schliemann's finds in the Shaft Graves at Mycenae.

Fig. 68. A Roman merchant ship. The ships that sank near Antikythera, Mahdia, and Grand Congloué were probably similar to this one. (Drawn from a relief showing commerce at Ostia, the port of Rome.)

Study of the finds, particularly the pottery, indicated that the ship at Antikythera had sunk during the early part of the first century B.C. It was known from written accounts that the Roman general Sulla had sacked Athens in 86 B.C. Was this one of his ships? Had it perhaps been caught in a storm on its way back to Rome with its load of booty? Some archaeologists thought so.

However, in 1958 a scholar showed that what had appeared to be just a corroded lump of bronze from the wreck was really an ancient astronomical computer. The device had interlocked gears and wheels that, when turned, indicated the correct relative positions of various heavenly bodies. Inscriptions on the "computer" proved that it had been made on the island of Rhodes in 82 B.C. Furthermore, astronomical calculations based on the positions of its gears demonstrated that the device had last been set in 80 B.C., probably shortly before the ship carrying it sank. The ship seemed to have gone down at least six years *after* Sulla's sack of Athens. The existence of such devices in ancient times had not been known previously. Thus, the Antikythera ship not only added to our knowledge of ancient art, but also to our understanding of Hellenistic astronomy and mechanics.

Seven years after the Antikythera find, Alfred Merlin, director of the Tunisian National Museum, made a discovery of his own. He was browsing in a bazaar in Tunis when he noticed what appeared to be genuine Hellenistic bronze statuettes. He traced the figurines back to Greek sponge divers who had found them offshore about three miles from Mahdia, a small Tunisian port. The Tunisian government, the French Institute, the Académie des Inscriptions, and private patrons quickly responded to Merlin's appeal for funds to investigate the site. In addition, the French Navy contributed the *Cyclope,* a tug equipped with heavy lifting cranes.

For five seasons between 1908 and 1913 helmeted Greek divers salvaged antiquities from the ancient wreck that lay beneath twenty fathoms (120 feet) of water. Frequent squalls interrupted the diving operation and swept away the marker buoys. There were difficulties below the surface too. The sunken ship had been carrying a cargo of about sixty marble columns on deck with the more fragile art works in its hold. To reach the statues divers had to dig between the columns or scoop out trenches beneath them. However, the wreck was lying in soft mud that blanketed the site with opaque black clouds at the slightest disturbance. Despite these difficulties enough art works were rescued to fill six rooms in the Bardo Museum in Tunis. The divers brought up bronze statues of the gods Dionysos, Hermes, and Eros, a satyr, a clown, three dancing dwarfs, and a herm signed by the famous Hellenistic sculptor Boethos of Chalcedon. Other bronze objects included large jars, candelabra, ornaments for furniture, and parts of a votive monument. The wreck also contained marble statues of Pan, Aphrodite, Niobe, and some satyrs, in addition to many pottery bowls, jars, and lamps.

Inscriptions on some of the recovered objects indicated that the cargo had come from Athens. The pottery on board suggested that the ship had sunk at the end of the second or early in the first century B.C., only slightly earlier than the Antikythera wreck. The destination of the ship remains a mystery, however. Some scholars have argued that it was carrying part of Sulla's spoils back to Italy when a storm blew it off course to its grave near the coast of Africa. Others have pointed out that what seem to be the vessel's anchors were found on the landward side of the wreck. This would indicate that the storm that caused the ship to sink was blowing from Africa toward the open sea and that an effort was made to prevent the ship from being blown back out into the Mediterranean. Thus, the cargo may have been intended for some Roman nobleman in Africa rather than Italy.

Whatever its original destination, the Mahdia ship, along with that of Antikythera, testifies to the traffic in Greek art works, columns, and architectural decoration during the period when Rome dominated the Mediterranean. In 1925 an original fourth-century B.C. bronze Apollo (probably by Praxiteles) was dredged up from the floor of the Bay of Marathon in Greece. And in 1928 a larger than life-size fifth-century bronze Zeus or Poseidon, as well as a Hellenistic bronze jockey and part of his horse were found by sponge divers off Greece's Cape Artemision. Such finds indicate that many undiscovered cargoes of masterpieces probably still repose on the bottom of the sea.

THE SACRED WELL AT CHICHÉN ITZÁ

Not all of the early underwater discoveries were made in Europe. Edward Herbert Thompson, American explorer and archaeologist, showed that excavations under water could also yield important information at inland Maya sites. Thompson became interested in Maya civilization after reading the reports of John Lloyd Stephens's discoveries in the Central American jungles. Then, in 1885, at the age of twenty-five, he was appointed U.S. consul at Merida, Yucatan. Naturally, he seized the opportunity to examine Maya remains.

Thompson was particularly intrigued by Diego de Landa's sixteenth-century account of a sacred well at Chichén Itzá:

> Into this Well they have and still have the custom of throwing men alive as a sacrifice to their gods in time of drought, and they believed they would not die, though they never saw them again. They also threw into it many other things like precious stones and things they prized, and so if this country had possessed gold it would be this Well that would have the greater part of it, so great is the devotion that the Indians show for it.[1]

One of the first acts of the new consul was a trip through the jungle to Chichén Itzá, where he found the well described by Landa. It was a *cenote,* a naturally formed circular hole in the limestone plateau. It had a diameter of about 180 feet, and there was a drop of seventy feet from the rim of the well's almost vertical walls to the surface of its

---

1. Quoted in Edward H. Thompson, *People of the Serpent: Life and Adventures Among the Mayas* (New York: Capricorn, 1965 [original edition, 1932]), p. v.

dark, stagnant water. The ruins of a small temple were still visible at its edge. As he stood on this spot Thompson thought about ancient priests and devotees bringing their precious offerings to the Well of Sacrifice. He visualized processions winding down the stairway of Chichén Itzá's great pyramid from the Temple of the Sacred Serpent, then along the Sacred Way to the small temple at the well. He could almost hear the deep booming of drums and the shrill notes of flutes and whistles. He could almost smell the sweet odor of the native incense, *copal,* as beautiful maidens or captive warriors were thrown into the abyss to disappear beneath the murky waters sacred to the rain god. It was a dramatic vision, but was it true? Thompson had to know.

Without special equipment, however, Thompson found it impossible to explore the *cenote.* Sadly Thompson put aside his dream and engaged himself in explorations and excavations in other parts of Yucatan. But he kept returning to Chichén Itzá. Finally, after many years in Yucatan, he bought the plantation on which the ruins stood. He resigned his office as consul and returned to the United States to secure financial backing for his plan to excavate the Sacred Well. He also took lessons in deep-sea diving and hired two Greek sponge fishermen to assist him in his underwater exploration. Finally, in 1904, he began excavating the well.

Thompson had previously established what he called the "fertile zone" of the well, the area most likely to contain offerings. He and some assistants had repeatedly heaved a log the approximate size and weight of a human body into the *cenote* from the temple platform on the rim. They thus determined how far sacrificial victims could have been thrown. A specially designed dredge was used to investigate this "fertile zone." Day after day the dredge's steel jaws plunged through eighty feet of water, bit into the deposit, and returned to the surface to empty their load onto the rim of the pit. Thompson carefully combed through the dead leaves, branches, soil, and other muck brought up from the well. But he found no evidence of ancient offerings. "Is it possible," he asked himself, "that I have let my friends into all this expense and exposed myself to a world of ridicule only to prove, what many have contended, that these traditions are simply old tales, tales without any foundation in fact?"[2]

Then one day the dredge brought up two yellow-white balls of resinous material. Thompson carefully examined the globular objects, even breaking one in half and tasting it. They were clearly man-made, but what were they? On impulse he put a piece into the embers of the campfire and immediately a sweet fragrance filled the air. The balls

2. Thompson, *People of the Serpent,* p. 272.

were *copal,* the sacred incense. They must have been thrown into the well as part of the offerings mentioned by Landa. The succeeding days brought additional confirmation of the early Spanish accounts. Flint, calcite, and obsidian implements and weapons, as well as vases, copper chisels and ornaments, gold bells, disks, and pendants, jade bowls and figurines, wooden spear-throwers, rattles, and sprinklers, and many other artifacts were recovered from the depths of the well. Finally, Thompson's faith in the trustworthiness of Landa's account was completely vindicated when human bones appeared in the debris brought up by the dredge.

After the dredge had raised all the material it could reach, Thompson and his Greek divers descended into the well to search for more artifacts. The water was pitch black and objects had to be located and "excavated" by touch alone. The risks were considerable, as Thompson explains:

> Every little while one of the stone blocks, loosened from its place in the wall by the infiltration of the water, would come plunging down upon us. . . . So long as we kept our speaking-tubes, air hose and lifelines and ourselves well away from the wall surface we were in no special danger. As the rock masses fell, the push of the water before and around them reached us before the rock did and even if we did not get away of our own accord, it struck us like a huge soft cushion and sent us caroming, often head down and feet upward, balancing and tremulous like the white of an egg in a glassful of water, until the commotion subsided and we could get on our feet again. Had we incautiously been standing with our backs to the wall, we should have been sheared in two as cleanly as if by a pair of gigantic shears and two more victims would have been sacrificed to the Rain God.[3]

No one died during the exploration of the well. However, Thompson later paid for his discoveries with the loss of his hearing due to diving-caused injuries.

The material Thompson recovered from the Sacred Well added much valuable information to our knowledge of Maya civilization. Of particular significance were the many wood and metal artifacts not usually found in land excavations at Maya sites. Scientists were able to trace the metal artifacts' gold and copper to their sources in Mexico, Colombia, Panama, Honduras, and Guatemala. This information threw new light on trade patterns in pre-Columbian America. Today, as a result of Thompson's daring, underwater exploration of the *cenotes* near Maya cities has become a regular part of Maya archaeology.

---

3. Thompson, *People of the Serpent,* pp. 283–84.

Part II—Underwater Archaeology Comes of Age (1952–64)

THE RESURRECTION OF THE *VASA*

Many historically important objects have been salvaged from the depths since the pioneering expeditions at Antikythera, Mahdia, and Chichén Itzá. However, the most spectacular archaeological salvage operation to date has been the raising of the *Vasa*. Construction of this great sixty-four-gun warship, intended as the flagship of the Swedish fleet, was completed in 1628. But as she sailed out of Stockholm harbor on her maiden voyage, a great gust of wind caught her. She heeled over so far to port that water poured in her open gun ports. Within minutes the ship went to the bottom in 110 feet of water.

Salvage attempts began soon after the sinking, but the *Vasa* resisted all efforts to bring her back to the surface. In 1664–65 Hans von Treileben, an ex-officer in the Swedish army, was able to recover fifty-three of the *Vasa*'s cannon through the use of a primitive diving bell. The lead bell, a little over four feet high, covered the upper body of a diver who stood on a platform hanging from the bell's lower rim. As the apparatus was lowered into the water, the pocket of air inside was compressed into the upper portion of the bell. This air pocket gave the diver enough oxygen for about fifteen minutes' work on the wreck. Through the bottom of the bell the diver manipulated a long wooden pole with an iron hook on the end. With this tool he pulled deck boards loose to allow access to the guns, and placed ropes around the cannon so they could be raised to the salvage vessel above. However, von Treileben's methods were not suitable for raising the ship itself. So, after his salvage of most of the cannon, the wreck was gradually forgotten.

It was not until the mid-twentieth century that the *Vasa*'s resting place was rediscovered by Anders Franzen, a Swedish petroleum engineer who studied naval history as a hobby. In his research Franzen came across accounts of the *Vasa*'s sinking, and he became convinced that of all the wrecks he had studied, this one would be the most valuable to salvage. The *Vasa* belonged to the seventeenth century, a period when detailed ship plans had not been made. So the *Vasa* could teach us much about ship construction in that age. Also, its wood was likely to be well-preserved because *teredos,* the shipworms that destroy the hulls of wooden vessels, do not live in the low-salt waters of the Baltic. Furthermore, *Vasa* had been new when it sank. It had not sustained damage from battle or a crash on rocks, so its hull should be reasonably intact. Finally, the ship had sunk in the sheltered waters of Stockholm harbor in close proximity to dockyards and naval support facilities. This would certainly ease salvage operations.

For three summers (1953–55) Franzen cruised around Stockholm harbor in a small boat using a core sampler to bring up bits of material from the bottom. However, he found no evidence of the *Vasa*. Then, in the archives, he uncovered a letter authorities sent to King Gustavus II Adolphus in 1628 giving the approximate location of the wreck. Franzen systematically searched the indicated area. Finally, in August 1956, the core sampler brought up a piece of black oak, the type of wood found in seventeenth-century ships. Swedish naval divers went below and soon verified that the object Franzen had located was a large wooden ship with two rows of gun ports on each side. The *Vasa* had been found.

She proved to be 165 feet long and 42 feet wide. Also, fortunately, she was sitting on the bottom in an upright position. Her upper deck and stern castle had been almost completely destroyed by the seventeenth-century salvagers and by ships' anchors that had gotten snagged on the wreck over the centuries.

However, the *Vasa*'s three lower decks, bottom, and sides were intact! Even so, could her waterlogged timbers stand the strain of being raised to the surface? Tests on samples of oak from the *Vasa* showed that her wood still retained 60 percent of its original strength. The committee of prominent men appointed to oversee the salvage operation decided to try to raise the vessel in one piece and asked for suggestions. Soon imaginative ideas began to arrive from all over the world. One inventor suggested that the hull be filled with ping-pong balls that would provide the buoyancy to raise the ship to the surface. Another argued that the water around and inside the vessel should be frozen into a block of ice that would then float to the top with the ship inside. The committee decided, however, that conventional salvage methods offered the best chance for success.

Since the *Vasa* lay at the entrance of a busy harbor, the salvage work was often interrupted by ships going in and out. But during the summers of the next three years divers dug tunnels beneath the wreck and passed two steel cables through each hole. They then secured these cables to the decks of two large pontoons on the surface. In August 1959 the *Vasa* was ready for her first lift. The salvagers filled the pontoons with water until their decks were almost flush with the surface. Workers drew the cables taut and slowly pumped the water out of the pontoons. As these vessels rose, the *Vasa*, supported by her cradle of steel cables, rose with them. She was towed to shallower water until she grounded. The salvage crew then refilled the pontoons with water, tightened the cables, and began another lift. It took eighteen lifts over almost two months to bring the *Vasa* from a depth of 110 feet to one of 45 feet just outside the dry dock she was to occupy.

Now the workers had to prepare the *Vasa* for her final lift. Divers went below to seal the gun ports and plug the more than ten thousand small holes where nails had rusted or dowels rotted. The *Vasa* had to be as watertight as possible so that the salvagers could pump water from the ship as she rose. This would make the *Vasa* lighter and lessen the strain on her timbers. Meanwhile, a special dry dock had been constructed and moved into position to receive the ghost from the deep. When all was ready, the final lift was made. On April 24, 1961, the *Vasa* broke the surface after more than three centuries on the floor of Stockholm's harbor. Pumps removed the water inside the *Vasa* and the vessel rose higher in the water until at last the cables from the pontoons could be released. The *Vasa* moved the last few yards into her dry dock floating on her own keel!

Archaeologists then began the arduous task of cleaning out the mud and debris inside the ship, keeping careful and extensive records of everything they found. The *Vasa* was a time capsule, a miniature seventeenth-century community. The well-preserved clothing, tools, dishes, and other objects found aboard her have already thrown valuable light on life during that time. The difficulties of the excavation were increased by the fact that the *Vasa* had to be almost continually sprayed with water to prevent her waterlogged timbers from drying out and shrinking.

While this work was going on, scientists were searching for a way to permanently preserve the ship and the objects found within and around her. After many experiments they found that a chemical called polyethylene glycol would penetrate the wooden beams and planks, replace the water within them, and prevent their warping or cracking. Once she had been thoroughly cleaned and moved to her temporary museum, the *Vasa* was sprayed with a solution of this chemical at least once a day for more than ten years. She then was allowed to gradually dry out. The numerous carved wooden figures that once adorned the ship's prow and stern were also preserved and restored. They then were replaced in their original positions. The *Vasa* now looks much as she did on that fateful day in August 1628.

SYSTEMATIC EXCAVATION UNDER WATER

The raising of the *Vasa* was a spectacular accomplishment. But the operation's success was due more to the remarkable state of preservation of the three-hundred-year-old ship than to the application of new or innovative methods of underwater archaeology. Most wrecks are not so well preserved, and many underwater remains cannot be brought to the surface for study. While the *Vasa* was being located, raised, and restored, other expeditions were developing systematic methods for completely excavating and recording remains under water.

In 1952 a French naval vessel equipped for underwater research set out to investigate reports of several amphora clusters on the bottom of the Mediterranean Sea near the coast of France. No one could foresee that forty years later the ship, the *Calypso*, and its captain, Jacques-Yves Cousteau, would be famous throughout the world. The expedition's divers were equipped with face masks, aqualungs, and rubber fins. This self-contained underwater breathing apparatus—"scuba" for short—had been developed by Emile Gagnan and Cousteau in 1942. It allowed divers more freedom of movement and greater visibility than did cumbersome helmeted diving suits. Furthermore, it was simpler to use and much less expensive.

The first site Cousteau checked was located at the eastern end of Grand Congloué island near Marseilles. Frédéric Dumas, a civilian advisor with the French Navy and a pioneer in underwater research, went down first. He searched the area until his air supply was almost completely exhausted, but he found nothing. Then it was Cousteau's turn. He too searched in vain until it was time to return to the ship. But just as he started to surface he spotted a low mound along the sloping bottom 120 to 180 feet below the surface. Amphora necks protruded through the sand, and pottery was scattered around the site. He quickly swam over to the mound, grabbed a few small pieces of pottery, and returned to the *Calypso*.

The chief archaeologist on board, Fernand Benoit, immediately recognized the objects as Campanian Ware. This was a well-known type of pottery produced near Naples during the latter part of the third and the early part of the second centuries B.C. This wreck, then, was older than the Antikythera and Mahdia ships and might throw valuable light on Mediterranean commerce during the Hellenistic Period. Without hesitation, Cousteau decided to eliminate the rest of the *Calypso*'s scheduled itinerary and instead use his allotted time and resources to excavate the wreck he had found.

Hundreds of amphoras, dishes, cups, and pieces of bronze were brought to the surface in the following days. When all of the loose objects around the wreck had been recovered, the divers' work became more difficult. They tried to dig out objects embedded in the mound covering the ancient ship. However, they found that the mud was too compact; special equipment would be needed. So, with its hold full of pottery and its deck covered with amphoras, the *Calypso* returned to Marseilles.

Early in the following year the research vessel was back at Grand Congloué. A platform was erected at the island's edge to serve as a permanent base for the expedition. And from this platform the Cousteau's crew deployed the first air lift to be used for the excavation of an underwater site. The air lift consisted of a large tube that ran from the platform to the wreck with a smaller air hose running alongside and entering the tube near its lower end. Compressed air was pumped down the small hose, entering the tube near its mouth. The air then rose up the tube, expanding as it went and creating a vacuum that produced suction at the tube's mouth. The water and mud sucked up by the air lift poured out of the tube's other end onto the platform. There strainers caught any small artifacts that might have been drawn up inadvertently. The air lift proved to be the solution to the problem of moving large amounts of sand and mud under water. It was so successful at Grand Congloué that it has become an essential tool of subsequent underwater excavations.

Cousteau's expedition also experimented with underwater telephones and closed-circuit television cameras. With these devices the archaeologists on the surface could observe the excavations and communicate instructions to the divers below. This system provided better supervision of the work than had been possible at Antikythera or Mahdia. However, it was still an inadequate substitute for the archaeologist's direct experience of his site.

Financed by the French government, the National Geographic Society, and private donations, the excavations at Grand Congloué continued until 1960. Hundreds of amphoras of an Italian type and over six thousand Campanian plates, cups, and jugs were taken from the wreck. Many of the jars were still sealed. Their seal impressions bore the inscription "L. TITI C. F."—Lucius Titius Caii Filius. Ancient Roman texts indicated that this individual's family had owned extensive vineyards in the Sabine area south of Rome.

In the hold of the ship were amphoras of an eastern Mediterranean type. Many of these jars had the letters SES incised on their necks followed by the symbol of a trident. Benoit surmised that the abbreviation stood for the Roman family name Sextius (Sestius in Greek).

He soon uncovered an interesting ancient reference to a merchant of that name. The Roman historian Livy mentioned that Marcus Sextius, a second-century B.C. wine dealer and shipowner, originally lived in the area of Naples. However, his love for Greek culture caused Sextius to move to the Aegean island of Delos and construct a luxurious villa for himself. Archaeologists followed this lead and carefully searched the excavated portions of the Roman quarter at Delos. There in the remains of a sumptuous villa they found a mosaic pavement bearing a trident design. On the trident were the letters SES!

Careful study of the amphoras from the Grand Congloué ship produced a problem, however. Some of the jars from the bottom of the wreck were of a type produced on Rhodes and at Cnidus. They seemed to be at least seventy years older than the types from Delos and Italy bearing the inscriptions of Lucius Titius and Marcus Sextius. This fact led some scholars to suggest that there had been *two* ships at Grand Congloué. The one belonging to Marcus Sextius must have been lying almost directly on top of the remains of an earlier vessel. In support of this theory these scholars noted that divers at Grand Congloué had reported finding lead sheathing on the underside of one of the ship's decks as well as on the bottom of the hull. The bottoms of the Lake Nemi, Antikythera, and Mahdia ships had also been sheathed in lead to protect their hulls from barnacles and shipworms. But their decks had not been. Thus, what the *Calypso*'s divers took to be a deck was possibly the bottom of the upper ship. The cargo found below that "deck" would then have belonged to an earlier vessel. Benoit and Dumas, however, remained convinced that there was only one ship at Grand Congloué.

This controversy could have been settled by careful study of detailed plans showing the exact positions where objects from the site were found. However, the excavators drew no such plans, nor did they make detailed measurements of the site during the various stages of the excavation. The work at Grand Congloué demonstrated the value of scuba divers, carefully planned diving schedules, and the air hose in underwater archaeology. By default it also showed the importance of careful measurements, photographs, and plans of all objects *in situ*.

In 1957 Commandant Philippe Tailliez of the French Navy developed one method of producing a plan of an underwater site. During his excavation of a wreck at Ile du Levant near Toulon, Tailliez had his divers take overlapping photographs of the entire site. He planned to piece these together to produce a photo-mosaic of the wreck from which a plan could be drawn. A measuring tape stretched along the length of the wreck provided the basis for measuring the position of each object in the photographs. Tailliez eventually succeeded in producing a photo-mosaic and plan for this site. But he found the task much more formidable than he had anticipated. Underwater currents made it difficult for the divers to remain the same distance above the wreck for each photograph. If the photographer's depth varied by only a couple of feet between pictures or if the camera lens was not kept absolutely horizontal, scale and perspective would change. The resulting photographs could not be joined together properly, nor could pictures of different stages of the excavation be easily compared.

During the late 1950s two other scholars also developed methods for mapping underwater remains. One was Frédéric Dumas, Cousteau's friend and coworker. Dumas stressed the need for preliminary test borings into an underwater mound to determine the area in which the ship itself was located. Once the position of the ancient vessel had been determined and excavation begun, Dumas placed a five-meter-square metal frame over part of the site. This frame would provide the means for measuring and plotting the location of all objects within that five-meter-square area. A beam marked in centimeters stretched across the frame. It could slide from one end of the frame to the other. Attached to it was a movable vertical pole also calibrated in centimeters. Thus, the beam and pole could be positioned over any spot within the square, and the pole could be raised or lowered until its bottom rested on the object to be measured. Each object was tagged with an identifying label so that an architect could plot its position, draw it on a plan, and indicate its relative elevation. The frame would be moved around until the entire site with all its artifacts had been measured and planned.

At about the same time, Nino Lamboglia, an Italian archaeologist, independently developed an underwater recording method similar to that of Dumas. Lamboglia had first become interested in underwater archaeology in 1925, when an early first-century B.C. wreck was found off the coast of Italy near Albenga. He was unable to persuade the Italian government to give him funds or divers to excavate the site, so he had to salvage the remains with a grappling dredge operated from a boat borrowed from a salvage company. He recovered over seven hundred amphoras from the wreck in only two weeks. But many objects were destroyed by the steel jaws of the dredge as it cut through the underwater mound. The dredge also brought up parts of the ship itself. However, since they could not be studied in their original positions, the parts provided little information on the ship's construction. Lamboglia was the first to admit that mechanical grabs were unsuitable for proper underwater excavation.

The Italian archaeologist then began studying the problems of excavating under water. In 1957 at a wreck near the island of Spargi between Corsica and Sardinia, he was able to test the ideas he had developed. Divers drove iron pegs into the sea floor and attached yellow canvas tapes to them, forming a grid of two-meter squares over the wreck. Black cords divided each of these squares into four smaller units. From photographs of each square, draftsmen made a plan of all objects on the site. However, Lamboglia's divers, like those at Ile du Levant, had difficulty maintaining a constant depth while photographing the site.

Two University of Pennsylvania expeditions in the early 1960s modified and improved the methods of underwater excavation and recording pioneered by Cousteau, Tailliez, Dumas, and Lamboglia. These expeditions excavated wrecks at Cape Gelidonya on the southern coast of Turkey (1960) and at Yassi Ada, a small island near Turkey's southwest corner (1961–64). George Bass, the leader of both expeditions, was a young archaeologist who had participated in land "digs" at Classical sites. However, he had no previous experience in diving. He took classes at the Philadelphia YMCA and quickly mastered the use of scuba equipment. For the first time, excavations of ancient Mediterranean wrecks were directed by an archaeologist who could experience the site firsthand. Bass was able to devise solutions to excavation problems that were acceptable from archaeological as well as technical diving standpoints.

Early in the excavations at Cape Gelidonya, there was some friction between Bass and the professional divers on the expedition's staff. Peter Throckmorton, the American journalist and diver who had discovered the Gelidonya and Yassi Ada wrecks in 1958–59, described the reason for this conflict:

> George infuriated ,us by violating the rules of efficient diving work on the bottom. When he came to a problem or question of whether the plan was correct, whether the material had been recorded in place thoroughly enough to permit its raising, George always stopped to check. He was capable of holding up the entire job for days, while he used up his diving time mulling over how best to raise a small object. He was, of course, absolutely right. If we were attempting a correct archaeological excavation under water, then it was just that, and not a diving job in the ordinary sense of the term.[4]

---

4. P. Throckmorton, *The Lost Ships: An Adventure in Undersea Archaeology* (Boston: Little, Brown, 1964), p. 206.

The Cape Gelidonya wreck proved to be the oldest known up to that time—a ship belonging to the end of the Bronze Age, about 1200 B.C.[5] This vessel had been carrying a cargo of bronze ingots, tools, and molds rather than the usual amphoras. Unfortunately, these objects had become concreted together into rock-hard lumps. It was necessary to measure and record entire lumps on the bottom, then to pry loose the concretion and send it to the surface. There the objects within the lump could be treated, separated, and individually drawn. The divers carefully labeled, plotted, and placed on a plan every object found, including fragments of the wooden hull of the ship. Because of such careful excavation and recording, the archaeologists could later determine which objects had belonged to the ship's cargo and which had probably been possessions of the crew. This distinction was useful in determining the vessel's probable place of origin and its trade route. Such information is important for historians seeking to reconstruct the patterns of commerce and cultural interrelationships of the eastern Mediterranean some three thousand years ago.

The wreck at Yassi Ada was that of a Byzantine ship from the first half of the seventh century A.D. During its excavation Bass and his staff made further advances in underwater excavation techniques. The ideas of Dumas and Lamboglia were combined. A rigid grid frame of two-meter squares was assembled over the entire wreck. Each square was leveled horizontally, and frequent checks were made to be sure that the frames remained level. A portable tower two meters square at its base and four meters high held a camera in a fixed position. This tower could be placed on top of each of the squares that formed the basic grid frame. In this way the problem of Tailliez and Lamboglia was solved. The camera was always the same distance above the objects being photographed, and the lens was kept absolutely horizontal. The base of the photo-tower contained a wire grid with much smaller squares. This wire grid simplified measurements and allowed photographs to indicate the exact positions of objects within the two-meter square area.

Yassi Ada was the first underwater site to be excavated with the same standards of precision and exactitude as those used in modern land excavations. Not only did underwater excavation technique come of age there, but Yassi Ada also foreshadowed the end of underwater archaeology as an archaeological specialty. Heretofore underwater

---

5. In recent years Bass has found and excavated an even older wreck at Ulu-Burun off the southern coast of Turkey. The Ulu-Burun ship sank around the middle of the fourteenth century B.C.

excavation had been performed primarily by professional divers with only minimal direction by archaeologists. But at Yassi Ada the work was done by professional archaeologists, draftsmen, architects, and other specialists who learned to dive at the site. Bass proved that it is easier to teach archaeologists to dive than it is to teach divers to be archaeologists. It takes years to train an archaeologist, and the temperament of most professional divers does not make them well-suited for such methodical and often boring work. On the other hand, a reasonably healthy individual can be taught to dive and work safely under water in a matter of weeks.

Hopefully, in time, there will be few, if any, "specialists" in underwater archaeology. Rather, Classical archaeologists should excavate Greek and Roman remains that happen to be under water just as they do those on land. Likewise, submerged Phoenician harbor installations should be excavated by specialists in the archaeology of Syria-Palestine. As Bass has pointed out, archaeology under water should be no different from archaeology in any other environment.

> We do not speak of those working on the top of Nimrud Dagh in Turkey as mountain archaeologists, nor those at Tikal in Guatemala as jungle archaeologists. They are all people who are trying to answer questions regarding man's past, and they are adaptable in being able to excavate and interpret ancient buildings, tombs, and even entire cities with the artifacts they contain. Is the study of an ancient ship and its cargo, or the survey of toppled harbour walls somehow different? That such remains may lie under water entails the use of different tools and techniques in their study, just as the survey of a large area on land using aerial photographs, magnetic detectors, and drills, requires a procedure other than excavating the stone artifacts and bones in a Paleolithic cave. The basic aim in all these cases is the same. It is all archaeology.[6]

---

6. George Bass, *Archaeology Under Water* (New York: Frederick A. Praeger, 1966), p. 15.

Part II

Modern Archaeology

Phase III—Systematizing and Organizing the Past (1925–60)

and

Phase IV—Toward a Scientific Archaeology (1960–Present)

9

Phase III—Systematizing and Organizing the Past (1925-1960)

Building Area Syntheses

One of the primary concerns of archaeologists in the period between the First and Second World Wars was organizing archaeological discoveries into meaningful patterns. They wanted to use archaeology to understand the history of various areas, especially those without early written sources. To accomplish this goal they created area syntheses that defined specific archaeological cultures and attempted to describe their growth temporally and spatially.

The concept of separate cultures, each defined by a network of shared traits, had been around for some time. At the end of the nineteenth century anthropologists and students of human geography had begun distinguishing groups of people by differences in their customs, ideas, and material culture. Max Uhle, for one, applied this approach to archaeological remains in the 1890s and early 1900s. He frequently wrote about the "cultures" of pre-Columbian Peru. But Uhle and the others who used the term did not clearly define its archaeological meaning. The culture complex idea did not become widespread in archaeology until the 1920s.

One of the first to carefully delineate the features of an archaeological culture and create an area synthesis was Alfred Kidder. In *An Introduction to the Study of Southwestern Archaeology* (1924) he

251

divided the Southwest into nine cultural areas. He then traced the development of each culture area through four chronological stages. However, the description of some of his culture areas consisted of little more than a listing of types of pottery and buildings found in the region.

Others were soon at work producing similar syntheses for other areas of the New World. Herbert Spinden attempted to define and chronologically order the Middle American cultures in his *Ancient Civilizations of Mexico and Central America* (1928). However, Spinden believed that the Classic Maya civilization had preceded the Teotihuacan and Monte Alban cultures. This erroneous view was corrected through George Vaillant's work in the 1930s and in his *Aztecs of Mexico* in 1941. That year also saw the publication of an article by James Ford and Gordon Willey that provided the first major spatial and chronological synthesis for the prehistoric cultures of the eastern United States. In the late 1930s and early 1940s scholars also developed area syntheses for the Arctic and the West Indies.

Similar work was taking place in Old World archaeology as well. Vere Gordon Childe, an Australian who spent all of his professional life in Great Britain, applied the culture-complex idea to European prehistory in *The Dawn of European Civilization* (1925) and *The Danube in Prehistory* (1929). Childe tried to show how the cultures of early Europe incorporated and modified ideas from the ancient Near Eastern civilizations, producing a new civilization in the process. His explanation of the development of European civilization contained many nuances as it tried to balance evidence for diffusion with indications of European creativity. It was in sharp contrast to many oversimplified works of the time that tried to trace all elements of civilization to one source (usually Egypt).

But if European civilization's development had been stimulated by elements from the Near East, how had civilization arisen in the Near East itself? Childe, influenced by Marxist ideas, saw the answer in terms of a materialist determinism. In works like *Man Makes Himself* (1936) and *What Happened in History* (1943), he argued that a series of technological discoveries had provided the foundations for new cultural organization. The discovery of agriculture and domestication of animals caused a dramatic change, called by Childe the Neolithic Revolution. During this era at the end of the Neolithic Period populations in the Near East had become sedentary and villages had arisen. Population growth and further discoveries such as metallurgy, the wheel, and the sailing ship produced, in turn, an Urban Revolution in which the first towns and cities appeared. The terms "Neolithic Revolution" and "Urban Revolution" soon became part of the regular vocabulary of those writing about the beginnings of civilization in the Near East. Gordon Childe continued to produce influential syntheses of European and world archaeology until his death in 1957.

Another early area synthesis that has had lasting impact was that created for the Syro-Palestinian region by William Foxwell Albright. Albright, an American, excavated Tell el-Ful (1922-23, 1933), Bethel (1927), and, most importantly, Tell Beit Mirsim (1926-32). By comparing the stratified pottery from Tell Beit Mirsim with materials then being excavated at Megiddo and other sites, Albright produced the basic pottery chronology for Syria and Palestine. Albright's pottery classifications and chronology have needed only minor modifications and are still in use today.

Even more significant was the fact that Albright was a "Renaissance man," one of the last scholars to be expert in and make significant contributions to several different scholarly disciplines. He knew virtually all of the ancient languages of the Near East. While his primary interest was in West Semitic languages, the Hebrew Scriptures, and Palestinian history and archaeology, he also made important contributions to Assyriology, Egyptology, and Hittitology. In addition, Albright was an expert in several other esoteric fields, such as historical geography, epigraphy (the study of writing), and historical linguistics. His wide-ranging knowledge and interests made him uniquely qualified to synthesize the results of Near Eastern research. Through hundreds of articles and books including *The Archaeology of Palestine and the Bible* (1932), *Archaeology and the Religion of Israel* (1942), and *The Archaeology of Palestine* (1949), Albright created what became known as biblical archaeology. This field integrated the results of historical geography, biblical studies, and research in Egypt, Mesopotamia, and other parts of the Near East with the archaeological evidence from excavations and surface surveys in Syria-Palestine. Albright's students and his ideas dominated Syro-Palestinian archaeology into the 1970s, and his influence is still strongly felt today.

R. E. M. Wheeler (later Sir Mortimer Wheeler) also revolutionized an entire field of archaeology, that of the Indian subcontinent. In 1943 Wheeler became director-general of antiquities in India and introduced his new excavation methods there (see below). His excavations at Taxila and Chandragupta closed the gap between the prehistoric and historical cultures in India. These sites and the trading post at Arikamedu had been centers of East-West trade in Greco-Roman times. Through them Wheeler was able to date some of the previously undated Indian cultures. Wheeler's work, in turn, made possible Stuart Piggott's *Prehistoric India* (1950), a masterful synthesis of the archaeological evidence.

Conflict Over Archaeological Theory

Archaeologists' descriptions of the cultures they had uncovered were obviously more complete when there were written sources like classical Greek and Roman works or the Bible to aid in the interpretation of the physical remains. But how could archaeologists understand vanished cultures from areas or periods without writing? How could they be expected to provide anything more than a listing of various types of artifacts for prehistoric societies?

One way, frequently used in the late nineteenth century, was to arrange archaeological finds into some system of unilinear cultural evolution. Two of these theoretical constructs became especially influential. The first was the social development scheme of Edward B. Tylor (*Primitive Culture*, 1871) and Lewis Henry Morgan (*Ancient Society*, 1877). This theme posited a progression from savagery to barbarism to civilization. The second was the economically determined progression proposed by Karl Marx and Friedrich Engels: a progression from egalitarian society to feudalism to capitalism (eventually, they believed, leading to communism).

Unilinear evolutionists usually argued for the psychic unity of mankind. Uniformity in the operation of the human mind supposedly caused different cultures to develop independently along parallel lines (though often at different rates). Such development, the theorists felt, was always in one direction, towards the complex "civilized" culture of the late-nineteenth-century West, or in the case of Marx and Engels, toward the inevitable future stage of pure socialism. Unilinear evolutionists also tended to create fanciful reconstructions of early prehistory based on the features their theory led them to expect.

By the end of the century, however, critics had burst the unilinear evolution bubble. Some scholars pointed out logical inconsistencies within the theories themselves. But archaeologists provided the most devastating evidence against unilinear evolution. They showed that the American Mound-Builders had been Indians, not remnants of some lost civilization. Furthermore, the Indian cultures that erected the mounds had been *more* advanced than those that succeeded them. Clearly culture did not always develop upward and onward in a straight line!

Theories like those of Morgan, Tylor, Marx, and Engels, however, had identified some important aspects of social and cultural development. Once critics eliminated their oversimplifications and claims of "inevitability"—the elements that made them unilinear and doctrinaire—these theories made great contributions to archaeological interpretation. In modified form they continued to have great influence on the social sciences into the 1930s and beyond.

However, forcing prehistoric data to conform to a preconceived theoretical scheme was not the only way to make sense of such data. As early as the eighteenth and nineteenth centuries some perceptive scholars had interpreted archaeological evidence through analogies drawn from historical sources or modern ethnological studies. Thus, for example, in the 1850s Ferdinand Keller argued that pilings found in Swiss lakes were the foundations of dwellings built out over the water for protection. His models for this reconstruction were stilt-villages that explorers had observed on some Polynesian islands.

In the United States during the 1930s W. D. Strong and W. R. Wedel went beyond ethnological analogy to develop what came to be known as the "direct historical approach" to archaeology. They started by studying the settlements and artifacts of modern American Indian groups. Then they traced the material culture traits of these groups backward into prehistoric times through the archaeological record. This method was successfully used in the Great Plains area and was soon being applied elsewhere in the United States as well.

Of course, "the direct historical approach" has its limitations. It can only be used in places where there was a direct and continuous link between the modern inhabitants and the prehistoric occupants. Also, as J. Ned Woodall has pointed out, "Sooner or later (usually sooner) the artifacts characteristic of a particular group had been so modified that it could no longer confidently be asserted that they belonged to the direct cultural ancestors of the historic people being studied."[1] Nevertheless, the method has proved valuable in American archaeology. Through it Strong and Wedel established the existence of some important cultural trends while tracing the development of the Pawnee and Cheyenne. Their work also laid the foundation for later archaeological study of the Great Plains.

While archaeologists of the 1930s and 1940s disagreed about the models and methods for understanding prehistoric societies, most would have agreed that their goal was to write cultural history. Archaeologists at this time were primarily concerned with chronology, and this was especially true for those developing area syntheses. But in the late 1940s a young scholar, Walter W. Taylor, took the profession to task for that emphasis.

Taylor's book, *A Study of Archaeology* (1948), was a revised ver-

---

1. J. Ned Woodall, *An Introduction to Modern Archaeology* (Cambridge, Mass.: Shenkman, 1972), p. 30.

sion of his 1943 Harvard doctoral dissertation. In it he complained that too much of what was passing for archaeology in the 1940s was mere chronicle, the arranging of artifacts and cultures in chronological order. Taylor admitted that chronology and historical reconstruction of cultural contexts were part of archaeology. But to him they were only a preliminary phase. What should follow, he argued, was a cultural anthropological approach, a "comparative study of the statics and dynamics of culture, its formal, functional, and developmental aspects."[2]

To accomplish this, Taylor advocated what he called the "conjunctive approach." This method would bring together many different ways to study the complete range of information about an archaeological culture system. It would aim at fully synthesizing ecological and archaeological data. Using the conjunctive approach, Taylor felt, archaeologists should be able to provide reconstructions of prehistoric cultures that were almost as complete as ethnographic descriptions of present-day cultures.

Few archaeologists were happy with Taylor's book. Those concerned with protohistoric or historic cultures of ancient Europe, the Near East, and Asia ignored it. Its emphasis on anthropological rather than historical goals would have been foreign, if not objectionable, to them. Even anthropologically oriented American archaeologists did not embrace Taylor's work. He had criticized most of the leading figures in American archaeology, so they (and their students and friends) reacted defensively. They claimed his ideas were unrealistic. More data had to be collected before such a complete contextual reconstruction could take place.

Despite this largely negative response, Taylor's critique caused some archaeologists to spend more time thinking about the functional aspects of past cultures, their ecological adaptations, and inferences about processes of cultural development. In due time Taylor's ideas burst forth again in the "New Archaeology" of the 1960s and 1970s.

Improvements in Excavation Techniques

We have already seen how archaeologists in most areas had begun to excavate stratigraphically by the mid-1920s. But some were "leveling" sites by taking off slices of earth of predetermined thickness. Others were attempting to follow sites' natural stratigraphy by removing all

---

2. *A Study of Archaeology* (American Anthropological Association Memoir No. 69), p. 39.

of the material belonging to one period of occupation before proceeding to the next. Obviously, the first procedure was easier than the second, especially at large, complex mounds that had been occupied for thousands of years. However, important new techniques of excavation were devised and promoted in the late 1920s, the 1930s, and the 1940s by Mortimer Wheeler.

Wheeler was a British disciple of Pitt Rivers. His early excavations in the 1920s and 1930s were of Roman and Celtic sites in Great Britain. The best known of these excavations was Maiden Castle, an Iron Age earthwork fortress in Dorsetshire, England. Wheeler's publication of this site (*Maiden Castle*, 1943) provided an effective illustration of the methodology that he later put to good use in deeply stratified sites in India. It generally became known as the Wheeler method or the Grid method of excavation.

Wheeler insisted that excavation should discover and follow a site's natural stratigraphy. To facilitate this, the site would be surveyed and a grid placed over it. Areas to be excavated would follow this grid layout. Large excavation areas were divided into smaller units (usually five meters square) separated by unexcavated walls of earth called balks. Excavation proceeded downward by scraping off layer after layer, using the balks to check the excavators' observations of the strata and as records of each square's stratigraphy. Everything was to be carefully recorded, including the stratigraphy visible in the balks.

Order and neatness were the watchwords in this system. The balks' sides had to be kept vertical for their stratigraphy to be observed correctly. Also, excavation surfaces had to be frequently swept so that any changes in texture or color were not obscured by piles of drying dirt. Because of the constant necessity of careful observation and recording, trained archaeologists or archaeological students were supposed to supervise no more than two or three squares at a time. This idea was particularly revolutionary in the East, where hundreds of workers had often excavated large sites with only minimal supervision by a few archaeologists.

One of Wheeler's students, Kathleen Kenyon, used these techniques during her important excavations at Jericho in the Holy Land during the 1950s. She was able to demonstrate that many of the conclusions reached by earlier excavators of the site were erroneous. For example, the city walls thought to belong to Joshua's time were actually Early Bronze Age structures destroyed about a thousand years before the Exodus. Kenyon became a champion of the new system in the Near East (where it generally became known as the Wheeler-Kenyon method). Others modified the method for use in excavating circular burial

Fig. 69. The grid method of excavation being used in Jordan in the mid-1960s. (Photograph by the author.)

mounds or other types of small sites. By the 1960s excavators in most parts of the world were using the basic principles and techniques of Wheeler's grid method.

Advances in Archaeological Surveying

The discovery, classification, and mapping of archaeological sites has always been a basic and necessary type of archaeological field work. Like excavation, surveys of archaeological sites became more thorough and systematic in the latter part of the nineteenth century. However, dramatic strides were made in this field during the first half of the twentieth century, when new technology began to be applied.

One of the earliest applications of modern technology to archaeology was the use of aerial photography to locate and determine the nature of archaeological sites. Often features that are difficult or impossible for pedestrians to notice show up very clearly when seen from above. This fact was recognized as early as the 1860s, when hot-air balloons began to be used for military reconnaissance. However, aerial reconnaissance and aerial photography came into their own during World

War I, the first war in which combat aircraft were used.

After the war O. G. S. Crawford, a British geographer and a pilot during the war, demonstrated the archaeological value of aerial reconnaissance. Archaeological remains such as roads, walls, earthworks, and ditches covered with earth and vegetation are often difficult if not impossible to notice on foot. But they frequently produce slight undulations in the ground's surface, or variations in soil color, or differences in the height and coloration of vegetation above them. Even if someone on the ground were to notice these discrepancies, they would seem random and meaningless. However, from the air not only can these shadows, soil marks, and crop marks be seen, but their patterns can be recognized. Thus, photographs taken from the air often reveal unsuspected archaeological remains or relationships between features.

World War II produced another aid for aerial surveying—infrared photography. Infrared film reacts to variations in water absorption by different materials. It was developed during the war to spot camouflaged military equipment or installations, but it also revealed hidden archaeological features. For example, infrared photographs of northern Italy revealed hundreds of Etruscan tombs just beneath the surface. This type of aerial photography has since been used frequently for archaeological surveys, especially in the Americas.

Buried remains have also been discovered through the use of electrical resistance meters. These devices measure differences in the electrical conductivity of materials just beneath the surface. Soil and rock are themselves poor conductors of electricity, but when the air spaces they contain are permeated by water containing dissolved mineral salts, they become capable of conducting an electric current. The soil in filled-in pits or ditches is usually less densely packed than the surrounding earth. It thus usually contains more moisture, giving it a lower resistance to electricity. Stone or brick walls, on the other hand, contain less water than neighboring soils. Therefore, they are more resistant to the flow of an electrical current. By measuring the current flow between properly spaced electrodes inserted into the earth, the surveyor can determine the positions of underground remains. However, the archaeological use of resistivity equipment is limited by the fact that it takes a lot of time to set up and operate. Also, it is usually unable to locate features that are more than three to six feet below the surface.

In the 1950s scientists developed another instrument to locate buried remains, the magnetometer. This device measures minute anomalies in the earth's magnetic field due to subsurface features. Objects that have been subjected to intense heat such as kilns or fire pits develop a weak permanent magnetism. Iron artifacts, or filled pits or ditches with a high humus content also distort the magnetic field around them from the normal. On the other hand, walls and stone constructions are less susceptible to magnetization by the surrounding magnetic field, so they display a reverse anomaly. Magnetometers have proved very successful in locating such buried remains. The most commonly used magnetic survey device is the proton magnetometer, which can locate objects up to ten feet below the surface. (However, in the 1960s and 1970s even more sensitive rubidium and cesium magnetometers have been developed. These devices have the ability to detect remains fifteen to twenty feet deep.) A single proton magnetometer cannot be used near wire fences, overhead electrical wires, or metal sheeting of any kind because of the "noise" they produce. But where such features are present two similar instruments, the differential fluxgate magnetometer and the fluxgate gradiometer, can be used. Magnetometers not only have a deeper range than electrical resistance equipment, they are also easier to use. Small, portable magnetometers allow one individual to survey between ten and twenty acres in a single day.

In Italy, many hundreds of Etruscan tombs have been discovered by use of these new survey devices. However, there are not enough Etruscologists or sufficient funds to excavate all of these burial chambers. So, in 1956 an Italian engineer named Carlo Lerici developed a method for exploring the ancient cemeteries that allows archaeologists to make the best use of their time and money. Lerici drilled a small hole through the earth into the chamber of an unexcavated tomb and inserted a periscope with a miniature light and camera on it. If the tomb was relatively intact and its wall paintings and other features could be seen, he took photographs of the interior. In this way he could explore about four tombs a day. Only those that were well preserved or that had not been robbed in antiquity would be excavated.

New Ways to Date the Past

By the 1920s scholars had developed generally reliable chronologies for those ancient societies that had possessed writing. Montelius, Arthur Evans, and others were also able to provide dates for contemporaneous non-literate cultures (or those whose writing could not be read) through their contacts with one or more of the literate civilizations. But absolute dates[3] for the period before about 3000 B.C. (when writing was

---

3. Absolute dates are dates that are fixed in relation to a single date or event. In the West, for example, we use a chronology that numbers years in terms of the birth

invented) were only educated guesses.

In the decades following the end of World War I, however, researchers devised several new methods of dating archaeological remains. Dendrochronology, or tree-ring dating, was one of these "new" dating systems, although its roots go far into the past. The reader will remember that in 1788 Rev. Manasseh Cutler counted the rings of trees growing on mounds at Marietta, Ohio, to determine how old the mounds were. Others used tree rings in a similar way in subsequent decades. But it was Charles Babbage, an Englishman, who laid the foundations for a more useful tree-ring chronology in 1838. He noted that the width of a tree's rings varies with climatic conditions and that exceptionally wide or narrow rings could provide a means of correlating rings of one tree with those of another. This would allow the development of a chronology longer than the lifespan of a single tree.

Little was done with Babbage's idea until the early twentieth century, when A. E. Douglass and other American scholars began working out the method of analysis in detail. They determined the best trees to use and found ways to overcome difficulties in relating ring sequences to one another. Then they began comparing the sequences of wide and narrow rings in the inner part of recently cut trees with the outer bands in old tree stumps. The inner bands of the tree stumps were then linked with bands in still older beams in archaeological sites. In this way they slowly extended their tree-ring count backward in time. Their work reached fruition in the 1930s and 1940s with the creation of a tree-ring sequence for the southwestern United States that reached back some two thousand years. Archaeologists were then able to use this sequence to date wood from pre-Columbian Indian sites in the region.

Because tree-ring sequences are dependent upon climate, wood specimens used for cross-dating must be gathered within a limited geographical area and usually from the same type of tree. The resulting chronology can only be applied within that same limited area. So far, dendrochronology has been used most extensively in the area where it was first developed, the southwestern United States. But relative tree-ring sequences, ones that cannot be linked to trees cut at a known time, have also proved to be valuable dating tools in excavations at Gordion in Turkey and Novgorod in Russia. Scholars are presently

---

of Jesus. Year dates are designated either B.C. ("Before Christ") or A.D. (*Anno Domini,* Latin for "the year of our Lord"). According to the calculations of the Christian monk who created this system, A.D. 1 was the year Jesus was born and began his reign as the Christ. All subsequent years he dated as Christ's "regnal years." For example, A.D. 325 means "the three hundred and twenty-fifth year of [the reign of] our Lord."

working to develop tree-ring chronologies for most areas of Europe and for other areas of the world.

The best-known of the new scientific dating techniques is radiocarbon or carbon-14 (C14) dating. This method was developed between 1946 and 1949 by Willard Libby of the University of Chicago. It was an offshoot of research done during World War II as part of the Manhattan Project to produce the atomic bomb. Carbon-14, a radioactive isotope of carbon (which has a normal atomic weight of 12), is produced in the upper atmosphere due to constant bombardment by cosmic rays. It has all of the chemical properties of ordinary carbon, but it is unstable. It eventually becomes nitrogen (N14) by the emission of an electron. Libby discovered that C14 formed a very small but fixed proportion of the carbon in the atmosphere and the oceans, and thus in all living things. As long as an organism is alive the proportion of radioactive carbon it contains remains constant. But when an organism dies it ceases to receive new carbon-14, causing the ratio of C14 to C12 to decrease gradually as the radioactive carbon decays into nitrogen. Libby determined that it takes 5,568 years plus or minus 30 years for half of the carbon-14 in an object to become nitrogen, another 5,568 years plus or minus 30 years for half of the remaining C14 to decay, and so on.[4] By determining the percentage of radioactive carbon remaining in material of animal or vegetable origin and comparing it with the percentage found in presently living organisms, scientists can tell how long the C14 has been decaying and thus, how long it has been since the organism in question died.

The discovery of radiocarbon dating revolutionized archaeological chronology in the 1950s. It could be applied to almost all archaeological sites, and it provided absolute dates for materials from pre-literate or non-literate groups. Its range of over forty thousand years (since extended to more than seventy thousand years) made it particularly useful for dating early prehistoric remains. Ongoing improvement of laboratory equipment and procedures and additional testing of C14 dates for tree rings and other firmly dated materials promise continued refinement of radiocarbon dating.[5] This will make the method even more

---

4. The time needed for half of a radioactive substance to decay into a non-radioactive substance is known as its half-life. More recent tests indicate that the half-life of carbon-14 is 5,730 years plus or minus 40 years.

5. Libby's assumption that the ratio of C14 to C12 has always been constant turned out to be wrong. Testing of selected rings from tree-ring sequences stretching back more than six thousand years showed that radiocarbon dates often deviated from the real dates by hundreds of years. However, scholars have been able to create tables by which one can correct a radiocarbon date to more accurately reflect the true age of a given sample. Radiocarbon dates appearing in recent publications have usually been corrected.

useful in the future.

Closely related to radiocarbon dating are methods for determining the geological age of rocks or strata by measuring the decomposition of radioactive elements such as uranium, rubidium, or potassium they contain. These elements decay at a much slower rate than carbon-14, so they can date deposits millions of years old. This fact is useful to archaeologists studying the emergence of man, since the oldest human fossils are too early to be dated by radiocarbon dating. The potassium-argon method was used to date a basalt layer in Java (and the bones of *Homo erectus* associated with it) to half a million years ago. At Olduvai Gorge in Tanganyika the method provided a date for the lowest levels of a fossil-covered volcanic ash bed, allowing scholars to determine that the hominid skull found there by Mary Leakey in 1959 was about 1.5 million to 2 million years old.

These scientific dating techniques revolutionized our understanding of prehistory and early history. The date of the origin of man was pushed back while the end of the Ice Age was brought forward in time. The beginnings of agriculture and urbanization were earlier than had been thought, the emergence of full civilization more recent. European megalithic monuments like Stonehenge turned out to be older than the pyramids of Egypt. For the first time archaeologists had the means for studying comparative rates of cultural change and the hope of learning something of the nature of cultural evolution.

10

Phase IV:
Toward a Scientific Archaeology
(1960-Present)

The "New Archaeology"

Despite W. W. Taylor's 1948 call for a conjunctive approach to archaeology and a 1958 plea for more explanation and interpretation of cultural process,[1] there was little change in the practice of archaeology into the 1960s. But the message of these voices crying in the wilderness did not go completely unheeded. In the 1960s, led by Lewis Binford, a new group of young American archaeologists issued another summons for their colleagues to adopt a more explicitly scientific approach and to concern themselves with cultural process. These Americans were soon joined by British archaeologists David Clarke and Colin Renfrew in espousing what became known as the "New Archaeology."

The new archaeology, rooted in cultural anthropology, renounced the historical orientation of traditional archaeology. Its supporters accepted the concept of cultural evolution and the use of systems theory. They strove to emulate the sciences by seeking to *explain* cultural proc-

---

1. Gordon R. Willey and Philip Phillips, *Method and Theory in American Archaeology* (Chicago: University of Chicago Press, 1958).

ess rather than just to describe it. They were very optimistic that they could deduce valid *laws* of cultural development and change. To accomplish this, they adopted the scientific method—formulating explicit hypotheses or models, deducing how they would work, then testing them by carefully designed research projects. Their search for objective, demonstrable explanations also led the new archaeologists to stress quantative analysis of data, using computers for random sampling, significance testing, and other types of statistical analysis.

The writings of Binford and his followers produced a heated debate. Some criticism even came from W. W. Taylor, who objected that the "new" archaeology wasn't really new! He pointed out that he had presented many of the new archaeology's ideas in *A Study of Archaeology* in 1948.[2] But most of the attacks were launched by traditional, historically oriented archaeologists, especially those in Europe.

Jaquetta Hawkes, a British prehistorian, was afraid that science and technology were going to "usurp the throne of history."

> We are now all getting terrified of our way of life being more and more dominated by the machine and by the statistical outlook. And it seems to me sad, if this is also going to affect our understanding of the past. . . . I feel they ["fanatical" science-oriented archaeologists] are quite content to become skillful with their machines and they don't realize perhaps how difficult it is to serve two masters or two values at the same time. And I think there's a great danger of completely branching off into doing these technical investigations which have no relation to history at all.[3]

Glyn Daniel, another British prehistorian, also had little use for the ideas of the new archaeologists. According to Daniel, the movement derived from the unexciting nature of pre-Columbian North American archaeology, which had "driven archaeologists into the welcoming arms of anthropologists who are all, vainly in my view, hoping to adumbrate laws of human behavior."[4] Daniel further predicted that "after the turmoil and heart-searching discussion prompted by the 'new' archaeology, archaeology will return, strengthened and refreshed, to

---

2. See Taylor's review of L. Binford and S. Binford, eds., *New Perspectives in Archaeology* in *Science* (1969): pp. 382–84.

3. Jaquetta Hawkes on a BBC program on modern archaeology in November 1971, quoted in David Wilson, *The New Archaeology* (New York: New American Library, 1974), pp. 275–76.

4. G. Daniel, *A Short History of Archaeology* (London: Thames and Hudson, 1981), p. 190.

its proper role of writing the history of man in the fullest possible sense."[5]

Robert Braidwood, an American specialist in Near Eastern prehistory, had a different explanation for the rise of the new archaeology, with its use of scientific jargon and its claims to being a science.

> In the U.S. at least, the growth of the "new" archaeology, with all its scientism, will eventually be understood in part as a response to the growth of the National Science Foundation as a source for substantial financial support for archaeology in the anthropological tradition. It was important to behave and to talk like a scientist. . . . I feel certain, too, that in the U.S., the obstreperous spirit of many of the "new" archaeologists reflected the unrest of the Vietnam years. These people belonged to the "don't trust anybody over thirty" generation (they are, of course, themselves well beyond that now!). It was declared publicly at association meetings, for example, that "nothing written before 1960 is worth reading" and, given the development of the movement's own new jargon, it was difficult for many of the "new" archaeologists and their students to *understand* anything written before 1960.[6]

Fortunately, the rhetoric on both sides has become more moderate over the years. Nevertheless, differences remain. Archaeologists from the historical/humanist tradition (I number myself in this group) still have doubts about whether anthropological archaeology will ever be able to discern laws of cultural dynamics. They also do not concede that archaeology is the "past tense of cultural anthropology."[7] Even so, today some of the elements of the new archaeology are commonplace in historically oriented archaeology as well.

The use of computers and statistical analysis has become virtually universal (see below), and more attention is paid to recovering data necessary for reconstructing the environment and ecology of the past. In addition, most archaeologists have come to recognize that they need to clearly state the problems they seek to solve or the questions they seek to answer. Then they need to plan their excavations or other research projects so that they will be relevant to those concerns. The use and testing of "models" of the past has also become widespread. There are still times when excavations are undertaken just "to see what

---

5. *A Short History of Archaeology*, p. 192.

6. R. Braidwood, "Archaeological Retrospect 2," *Antiquity* 55 (1981): pp. 24–25 (emphasis in the original).

7. C. Renfrew and P. Bahn, *Archaeology: Theories, Methods, and Practice* (New York: Thames and Hudson, 1991), p. 9.

is there." But as costs continue to increase, such expeditions are becoming fewer and fewer.[8] The impact of the new archaeology has been significant, even on those who most strongly opposed it initially.

Computers in Archaeology

As we have seen, one of the major features of the "new archaeology" was its emphasis on quantitative analysis of archaeological data, an emphasis made practical by the contemporaneous computer revolution. It was possible to do statistical analysis of archaeological finds before the advent of the digital computer, but the procedures were very difficult and time consuming. Such analysis was therefore seldom attempted, even when the number of finds was small. On the other hand, the ability to perform various types of statistical analyses, such as multivariate factor analysis, cluster analysis, or principle component analysis, is one of the strengths of computers. They can easily sort through massive volumes of data to reveal recurring patterns of association that otherwise might go unnoticed.

An example of the impact of computers can be seen in the way pottery and other artifacts are now recorded and analyzed. Classic typological sequence dating as developed by Montelius and Petrie utilized observation of changes in the form or decoration of pottery or other implements. When stratigraphical excavations became common, the emphasis was still on noting changes in types of objects from layer to layer. Thus, in most large-scale excavations of the 1930s to 1950s only the *types* of artifacts found in each layer were recorded. But sometimes artifact styles change very slowly. At some sites archaeologists found two, three, or more stratified occupation layers containing basically the same types of artifacts. If another site had only a single layer with these same types of artifacts, how could the excavator determine whether his layer dated from the beginning, middle, or end of the period when the artifacts were in use?

Actually, the work of Nels Nelson and Alfred Kidder in the American Southwest during the early decades of the twentieth century had already supplied an answer to this problem. They excavated stratified

---

8. Of course, an exception to this statement is salvage archaeology. This is the excavation and study that must be done (often very hurriedly) when sites are threatened by destruction, usually by the construction of roads or buildings. The goal of such work must, of necessity, be to discover what is there and to recover as much information as possible before the site is destroyed.

	Number of Sherds							Approximate Percentages						
Level:	1	2	3	4	5	6	7	1	2	3	4	5	6	7
Type A	63	65	20	28	9	10	12	22	20	6	7	5	3	5
Type B	108	137	143	126	70	64	39	38	41	43	30	36	21	15
Type C	30	23	27	129	59	106	78	10	7	8	30	30	34	31
Type D	82	104	141	144	58	129	127	30	32	43	33	29	42	49
Totals	283	329	331	427	196	309	256	100	100	100	100	100	100	100

Fig. 70. Kidder's chart showing percentage changes of four types of pottery by level. (Modified version of a chart given in A. Kidder, The Pottery of Pecos, vol. 1, 1931.)

refuse dumps at their sites in New Mexico and recorded not only the changes in types of pottery from layer to layer, but also the number of each type found. For each level Kidder even calculated the percentage of the whole each type represented (see Fig. 70). It was clear that even though several layers contained the same types of pottery, the frequency of each type varied stratum by stratum. Thus, changes in the percentage of the whole assemblage that each type of artifact represented could be a valuable indication of relative chronology.

Other archaeologists began using pottery frequency graphs at North American sites excavated in the 1940s and 1950s. Unfortunately, however, this work had little or no impact on European archaeologists or on American specialists in the various fields of Old World archaeology. The number of pottery sherds in each stratum at most American sites was small, usually only a few hundred. But in a large-scale excavation of an occupation site in the Near East or parts of Europe the sherds found in a single stratum often numbered in the thousands and sometimes in the tens of thousands. So, until computers became common in the late 1960s and early 1970s most excavators of large Old World occupation sites only recorded the types of pottery found in each stratum, not the numbers or percentages of each type.

In 1962 James A. Ford showed how remains from several different sites could be placed in proper sequential order by combining their frequency graphs into one seriation chart.[9] The use of frequency graphs as seriation or dating tools was based on the assumption that a diagram of the popularity of each artifact type or style would look much the same. The numbers (and percentage) of a given artifact type would be small when it was first introduced. They would gradually increase over time until the type reached its maximum popularity. Then the numbers and percentages would slowly decrease until the type stopped being used. The resulting graph would form what is known as a battleship-shaped curve, wide in the middle and tapering to points at beginning and end.

The validity of this assumption was shown in the late 1960s by James Deetz and Edwin Dethlefsen.[10] They studied dated eighteenth- and early nineteenth-century tombstones in New England cemeteries. There were three predominant decorative motifs used on the headstones: death's head, cherub, and urn and willow. When the percentages of these types were graphed decade by decade, each type exhibited a battleship-shaped distribution curve (Fig. 71). Such controlled studies and the increasing availability of computers led specialists in Old World archaeology to join the Americanists in using artifact frequency analysis.

Today at almost all digs the archaeologists record *every* artifact, even when there are large numbers of pottery sherds, noting type and special features. This information is then fed into computers for analysis. Or, more commonly today, the records are entered directly into notebook computers in the field.

Computers not only supply frequency tables and charts, but they also discover various patterns of recurrence. That is, they note common groupings of items in the data being studied. Such recurring relationships as well as changes in the frequency of occurrence of certain objects may provide valuable clues about a culture's lifestyle, economy, social structure, and beliefs.

---

9. J. A. Ford, *A Quantitative Method for Deriving Cultural Chronology* (Washington: Pan American Union, 1962).

10. E. F. Dethlefsen and J. Deetz, "Death's Heads, Cherubs, and Willow Trees: Experimental Archaeology in Colonial Cemeteries," *American Antiquity* 31, no. 4 (1966): pp. 502-10.

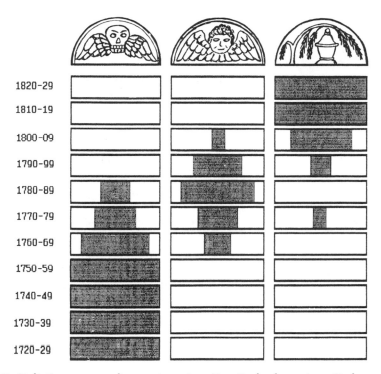

Fig. 71. Stylistic sequence of gravestones in a New England cemetery. (Redrawn from a figure in James Deetz, *Invitation to Archaeology*, Garden City, New York: The Natural History Press, 1967, p. 31.)

At a small cave site in the Oaxaca valley of Mexico, archaeologists plotted their finds on a grid and then had a computer analyze their spacial relationships. In the lowest levels of occupation, the remains indicated that the inhabitants were a small band of hunters and gatherers without knowledge of agriculture. The computer's analysis of the finds, however, allowed valuable information to be added to this description. The various types of plant remains proved to be grouped together by the habitat in the foothills from whence they came. The materials from different habitats were found in different areas of the cave. This suggested that the cave's inhabitants went on trips to different habitat zones in the foothills at different times of year. On each expedition they brought the materials they gathered back to their cave and together they processed them, using a different area of the cave each time. So each habitat grouping of plants in the cave represented the results of a particular foraging trip into the foothills by the hunter-gatherers.

However, the remains of animals from very different habitats were all found in the same area of the cave. The difference between the treatment of vegetable and animal remains suggested to the excavators that hunting and processing of meat was the job of only one group, probably the males. On the other hand, plant gathering was probably performed by the women or by both sexes together.

Like workers in other fields, archaeologists have discovered that computers are useful for much more besides word processing and statistical analysis. One expedition, the Akhenaton Temple Project, has used computers to reconstruct a demolished Egyptian temple. The stones from this temple had been used as fill in later construction. But archaeologists recovered thousands of the stone blocks, most having parts of sculptured scenes on one or more of their sides. The sculptures were carefully photographed at the same scale. Then information on figures in the scenes, angles of the rays of the Aton (if shown), and other details were entered into a computer. The computer listed in groups all of the stones that had similar features. Thus, scholars were able to compare the photographs of the stones in each group and place them in the proper relationship to one another.

Other expeditions are using computer-aided design programs to make plans and reconstructions of the architectural remains they find. Such programs also allow archaeologists to visualize objects from several different perspectives. Computers can also analyze and enhance faded images or writing, helping reveal a painting or a text's original appearance. They can perform cultural simulations based on data fed into them, enabling archaeologists to test some of their assumptions about ancient cultural development. The list of their uses goes on and on, but enough has been said to make it clear that the computer has become, and for the forseeable future will remain, the archaeologist's most useful tool.

Other Recent Developments

Archaeology has continued to make valuable use of high-technology scientific equipment, although it was usually designed for other purposes. One of the most important applications of this technology continues to be in the area of remote sensing. For example, ground-penetrating radar, developed for use in the search for oil and gas, has aided archaeologists surveying and mapping sites in Egypt, Britain, New Jersey, and other areas. Recently, it was able to locate a Maya village buried under volcanic ash. Magnetometers could not be used in this instance because of the magnetic intensity of the volcanic covering.

The values of aerial photography have been expanded with the use of photographs taken from space! Mapping satellites send back pictures made with both visual and infrared light. The American LANDSAT satellites show features ninety feet wide or larger, and the French SPOT satellites reveal objects as small as sixy feet wide. Military satellites can spot features much smaller than that, but almost all of their photographs are classified. Some have been released, however, and have proved useful in locating fossil beds in Africa.

Satellite images have the potential to revolutionize archaeological exploration and surveying. Recently, archaeologists located a long lost city in the Arabian desert by noting the convergence of ancient roads and caravan trails detected on a photograph taken from space. This technology cannot yet be used routinely, for the cost is still too high (about $3,000 per photograph). But it holds great promise for the future, especially when the military begins releasing photographs whose contents no longer need remain secret.

Underwater archaeology has also made use of devices created by scientists and engineers. In archaeology under water, as on the surface, surveying and mapping consume a large portion of the archaeologist's time. Of course, working time is even more precious under water than on land. This led the university museum of the University of Pennsylvania to try to speed up the process of underwater exploration and surveying. With financial support from the National Science Foundation and the National Geographic Society, the museum commissioned the construction of a small, electric, two-person submarine. The *Asherah,* launched in 1964, could cruise under the sea at four knots (4.6 miles per hour) and at depths up to six hundred feet. The miniature sub's two motors and propellers could be rotated to enable it to go forward, backward, up, down, or to hover motionless over a given spot. It carried two specially mounted and synchronized underwater cameras for taking stereo photographs from which detailed maps and plans could be made.

The museum used the *Asherah* for several years at various sites in the Mediterranean. While it was good for some specialized tasks, especially producing photographic plans, it proved to be too expensive to maintain and operate. Eventually the small submarine was sold to a private corporation for use in servicing offshore oil rigs.

Since the 1960s engineers have produced other technological aids for underwater research. These include side-scanning sonar, which shows the contours of the sea bed, and small, unmanned, remote-controlled, submersible devices equipped with grabs and cameras. It remains to be seen whether any of the newer instruments will prove cost-effective and become regularly used in underwater archaeology.

Radiocarbon dating and other scientific dating methods developed in the 1940s and 1950s have continued to be improved and made more accurate. Scientists have also developed other methods for dating archaeological remains. Fission-track dating uses microscopic evidence of the fission of trace amounts of a uranium isotope (U^{238}) to date glass and inclusions in clay. Archaeomagnetic or paleomagnetic dating obtains dates by comparing the magnetic orientation of particles in clay ovens, burned walls, and other fired materials with past positions of the earth's magnetic pole. Obsidian hydration dating determines when an obsidian tool was last used by measuring the amount of water its surface layers have absorbed. And thermoluminescence dating determines when clay objects were last fired by measuring the amount of light emitted when they are subjected to high heat.[11]

Moreover, the scientist's contribution to archaeology is not finished once remains have been located, excavated, and dated. As archaeologists became more concerned with providing a complete picture of the vanished cultures they uncovered, they realized the necessity for scientific analysis of the finds. The materials submitted for study began to include everything from soil and bones to metal and pottery artifacts.

Many cultural features result from adaptation to the physical environment. So, if we are to fully understand vanished cultures, we must know the ecological conditions in which they developed. For such information, archaeologists again call on their colleagues in the natural sciences. Through analysis of a site's soil and rock formations, animal bones, pollen, seeds, and other remains of vegetation, scientists can reconstruct the ancient climate, flora, and fauna of the area. They can determine what animals were hunted or domesticated, and what crops were gathered or grown.

Even the bones of ancient people can contribute to our understanding of former ways of life. Too often in the past, skeletal remains were ignored or studied only to determine the population's racial type. But careful analysis of human physical remains can provide much more important information about a culture. It can supply information on

---

11. When its accuracy improves and its price declines, this method promises to be the most useful for the archaeologist, since pottery sherds are among the most plentiful artifacts at almost all post-Neolithic sites. Even in its present state, however, this method has been used to unmask several modern forgeries of clay plaques and statues.

diet, reveal some of the diseases that beset the population, and indicate the average life expectancy and genetic relationships within the culture and with other cultures. Such study can also throw light on the nature and quality of the available medical and dental care.

Scientific study of human remains can even throw new light on historical periods. In the late 1960s and early 1970s scholars X-rayed the mummies of ancient Egyptian pharaohs preserved in the Cairo museum. They used much better equipment than that available when the bodies were found late in the nineteenth century and early in this century. The X-ray project provided independent evidence for genetic relationships between the pharaohs and their ages at death that sometimes did not agree with information derived from written sources. The study also shed light on matters of customs, health, and hygiene little mentioned in texts. For example, it was learned that circumcision was not universal among the ancient Egyptians, as had been thought previously.

However, as Grahame Clark has pointed out, the archaeologist is still primarily concerned with artifacts. Even here, however, in the study of tools, weapons, buildings, and other examples of human handiwork, scientific analysis has its place.

> All too commonly these have been studied from a merely morphological point of view, as a means of distinguishing one culture from another and successive stages of development within each. Such methods of analysis, proper to art history, while sure of a place in the archaeologist's armoury, are no longer his principal weapon even in the most backward areas. Today the emphasis falls more on the effort to understand how the various peoples of antiquity in fact lived and artifacts are being studied more and more as sources of information about such broad topics as economy, technology, warfare, settlement, social organization and religion. The effect of this shift of emphasis has once more been to draw archaeology and the natural sciences closer together: whereas stylistic analysis requires no more than intuitive appreciation, it requires a wide range of more or less highly specialized scientific techniques and procedures to elicit full information about such things as the precise character and sources of raw materials, the techniques used to convert these into artifacts and the uses to which the finished objects were put.[12]

One of the most important pieces of information provided by scientific analysis of clay or metal artifacts is an indication of place of

---

12. G. Clark, in E. Brothwell and D. Higgs, eds., *Science in Archaeology* (London: Thames and Hudson, 1963), pp. 18–19.

manufacture. Every clay deposit or source of ore has its own distinct combination of minerals and trace amounts of rare elements. Scientists can determine the exact chemical composition of an artifact through the use of equipment such as the spectograph, flame photometer, petrological microscope, spectrophotometer, or electron probe microanalyzer. Comparison with deposits from the site where the artifact was found will then reveal whether the implement was produced locally or imported. When a sufficient number of sites has been studied in this way, it becomes possible to pinpoint exactly the sources of imported items. This information, in turn, throws much light on ancient trade patterns and cross-cultural contacts.

The techniques utilized to excavate the materials submitted for scientific study have also continued to evolve. By the 1970s many archaeologists were dissatisified with Wheeler's grid method of excavation. The method provided excellent information on stratigraphy and chronology, but it was so time-consuming that only a few small areas of large sites could be dug. As archaeologists turned more and more from concerns with chronology to attempts to reconstruct past ways of life, they wanted to uncover larger areas of each stratum. This concern with the spacial relationships of the remains led to the development of what is known as open-area or simply area excavation. Archaeologists using this method uncover large areas of a site and cut vertical sections only when they are needed to clarify the stratigraphy of a particular locus or feature. This is combined with more detailed recording of remains made possible by the use of notebook computers.

Today, archaeologists use both excavation methods, as well as combinations of the two designed to fit individual sites. In addition, because of their interest in ancient ecology, excavators spend more time trying to recover animal and plant remains. They often put large amounts of soil through screens or sieves to find small animal bones and other tiny artifacts. And some use elaborate water flotation systems to recover even smaller and lighter carbonized vegetable, insect, and molluscan remains.

Employment of careful excavation techniques, high-tech equipment, and scientific analysis of finds have made archaeologists much less colorful than they were in days gone by. The likes of "Indiana Jones" have no place in the profession today. But that does not mean that dramatic and spectacular discoveries have come to an end. In recent decades the Leakeys and others have uncovered fossils of earlier and earlier human ancestors in Africa. Cuneiform specialists discovered a previously unknown early Semitic language when Italian archaeologists found an archive of tablets at Ebla in Syria. On the island of

Thera in the Aegean, Greek archaeologists are unearthing a Minoan town buried in a volcanic eruption that occurred some 1,600 years earlier than the one that destroyed Pompeii. Chinese archaeologists continue to excavate the army of life-size terra cotta statues found guarding the tomb of China's first emperor. Maya hieroglyphic writing has finally been deciphered, allowing scholars to write the first true history of the Maya.

Such discoveries still thrill not only the archaeologist, but the general public as well. Today, as in the past, there is a widespread feeling of mingled excitement, exultation, and awe whenever a new find unlocks a door to the past and restores to us a portion of our heritage as human beings. Some intellectual purists have decried archaeology's capacity to "entertain" the masses. Thankfully, it continues to do so. Only the interest and support of the public will continue to ensure archaeology's growth, political support, and funding.

Looking to the Future

Archaeology is still a young discipline. Despite over a century and a half of excavation, archaeologists are still in the initial stages of their quest for an understanding of humanity's past. Many areas of the world have not received more than the most rudimentary investigation. Even in those areas that have been most intensely studied, the number of uninvestigated sites still outnumber by a large margin those that have been excavated. In addition, previous excavations and published reports must be reexamined periodically in the light of new techniques, new discoveries, and new questions.

There are also many challenges facing the present generation of archaeologists. Population growth, industrialization, neglect, and looting are causing widespread devastation to archaeological sites. Thousands of sites around the world have been destroyed by developers before being excavated. In addition, well-known monuments like the Parthenon in Athens and Egypt's Great Sphinx, temples, and tomb paintings are now slowly deteriorating, victims of air pollution, changes in the underground water table, and other changes in the environment brought about in recent times. Some way has to be found to balance the need for study of the past with the need for growth and development for the future. We need to devise measures that will protect archaeological monuments both from their environments and from increasing

Fig. 72. Garden of the restored House of the Vettii at Pompeii. The sculptures that once stood in this garden were stolen by professional antiquities thieves in 1978. (Photograph by the author.)

numbers of tourists, while still keeping them somewhat accessible to the public.

Another problem is the worldwide antiquities market. Although antiquities collecting and traffic in artifacts were responsible for some of the early growth and development of archaeology, they have usually resulted in more loss than gain. Objects taken from a site and sold individually lose their context and cultural associations. Today, the market for antiquities is leading some individuals to loot and vandalize archaeological sites on a scale comparable to that of the early and mid-nineteenth century, before most countries passed antiquities laws.

For example, although the site was guarded, in 1978 thieves entered Pompeii during the night, stole coins and other objects from the museum on the site and carried off a number of sculptures from the garden of the House of the Vettii (Fig. 72). In the past, all such sculptures had been placed in the museum in Naples. But archaeologists had decided to leave the original statues and herms in the garden of this one restored dwelling. The works that were taken were quite heavy, so obviously the thieves came well-prepared with the proper equipment.

In recent years professional antiquities thieves have also cut reliefs out of Etruscan tombs, French megalithic tombs, and Egyptian tombs.

They have hacked off parts of Asian temples and Maya stelae. And they have robbed several major museums, including the National Museum of Anthropology in Mexico City.

Because of the connection between the antiquities trade and such looting and stealing, in 1970 the University Museum of the University of Pennsylvania announced that it would no longer buy or accept objects that lacked a reliable provenance and proof of legitimate excavation. The British Museum and other museums in Britain's Museums' Association followed suit. They too now refuse to buy antiquities lacking dependable documentation. However, this is only a first step in ending the profitable trade in antiquities.

The past two decades have also seen several conflicts between archaeologists and various ethnic groups over the treatment of finds, especially burial remains. As nationalism and ethnic consciousness continue to increase, such conflicts will become more common. In the future, various archaeological associations will probably follow the lead of the Society for American Archaeology, which, while recognizing the need for continued study of human remains, has stated that the concerns and beliefs of different cultures should also be respected.

> Human skeletal materials must at all times be treated with dignity and respect. Commercial exploitation of ancient human remains is abhorrent. Whatever their ultimate disposition, all human remains should receive appropriate scientific study, should be responsibly and carefully conserved, and should be accessible only for legitimate scientific or educational purposes.[13]

Clearly, there is much left to be done. But the future of archaeology is bright. The application of scientific techniques to archaeological problems has already produced results that not only were unknown, but in some instances were considered unknowable, only a generation ago. Undoubtedly, such advances will continue to be made.

Archaeology has made great strides over the last two centuries, and sometimes we moderns are tempted to be smug about the superiority of our methods and technology. But reviewing the story of archaeology's past should teach us humility. The excavation techniques, explanatory models, and scientific approach of which we are so proud are the end products of a long development. It is important to remember that we can see so much better than even the greatest of our fore-

---

13. Statement concerning the treatment of human remains adopted by the Society for American Archaeology.

bears because we are standing on their shoulders.

The preceding pages have recorded many blunders and missed opportunities as well as triumphs and advances. It is natural to feel regret when we consider the many false turns of scholarship and all of the evidence that has been destroyed. But it is sobering to realize that the future probably will judge our era in the same way. Undoubtedly historians in coming generations will decry the "primitive" archaeological methods of the 1990s as we do those of the eighteenth and nineteenth centuries. We can only hope that they also will recognize that, like most of our predecessors, we were doing the best we could with what we had.

Appendix

Major Events and Discoveries in the History of Archaeology

1446   Alberti finds two Roman ships at the bottom of Lake Nemi, Italy

1517   Hernandez de Córdoba discovers Maya cities in Yucatan

1519   Hernando Cortéz begins his conquest of the Aztec empire in Mexico

1532   Pizarro invades Peru and destroys the Inca empire

1535   Demarchi uses an early diving suit to investigate the Lake Nemi ships

1539   Hernando de Soto explores the southeastern United States noting many mounds

1553   Etruscan bronzes ("the Chimera" and "Minerva") found at Arezzo

1556   Etruscan bronze statue, "The Orator" found

1563   Leo Africanus's description of Africa published

1566   Diego de Landa, *Relacion de las casas de Yucatán*

1583   J. Eldred, *The Voyage of M. John Eldred to Trypolis in Syria by Sea and from Thence by Land and River to Babylon and Balsara*

1609   Garcilaso de la Vega, *The Royal Commentaries of the Incas*

1628   The *Vasa* sinks on her maiden voyage out of Stockholm harbor

1646   John Greaves's *Pyramidographia* summarizes what was then known about the pyramids of Egypt

1650   Archbishop Ussher publishes his biblical chronology; William Dugdale, *History of Warwickshire*

1663   Pietro della Valle describes Mesopotamian sites and brings inscribed bricks back to Europe

1664   Hans von Treileben salvages most of *Vasa's* cannon

1669   Nicholas Steno ascribes geological features to natural causes

1678   Jean Tavernier, *The Six Voyages of Tavernier through Turkey into Asia*

1681   R. Knox, *An Historical Relation of Ceylon, together with Somewhat Concerning Remarkable Passages of My Life*

1690   John Conyers finds the bones of an "elephant" with a stone axe in England

1707   Edward Lhwyd, *Archaeologia Britannica*

1709   The theater of Herculaneum found near Naples—D'Elbeuf's excavations begin

1723   Dempster's *De Etruria Regali*

1726   Academia Etrusca founded at Cortona in Italy

1737   Antonio Gori, *Museum Etruscum*

1738   Excavations resumed at Herculaneum under Alcubierre

1740   William Stuckeley, *Stonehenge, A Temple Restored to the British Druids*

1743   Richard Pococke, *A Description of the East, and Some Other Countries*

1748   Alcubierre begins excavations at Pompeii

1751   Society of Antiquaries of London founded

1757   Frederick Norden, *Travels in Egypt and Nubia*

1764   J. Winckelmann, *History of Ancient Art*

1774   J. Esper uncovers human remains with those of an extinct bear in a German cave

1775   James Adair, *History of the American Indian*

1776   Karsten Niebuhr, *Voyage en Arabie*

1780   Thomas Jefferson excavates an Indian burial mound near Monticello; L'Abbe de Beauchamp examines Mesopotamian mounds

1784   The Asiatic Society of Bengal founded in Calcutta, India

1785   James Hutton, *Theory of the Earth*

1787   Del Rio explores Palenque; Rufus Putnam studies mounds near Marietta, Ohio

1789   Lanzi's *Saggio di Lingua Etrusca*

1790   A Hindu temple containing a pot of Roman coins discovered north of Madras in India

1797   J. Frere finds stone tools stratified beneath a layer containing fossils of extinct species

1798   Napoleon's Egyptian expedition
1802   Grotefend deciphers twelve Persian cuneiform signs
1803   Lord Elgin begins removing the Parthenon sculptures; Vivant Denon, *Travels in Upper and Lower Egypt*
1805   Dupaix and Castaneda explore pre-Spanish ruins in Mexico
1808   C. Rich appointed British resident in Baghdad
1809   Publication of *Description de l'Egypte* begun
1810   Humboldt's survey of the pre-Spanish monuments of the Americas appears; J. Seely visits the cave-temples of Ellora in India
1811   Cockerell and von Hallerstein uncover a Greek temple on the island of Aegina
1812   Dr. J. McCulloh examines mounds in Ohio; the American Antiquarian Society founded; Burckhardt discovers Petra
1814   Thomas Young deciphers the hieroglyphic writing of the names Cleopatra and Ptolemy
1815   Belzoni begins his career in Egypt; C. Rich, *Memoir on the Ruins of Babylon*
1816   C. Thomsen arranges Danish antiquities according to the Three Age system; William Smith, *Strata Identified by Organized Fossils*
1818   Rich, *Second Memoir on the Ruins of Babylon*
1820   The Venus de Milo (or Aphrodite of Melos) found on Melos with other pieces of marble intended for a lime kiln; Caleb Atwater, *Description of the Antiquities Discovered in the State of Ohio and Other Western States*
1821   Rich visits Kuyunjik and Nebi Yunus across from Mosul in Mesopotamia; Lelorrain removes the Dendera zodiac from Egypt
1822   Champollion announces his decipherment of Egyptian hieroglyphics; Del Rio's *Description of the Ruins of an Ancient City, Discovered Near Palenque* published
1824   McEnery begins excavating in Kent's Cavern, England
1826   F. Cailliaud, *Voyage à Méroé*
1827   A large diving bell used in an attempt to excavate the Lake Nemi ships in Italy; Dupaix's report and Castañeda's drawings of Palenque used in Baradere's *Antiquités Mexicaines*
1829   Instituto di Correspondenza Archaeologica founded in Italy; a French expedition explores and excavates in the Peloponnesus in Greece; Schmerling finds human bones with those of extinct species beneath a stalagmite crust in a Belgian cave
1830   Charles Lyell, *Principles of Geology*: Lord Kingsborough begins publishing *Antiquities of Mexico*
1835   H. Rawlinson copies inscriptions on the Behistun rock

1836   Thomsen's guide book to the Danish Museum sets forth the Three Age system; Rich, *Narrative of a Residence in Koordistan*; A. Gallatin, *A Synopsis of the Indian Tribes Within the United States*

1837   Rawlinson deciphers and translates the first half of the Old Persian cuneiform inscription from Behistun; Greek Archaeological Society founded; J. Boucher de Perthes begins excavating in the Sommes gravel deposits

1838   W. Harrison, *Discourse on the Aborigines of the Valley of the Ohio*; Waldeck, *Voyage pittoresque et archaeologique dans . . . Yucatan*

1839   Stephens and Catherwood at Copán; S. Morton, *Crania Americana*

1841   J. Stephens, *Incidents of Travel in Central America, Chipas and Yucatan*

1842   J. Worsaae, *Danmarks Oldtid*; Byres, *Hypogaei, or the Sepulchral Cavarns of Tarquinia*; Lepsius leads the Prussian expedition in Egypt; the American Ethnological Society founded

1843   Botta begins his excavations at Khorsabad; Prescott, *History of the Conquest of Mexico*; Stephens, *Incidents of Travel in Yucatan*; the British Archaeological Association founded

1845   Layard begins excavating Nimrud

1846   The Smithsonian Institution founded; H. Rawlinson, *The Persian Cuneiform Inscription of Behistun* (a complete translation)

1847   Prescott, *History of the Conquest of Peru*

1848   G. Dennis, *Cities and Cemeteries of Etruria*; A. H. Layard, *Nineveh and Its Remains*; E. Squier and E. Davis, *Ancient Monuments of the Mississippi Valley*

1849   J. Worsaae, *Primeval Antiquities of Denmark*; P. Botta and E. Flandin, *Monument de Nineve*; Layard and H. Rassam excavate at Kuyunjik

1850   A. Mariette discovers and excavates the Serapeum in Egypt; W. Loftus works at Warka in Mesopotamia

1851   V. Place resumes the excavation of Khorsabad

1853   "Stilt-villages" found in Swiss lakes; Rassam finds Asshurbanipal's palace at Kuyunjik

1855   Alexander Rhind conducts careful excavations in Egypt; S. Haven, *Archaeology of the United States*

1856   C. Markham, *Cuzco: A Journey to the Ancient Capital of Peru*

1857   J. Messikommer's excavation of a stilt-village in Switzerland provides stratigraphical support for the Three Age system; F. Schwab salvages artifacts from the underwater mound, La Tène;

the decipherment of Akkadian cuneiform texts recognized; first
Neanderthal skull found
1858   Mariette named conservator of Egyptian monuments
1859   J. Evans and J. Prestwich recognize the antiquity of man; W.
Pengelly excavates Windmill Hill Cave; C. Darwin, *Origin of
Species*
1860   G. Fiorelli systematizes the excavations at Pompeii
1861   P. Rosa begins his excavations on the Palatine Hill in Rome;
A. Cunningham becomes first surveyor general of the Archaeological Survey of India
1863   E. G. Squier excavates at Moche, Peru; J. T. Wood discovers
ancient Ephesus in Turkey and begins excavations; the "Winged
Victory" statue found on Samothrace in the Aegean; R. Foote
finds Paleolithic artifacts near Madras, India; C. Lyell, *The
Geological Evidences of the Antiquity of Man*
1866   The Palestine Exploration Fund established
1867   J. Thompson, *The Antiquities of Cambodia*
1868   L. Lartet discovers a cave burial at Cro-Magnon in France
1869   H. Schliemann digs at Ithaca and publishes *Ithaka, the
Peloponnese and Troy*; J. Oppert identifies the Sumerians
1870   Schliemann begins excavating Hissarlik (Troy) in Turkey
1871   K. Mauch discovers Great Zimbabwe in southern Africa;
C. Humann finds the Altar of Zeus at Pergamon in Turkey;
C. Darwin, *The Descent of Man*; E. Tylor, *Primitive Culture*
1872   George Smith discovers the Mesopotamian flood story
1873   A. Conze excavates on Samothrace in the Aegean
1874   Schliemann excavates Grave Circle "A" at Mycenae
1875   E. Curtius begins work at Olympia, Greece
1877   E. de Sarzec begins excavating Telloh in southern Mesopotamia; E. Morse excavates Neolithic shell-mounds at Omori, Japan;
L. Morgan, *Ancient Society: or Researches in the Lines of Human
Progress from Savagery through Barbarism to Civilization*
1878   Schliemann returns to Troy; the Smithsonian Institution
establishes the Bureau of American Ethnology
1879   Paleolithic paintings found in a cave at Altamira, Spain; the
Archaeological Institute of America founded
1880   Pitt Rivers begins excavating Cranborne Chase; W. M. F. Petrie
begins his work in Egypt
1881   G. Maspero begins work in Egypt; A. Maudslay begins his study
of Maya sites
1882   The Egyptian Exploration Fund organized in London
1884   Schliemann and Dörpfeld excavate at Tiryns

1885   E. Thompson visits Chichén Itzá and locates the "Sacred Well";
        O. Montelius, *Sur la Chronologie l'Age du Bronze*
1887   The Amarna tablets discovered at el-Amarna in Egypt; Pitt
        Rivers begins publishing *Excavations at Cranborne Chase*
1888   The University of Pennsylvania begins its excavations at Niffar
        (Nippur) in Mesopotamia
1890   Petrie excavates at Tell el-Hesi in Palestine
1891   E. Dubois finds remains of Java Man in central Java; T. Bent
        excavates at Great Zimbabwe in Africa; the Harvard Peabody
        Museum expedition begins work in Honduras
1894   Cyrus Thomas, *Report on Mound Exploration*
1895   Engravings found on a cave wall at La Mouthe, France; Borghi
        retrieves some objects from the Lake Nemi ships
1896   Max Uhle begins stratigraphic excavations at Pachacamac, Peru
1897   Cave drawings found at Pair-non-Pair, France
1899   R. Koldewey begins excavating Babylon
1900   A. Evans begins work at Knossos in Crete; an ancient wreck
        is found beneath the Mediterranean Sea near the island of
        Anitkythera
1901   C. Tsountas excavates at Sesklo in Greece; J. Marshall becomes
        director of the reorganized Archaeological Survey of India
1902   W. Andrae begins work at Asshur in Mesopotamia; R. Hall
        and W. Neal, *The Ancient Ruins of Rhodesia*
1904   G. Reisner starts excavating the mastaba cemetery at Giza; E.
        Thompson begins exploring the well at Chichén Itzá
1906   H. Winckler begins excavating Boghazköy and uncovers a large
        Hittite cuneiform archive
1907   A. Merlin finds an ancient wreck off Mahdia, Tunisia; A. Stein
        discovers a library of early Chinese texts in one of the "Caves
        of the Thousand Buddhas" at Ch'ien Fo Tung, China
1908   C. Tsountas, *Prehistoric Acropolis of Dimini and Sesklo*
1911   H. Bingham discovers Machu Picchu in Peru; M. Gamio con-
        ducts stratigraphic excavations at Atzcapotzalco, Mexico
1913   N. Nelson excavates stratigraphically in the Galisteo Basin, New
        Mexico
1915   C. Blegen excavates Korakou near Corinth, Greece; A. Kidder
        begins work at Pecos Pueblo, New Mexico; F. Hrozný announces
        his decipherment of Hittite
1920   A. Wace begins his work at Mycenae
1921   The Archaeological Survey of India begins excavations at
        Harappa and Mohenjo-daro in the Indus Valley; J. G. Andersson
        finds the first evidence of "Peking Man" at Chou-kou-tien near

Beijing; A. Evans begins publishing *The Palace of Minos*

1922 H. Carter discovers Tutankhamun's tomb in Egypt; C. L. Woolley begins work at Ur in Mesopotamia

1924 A. Kidder, *An Introduction to the Study of Southwestern Archaeology*

1925 A bronze statue of Apollo dredged from the Bay of Marathon; Paleolithic flint points found at Folsum, New Mexico; the Oriental Institute of the University of Chicago begins its excavation of Megiddo in Palestine; V. G. Childe, *The Dawn of European Civilization*

1926 W. F. Albright begins his excavations at Tell Beit Mirsim in Palestine

1928 The Archaeological Section of the Institute of History and Philology of the Academia Sinica established and begins excavations at Anyang, a Bronze Age capital of China

1929 G. Caton-Thompson excavates at Great Zimbabwe and shows it is African in origin; excavations begin at Ras Shamra (ancient Ugarit) in Syria, where an archive of cuneiform tablets (including many in a West Semitic language) would be found; Childe, *The Danube in Prehistory*

1932 C. Blegen begins work at Troy; a royal burial ground with gold treasures found at Mapungubwe in South Africa; Lake Nemi ships exposed in Italy

1934 Excavations begin at Tell Hariri, Syria (ancient Mari), where a great cuneiform archive from the seventeenth century B.C. would be found

1936 V. G. Childe, *Man Makes Himself*

1939 C. Blegen discovers a Mycenaean palace and Linear B tablets at Pylos in Greece

1940 Paleolithic paintings found in the Lascaux Cave in France

1943 Mortimer Wheeler becomes director-general of antiquities in India

1947 Bedouin find ancient scrolls in a cave by the Dead Sea

1948 W. Taylor, *A Study of Archaeology*

1949 W. Libby announces the development of radiocarbon (C^{14}) dating

1952 J. Cousteau excavates a Roman wreck off Grand Congloué island near Marseilles; K. Kenyon begins her excavations at Jericho; M. Ventris announces his decipherment of the Mycenaean script, Linear B; A. Ruz Lhuillier discovers an unlooted Maya tomb inside the Temple of Inscriptions at Palenque

1956 A. Franzen locates the remains of the *Vasa* at the bottom of Stockholm harbor and plans are made to raise it to the surface

1959   Mary and Louis Leakey uncover remains of an early hominid in the Oduvai Gorge of Tanganyika

1960   G. Bass uses new methods to excavate a thirteenth-century B.C. wreck at Cape Gelidonya, Turkey; documents from the Second Jewish Revolt (A.D. 132–135) found in the Cave of Letters near the Dead Sea (Nahal Hever, Israel)

1961   Excavations begin at Çatal Huyuk, a Neolithic town in Turkey; Bass develops even better underwater methods during work at Yassi Ada, Turkey; a Viking settlement found at L'Anse aux Meadows, Newfoundland

1962   Excavations at Kata Zakros in eastern Crete reveal a Minoan palace; L. Binford's "Archaeology as Anthropology" (American Antiquity 28) heralds the start of the "New Archaeology"

1963   Y. Yadin begins his excavation of Masada in Israel

1967   S. Marinatos begins excavating Akrotiri, a Minoan town on the volcanic island of Thera in the Aegean

1969   Israeli excavations begin in the Old City of Jerusalem

1972   Many gold objects found in a Copper Age cemetery near Lake Varna in Bulgaria

1974   Chinese archaeologists find a terra cotta army guarding the tomb of the first Ch'in emperor near the city of Xian

1975   An archive of Early Bronze Age tablets, many of them in a previously unknown Semitic language, found at Tell Mardikh (ancient Ebla) in Syria

1976   D. Johanson finds remains of "Lucy," an early hominid, in Africa

1977   The tomb of Philip II of Macedon found intact at Vergina in Greece

1979   Underwater archaeologists begin work in Herod's harbor at Caesarea, Israel

1984   G. Bass finds a fourteenth-century B.C. shipwreck at Ulu-Burun, Turkey

1987   Excavation of the Villa of the Papyri at Herculaneum resumes after more than two hundred years

1990   The tomb of Caiphas found in Jerusalem

1991   Maya hieroglyphs fully deciphered

Recommended Reading

General Reading

Casson, Stanley. *The Discovery of Man: The Story of the Inquiry into Human Origins.* New York: Harper and Brothers, 1939.

Ceram, C. W. *Gods, Graves and Scholars.* 2nd ed. New York: Alfred A. Knopf, 1967.

———. *Hands on the Past.* New York: Alfred A. Knopf, 1966.

Cleator, P. E. *Lost Languages.* New York: John Day, 1959.

Daniel, Glyn. *150 Years of Archaeology.* London: Gerald Duckworth, 1975.

———. *The Origins and Growth of Archaeology.* Baltimore: Penguin, 1967.

———. *A Short History of Archaeology.* London: Thames and Hudson, 1981.

Deuel, Leo. *Testaments of Time: The Search for Lost Manuscripts and Records.* Baltimore: Penguin, 1965.

Fagan, Brian M. *The Adventure of Archaeology.* Washington, D.C.: National Geographic Society, 1985.

———. *Quest for the Past: Great Discoveries in Archaeology.* Prospect Heights, Ill.: Waveland Press, 1978.

Hawkes, Jacquetta. *The World of the Past.* Two volumes. New York: Alfred A. Knopf, 1963.

Heizer, Robert, ed. *Man's Discovery of His Past: Literary Landmarks in Archaeology.* Englewood Cliffs, N.J.: Prentice-Hall, 1962.

Norman, Bruce. *Footsteps: Nine Archaeological Journeys of Romance and Discovery.* Topsfield, Mass.: Salem House, 1988.

Trigger, Brian G. *A History of Archaeological Thought.* Cambridge: Cambridge University Press, 1989.

Winstone, H. V. F. *Uncovering the Ancient World.* New York: Facts on File, 1987.

Chapter 1: The Discovery of Prehistory

Bibby, Geoffrey. *The Testimony of the Spade.* New York: Alfred A. Knopf, 1956.

Bowden, Mark. *Pitt Rivers: The Life and Archaeological Work of Lieutenant-General Augustus Henry Lane Fox Pitt Rivers.* Cambridge: Cambridge University Press, 1991.

Daniel, Glyn, and Colin Renfrew. *The Idea of Prehistory.* New York: Columbia University Press, 1988.

Daniel, Glyn. *The Three Ages.* Cambridge: Cambridge University Press, 1943.

Gillispie, Charles C. *Genesis and Geology: A Study in the Relations of Scientific Thought, Natural Theology and Social Opinion in Great Britain, 1790-1850.* Cambridge, Mass.: Harvard University Press, 1951.

Gräslund, B. *The Birth of Prehistoric Chronology.* Cambridge: Cambridge University Press, 1987.

Grayson, D. K. *The Establishment of Human Antiquity.* New York: Academic Press, 1983.

Haber, Francis C. *The Age of the World: Moses to Darwin.* Baltimore: Johns Hopkins Press, 1959.

Klindt-Jensen, O. *A History of Scandinavian Archaeology.* London: Thames and Hudson, 1975.

Sklenár, K. *Archaeology in Central Europe: The First 500 Years.* New York: St. Martin's Press, 1983.

Thompson, Michael. *General Pitt Rivers: Evolution and Archaeology in the Nineteenth Century.* Bradford-on-Avon: Moonraker Press, 1977.

Walters, Henry B. *The English Antiquaries of the Sixteenth, Seventeenth and Eighteenth Centuries.* London: Edward Walters, 1934.

Wendt, Herbert. *In Search of Adam: The Story of Man's Quest for the Truth About His Earliest Ancestors.* Boston: Houghton Mifflin, 1956.

For what has been learned about human origins and prehistory:

Brothwell, Don. *The Bog Man and the Archaeology of People.* London: British Museum, 1986.

Campbell, Bernard G. *Humankind Emerging.* 6th ed. New York: HarperCollins, 1992.

Fagan, Brian M. *People of the Earth: An Introduction to World Prehistory.* 7th ed. New York: HarperCollins, 1992.

Gowlett, J. *Ascent to Civilization: The Archaeology of Early Man.* New York: Alfred A. Knopf, 1984.

Milisauskas, Sarunas. *European Prehistory.* New York: Academic Press, 1978.

Renfrew, Colin. *Before Civilization: The Radiocarbon Revolution and Prehistoric Europe.* New York: Cambridge University Press, 1979.

Wenke, Robert J. *Patterns in Prehistory: Humankind's First Three Million Years.* 3rd ed. New York: Oxford University Press, 1990.

Chapter 2: Retrieving Egypt's Distant Past

Baikie, James. *A Century of Excavation in the Land of the Pharaohs.* London: The Religious Tract Society, 1926.

Bratton, Fred G. *A History of Egyptian Archaeology.* New York: Crowell, 1968.

Cottrell, Leonard. *The Lost Pharaohs.* New York: Holt, Rinehart and Winston, 1961.

———. *The Mountains of Pharaoh.* New York: Rinehart and Co., 1956.

Davies, W. V. *Egyptian Hieroglyphs.* Vol. 6 of *Reading the Past.* Berkeley: University of California Press, 1987.

Fagan, Brian M. *The Rape of the Nile.* New York: Charles Scribner's Sons, 1975.

Greener, Leslie. *The Discovery of Egypt.* London: Cassell and Co., 1966.

Mertz, Barbara. *Temples, Tombs and Hieroglyphs: A Popular History of Ancient Egypt.* Rev. ed. New York: Dodd, Mead and Co., 1978.

Romer, John. *Valley of the Kings.* New York: Holt, Rinehart and Winston, 1981.

Wilson, John A. *Signs and Wonders Upon Pharaoh: A History of American Egyptology.* Chicago: The University of Chicago Press, 1964.

Wortham, John D. *The Genesis of British Egyptology, 1549-1906.* Norman, Okla.: University of Oklahoma Press, 1971.

For interesting and reliable summaries of what has been learned about ancient Egyptian history and civilization:

Aldred, Cyril. *The Egyptians.* Rev. ed. New York: Thames and Hudson, 1984.

David, A. Rosalie. *The Egyptian Kingdoms.* New York: Peter Bedrick, 1975.

James, T. G. H. *Ancient Egypt: The Land and Its Legacy.* Austin: University of Texas Press, 1988.

————. *The Archaeology of Ancient Egypt.* London: The Bodley Head, 1972.

————. *Pharaoh's People: Scenes from Life in Imperial Egypt.* London: The Bodley Head, 1984.

Kemp, Barry J. *Ancient Egypt: Anatomy of a Civilization.* New York: Routledge, Chapman and Hall, 1992.

Romer, John. *People of the Nile.* New York: Crown, 1982.

Ruffle, John. *The Egyptians.* Ithaca, N.Y.: Cornell University Press, 1977.

Chapter 3: The Rediscovery of Near Eastern Civilizations

Budge, E. A. Wallis. *The Rise and Progress of Assyriology.* London: Martin Hopkinson, 1925.

Ceram, C. W. *The Secret of the Hittites: The Discovery of an Ancient Empire.* New York: Alfred A. Knopf, 1955.

Duel, Leo. *The Treasures of Time: Firsthand Accounts by Famous Archaeologists of Their Work in the Near East.* New York: World Publishing, 1961.

Fagan, Brian M. *Return to Babylon: Travelers, Archaeologists and Monuments in Mesopotamia.* Boston: Little, Brown, 1979.

Gadd, Cyril J. *The Stones of Assyria.* London: Chatto and Windus, 1936.

Hilprecht, H. V. *Explorations in Bible Lands During the Nineteenth Century.* Philadelphia: A. J. Holman, 1903. (The section on Mesopotamia was reissued in 1904 as a separate volume, *The Excavations in Assyria and Babylonia.*)

Kubie, Nora B. *Road to Nineveh: The Adventures and Excavations of Sir Austen Henry Layard.* Garden City, N.Y.: Doubleday, 1964.

Lloyd, Seton. *Foundations in the Dust: A Story of Mesopotamian Exploration.* Rev. ed. London: Thames and Hudson, 1980.

Meade, C. W. *Road to Babylon: The Development of U.S. Assyriology.* Leiden: E. J. Brill, 1974.

Shepherd, Naomi. *The Zealous Intruders: The Western Rediscovery of Palestine.* San Francisco: Harper and Row, 1987.

Silberman, Neil Asher. *Digging for God and Country: Exploration, Archaeology, and the Secret Struggle for the Holy Land, 1799-1917.* New York: Alfred A. Knopf, 1982.

For interesting and reliable summaries of what has been learned about the archaeology, history, and civilization of various ancient Near Eastern cultures:

Aharoni, Yohanan. *The Archaeology of the Land of Israel.* Philadelphia: Westminster Press, 1978.

Akurgal, Ekrem. *Ancient Civilizations and Ruins of Turkey.* Istanbul: Haset Kitabevi, 1983.

Curtis, John. *Ancient Persia.* Cambridge, Mass.: Harvard University Press, 1990.

Gurney, Oliver R. *The Hittites.* Revised edition. New York: Penguin, 1981.

Hinz, Walther. *The Lost World of Elam: Re-creation of a Vanished Civilization.* New York: New York University Press, 1973.

Lloyd, Seton. *The Archaeology of Mesopotamia.* London: Thames and Hudson, 1978.

Macqueen, J. G. *The Hittites and Their Contemporaries in Asia Minor.* Revised edition. New York and London: Thames and Hudson, 1986.

Mazar, Amihai. *Archaeology of the Land of the Bible, 10,000–586 B.C.E.* New York: Doubleday, 1990.

Mellaart, James. *The Archaeology of Ancient Turkey.* Totowa, N.J.: Rowman and Littlefield, 1978.

Postgate, Nicholas. *Early Mesopotamia: Economy and Society at the Dawn of History.* New York: Routledge, Chapman and Hall, 1992.

Redford, Donald B. *Egypt, Canaan, and Israel in Ancient Times.* Princeton, N.J.: Princeton University Press, 1992.

Roux, Georges. *Ancient Iraq.* Revised edition. New York: Penguin, 1980.

Saggs, H. W. F. *The Greatness That Was Babylon.* Revised edition. London: Sidgwick and Jackson, 1988.

———. *The Might That Was Assyria.* London: Sidgwick and Jackson, 1984.

Chapter 4: The Growth of Aegean Archaeology

Cottrell, Leonard. *The Bull of Minos.* New York: Holt, Rinehart and Winston, 1958.

Deuel, Leo. *Memoirs of Heinrich Schliemann: A Documentary Portrait Drawn from His Autobiographical Writings, Letters and Excavation Reports.* London: Hutchinson, 1978.

Evans, Joan. *Time and Chance: The Story of Arthur Evans and His Forebears.* London: Longmans, Green, 1943.

Horowitz, Sylvia L. *The Find of a Lifetime: Sir Arthur Evans and the Discovery of Knossos.* New York: Viking Press, 1981.

Ludwig, Emil. *Schliemann: The Story of a Gold-seeker.* Boston: Little, Brown, 1932.

McDonald, William A., and Carol G. Thomas. *Progress Into the Past: The Rediscovery of Mycenaean Civilization.* 2nd ed. Bloomington, Ind.: Indiana University Press, 1990.

Michaelis, Adolf. *A Century of Archaeological Discoveries.* New York: E. P. Dutton, 1908.

Stoneman, Richard. *Land of Lost Gods: The Search for Classical Greece.* Norman, Okla.: University of Oklahoma Press, 1987.

Tsigakou, Fani-Maria. *The Rediscovery of Greece: Travellers and Painters of the Romantic Era.* New York: Caratzas Brothers, 1981.

Wood, Michael. *In Search of the Trojan War.* New York: Facts on File, 1985.

For summaries of the archaeology and history of Greece and the Aegean area:

Biers, William R. *The Archaeology of Greece: An Introduction.* Revised edition. Ithaca, N.Y.: Cornell University Press, 1987.

Blegen, Carl W. *Troy and the Trojans.* New York: Frederick A. Praeger, 1963.

Doumas, Christos. *Thera: Pompeii of the Ancient Aegean.* London: Thames and Hudson, 1983.

Grant, Michael. *The Classical Greeks.* New York: Charles Scribner's Sons, 1989.

———. *From Alexander to Cleopatra: The Hellenistic World.* New York: Charles Scribner's Sons, 1982.

———. *The Rise of the Greeks.* New York: Charles Scribner's Sons, 1987.

Hood, Sinclair. *The Minoans: The Story of Bronze Age Crete.* New York: Frederick A. Praeger, 1971.

MacKendrick, Paul. *The Greek Stones Speak: The Story of Archaeology in Greek Lands.* Rev. ed. New York: Norton, 1982.

Taylour, William. *The Mycenaeans.* Revised edition. London: Thames and Hudson, 1983.

Willetts, R. F. *The Civilization of Ancient Crete.* London: Batsford, 1977.

Chapter 5: Recovering the Remains of Ancient Italy

Brion, Marcel. *Pompeii and Herculaneum: The Glory and the Grief.* New York: Crown Publishers, 1960.

Corti, Egon C. *The Death and Resurrection of Pompeii and Herculaneum.* London: Routledge and Kegan Paul, 1951.

Deiss, Joseph J. *Herculaneum: Italy's Buried Treasure.* New York: Harper and Row, 1985.

Grant, Michael. *Cities of Vesuvius: Pompeii and Herculaneum.* London: Weidenfeld and Nicolson, 1971.

Grimal, Pierre. *In Search of Ancient Italy.* London: Evans Brothers, 1964.

Lanciani, Rudolfo A. *The Destruction of Ancient Rome.* London: Macmillan and Co., 1901.

Wellard, James. *The Search for the Etruscans.* New York: Saturday Review Press, 1973.

For information on the archaeological remains and history of the civilizations of ancient Italy:

Arnott, Peter. *The Romans and Their World.* New York: St. Martin's Press, 1970.

Finley, M. I. *Ancient Sicily.* London: Chatto and Windus, 1979.

Grant, Michael. *Cities of Vesuvius: Pompeii and Herculaneum.* New York: Macmillan, 1971.

———. *The Etruscans.* New York: Charles Scribner's Sons, 1980.

Holloway, R. Ross. *The Archaeology of Ancient Sicily.* New York: Routledge, Chapman and Hall, 1991.

MacKendrick, Paul. *The Mute Stones Speak: The Story of Archaeology in Italy.* 2nd ed. New York: Norton, 1983.

Macnamara, Ellen. *The Etruscans.* Cambridge, Mass.: Harvard University Press, 1991.

Chapter 6: Unearthing the New World's Past

Brunhouse, Robert L. *In Search of the Maya: The First Archaeologists.* Alburquerque, N.M.: University of New Mexico Press, 1973.

Deuel, Leo. *Conquistadors Without Swords: Archaeologists in the Americas.* New York: St. Martin's, 1967.

Fagan, Brian M. *Elusive Treasure: The Story of Early Archaeologists in the Americas.* New York: Scribners, 1977.

Fitting, James E., ed. *The Development of North American Archaeology: Essays in the History of Regional Traditions.* Garden City, N.Y.: Anchor Books, 1973.

Gallenkamp, Charles. *Maya: The Riddle and Rediscovery of a Lost*

Civilization. 3rd rev. ed. New York: Penguin, 1987.
Willey, Gordon R., and Jeremy A. Sabloff. *A History of American Archaeology.* San Francisco: W. H. Freeman, 1974.

For reliable information on pre-Columbian New World cultures:

Coe, Michael D. *Breaking the Maya Code.* New York: Thames and Hudson, 1992.
————. *The Maya.* 4th ed. New York: Thames and Hudson, 1987.
Davies, Nigel. *The Ancient Kingdoms of Mexico.* New York: Penguin, 1984.
Fagan, Brian M. *Ancient North America: The Archaeology of a Continent.* London: Thames and Hudson, 1991.
Moseley, Michael E. *The Incas and Their Ancestors: The Archaeology of Peru.* New York: Thames and Hudson, 1992.
Reader's Digest. *Mysteries of the Ancient Americas: The New World Before Columbus.* Pleasantville, N.Y.: The Reader's Digest Association, 1986.
Sabloff, Jeremy A. *The Cities of Ancient Mexico: Reconstructing a Lost World.* New York: Thames and Hudson, 1989.
Schele, Linda, and Freidel, David. *A Forest of Kings: The Untold Story of the Ancient Maya.* New York: William Morrow, 1990.
Stuart, George E., and Gene S. *The Mysterious Maya.* Washington, D.C.: The National Geographic Society, 1977.
Swanson, Earl H., Warwick Bray, and Ian Farrington. *The New World.* Oxford: Elsevier Phaidon, 1975.

Chapter 7: Discoveries in the Far East and Sub-Saharan Africa

Cheng, Te-K'un. *Archaeology in China.* Four volumes. Cambridge: W. Heffer & Sons, 1959.
Davidson, Basil. *The Lost Cities of Africa.* Boston: Little, Brown, 1959.
Robertshaw, P., ed. *A History of African Archaeology.* Portsmouth, N.H.: Heinemann, 1990.

For accounts of the archaeological remains and civilizations of the Far East and sub-Saharan Africa:

Agrawal, D. P. *The Archaeology of India.* Curzon Press, 1982.
Arkell, A. *History of the Sudan from Earliest Times to 1821.* 2nd ed. London: University of London, 1961.

Beach, D. N. *The Shona and Zimbabwe, 900-1850.* New York: Africana, 1980.

Clark, J. Desmond. *The Prehistory of Africa.* New York: Frederick A. Praeger, 1970.

Davies, Oliver. *West Africa Before the Europeans.* London: Methuen, 1967.

Fagan, Brian M. *Southern Africa During the Iron Age.* London: Thames and Hudson, 1965.

Garlake, P. *Great Zimbabwe.* New York: McGraw-Hill, 1973.

Hintze, Fritz and Ursula. *Civilizations of the Old Sudan.* Amsterdam: B. R. Grüner, 1968.

Johnson, Jerah. *Africa and the West.* Hinsdale, Ill.: The Dryden Press, 1974.

Kidder, J. E. *Japan Before Buddhism.* Rev. ed. New York: Frederick A. Praeger, 1966.

Mazzeo, Donatella, and Chiara S. Antonini. *Monuments of Civilization: Ancient Cambodia.* New York: Grosset & Dunlap, 1978.

Rawson, Jessica. *Ancient China: Art and Archaeology.* New York: Harper and Row, 1980.

Shinnie, P. *Meroe: A Civilization of the Sudan.* New York: Praeger, 1967.

Watson, William. *Early Civilization in China.* London: Thames and Hudson, 1966.

Chapter 8: Reclaiming Sunken History

Bass, George F. *Archaeology Beneath the Sea.* New York: Walker, 1975.
———. *Archaeology Under Water.* New York: Praeger, 1966.

Cleator, P. E. *Underwater Archaeology.* New York: St. Martin's, 1973.

Diole, Philippe. *4,000 Years Under the Sea.* New York: Julian Messner, 1954.

Dugan, James. *Man Under the Sea.* New York: Harper and Brothers, 1956.

Rackl, Hanns-Wolf. *Diving Into the Past: Archaeology Under Water.* New York: Charles Scribner's Sons, 1968.

Throckmorton, Peter. *The Lost Ships.* Boston: Little, Brown, 1964.
———. *Shipwrecks and Archaeology: The Unharvested Sea.* London: Victor Gollanz, 1970.

For exploration and excavation techniques used in archaeology under water:

Dean, Martin, ed. *Archaeology Underwater: The NAS Guide to Principles and Practice.* London: Nautical Archaeology Society and Archetype Publications, 1992.

Dumas, Frederic. *Deep-Water Archaeology.* London: Routledge and Kegan Paul, 1962.

Green, Jeremy. *Maritime Archaeology: A Technical Handbook.* San Diego, Calif.: Academic Press, 1990.

Peterson, M. *History Under the Sea: A Handbook for Underwater Exploration.* Washington, D.C.: Smithsonian Institution, 1965.

U.N.E.S.C.O. *Underwater Archaeology: A Nascent Discipline.* Paris: U.N.E.S.C.O., 1972.

Wilkes, Bill St. John. *Nautical Archaeology: A Handbook for Skin Divers.* New York: Stein and Day, 1971. (As an informative description of underwater excavation methods, this book is fine. However, skin divers should *not* attempt to excavate wrecks on their own, as Wilkes suggests.)

Chapter 9: Systematizing and Organizing the Past (1925–1960)

Aitken, M. J. *Thermoluminescence Dating.* San Diego, Calif.: Academic Press, 1985.

Bowman, S. *Radiocarbon Dating.* London: British Museum, 1990.

Brothwell, Don, and Eric Higgs, eds. *Science in Archaeology.* London: Thames and Hudson, 1963. (This first edition discusses scientific techniques known and used up to the beginning of the 1960s, which is the scope of this chapter. A revised edition with additional material was published in 1969.)

Eckstein, D. *Dendrochronological Dating.* Strasbourg: European Science Foundation, 1984.

Harris, M. *The Rise of Anthropological Theory.* New York: Thomas Y. Crowell, 1968.

Hawkes, Jaquetta. *Mortimer Wheeler: Adventurer in Archaeology.* London: Weidenfeld, 1982.

Taylor, R. E. *Radiocarbon Dating: An Archaeological Perspective.* San Diego, Calif.: Academic Press, 1987.

Trigger, Brian G. *Gordon Childe.* London: Thames and Hudson, 1980.

Wheeler, R. E. M. *Archaeology From the Earth.* Baltimore: Penguin, 1954.

———. *Still Digging.* London: Michael Joseph, 1955.

Willey, Gordon R., and Philip Phillips. *Method and Theory in Ameri-*

can *Archaeology*. Chicago: University of Chicago Press, 1958.
Zeuner, Frederick E. *Dating the Past*. 4th ed. London: Methuen, 1958.

Chapter 10: Toward a Scientific Archaeology (1960–Present)

Aitken, M. J. *Science-Based Dating in Archaeology*. New York: Longman, 1990.
Baillie, M. G. L. *Tree-ring Dating and Archaeology*. Chicago: University of Chicago Press, 1982.
Barker, Philip. *Techniques of Archaeological Excavation*. 2nd ed. New York: Humanities Press, 1983.
Binford, Lewis R., and Sally R. Binford, eds. *New Perspectives in Archaeology*. Chicago: Aldine, 1968.
Clarke, David L. *Analytical Archaeology*. London: Methuen, 1968.
Colwell, R. N., ed. *Manual of Remote Sensing*. 2nd ed. Falls Church, Va.: Society of Photogrammetry, 1983.
Doran, J. E., and F. R. Hodson. *Mathematics and Computers in Archaeology*. Cambridge, Mass.: Harvard University Press, 1975.
Mauch Messenger, P., ed. *The Ethics of Collecting Cultural Property: Whose Culture? Whose Property?* Albuquerque, N.M.: University of New Mexico Press, 1989.
Redman, C. L., ed. *Research and Theory in Current Archaeology*. New York: Wiley-Interscience, 1973.
Renfrew, Colin, ed. *The Explanation of Culture Change: Models in Prehistory*. Pittsburgh, Pa.: University of Pittsburgh Press, 1974.
Renfrew, C., M. J. Rowlands, and B. A. Segraves, eds. *Theory and Explanation in Archaeology: The Southampton Conference*. New York: Academic Press, 1982.
Wilson, David. *The New Archaeology*. New York: Alfred A. Knopf, 1974.
Woodall, J. Ned. *An Introduction to Modern Archaeology*. Cambridge, Mass.: Schenkman, 1972.

For information on the theory and methods of current-day archaeology:

Hayden, Brian. *Archaeology: The Science of Once and Future Things*. San Francisco: W. H. Freeman, 1992.
Hester, T. N., H. J. Shafer, and R. F. Heizer. *Field Methods in Archaeology*. 7th ed. Palo Alto, Calif.: Mayfield, 1987.
Joukowsky, Martha. *A Complete Manual of Field Archaeology*. Engle-

wood Cliffs, N.J.: Prentice-Hall, 1980.

McIntosh, J. *The Practical Archaeologist.* New York: Facts on File, 1986.

Renfrew, Colin, and Paul Bahn. *Archaeology: Theories, Methods, and Practice.* London: Thames and Hudson, 1991.

Sharer, Robert J., and Wendy Ashmore. *Archaeology: Discovering Our Past.* 2nd ed. Mountain View, Calif.: Mayfield, 1993.

Index